Telling the Other

Telling the Other

The Question of
Value in Modern and
Postcolonial Writing

PATRICK McGEE

Cornell University Press

Ithaca and London

First published 1992 by Cornell University Press.

International Standard Book Number 0-8014-2749-5 (cloth)
International Standard Book Number 0-8014-8027-2 (paper)
Library of Congress Catalog Card Number 91-48247

Printed in the United States of America

Librarians: Library of Congress cataloging information appears on the last page of the book.

⊗The paper in this book meets the minimum requirements of the American National Standard for Information Sciences—Permanence of Paper for Printed Library Materials, ANSI Z39.48-1984.

In Memory of
LILLIAN McGEE
June 18, 1927 – March 12, 1989

Contents

ACKNOWLEDGMENTS ix

Introduction 1

1 *Criticism as Symbolic Exchange:
Baudrillard, Hart Crane* 17

2 *Faulkner's Letter* 41

3 *Writing as a Forbidden Pleasure:
Irigaray, Lacan, Joyce* 64

4 *Woolf's Other* 94

5 *. . . and the Other Modernism:
From Conrad to Rushdie* 116

6 *Texts between Worlds:
African Allegories* 147

7 *Apocalypse and Sexual Difference:
Monique Wittig in the Post-
structuralist Context* 172

WORKS CITED 205

INDEX 213

Acknowledgments

This book owes a debt to scholars whose work and presence have nourished my thinking and compelled me to write. At the top of the list are Jacques Derrida, Fredric Jameson, Jerome McGann, Edward Said, Gayatri Spivak, and Monique Wittig. During a period when I felt that I was working largely without institutional support, I depended on the intellectual and personal commitment of my colleagues and friends: Granger Babcock, Anthony Barthelemy, Morris Beja, Bernard Benstock, Shari Benstock, Robert Con Davis, Daniel Fogel, Prabhakara Jha, Ellen Carol Jones, Karen Lawrence, Veronica Makowsky, Jerome McGann, Susan Miller, Janet Montelaro, Ronald Montelaro, Richard Moreland, Leslie Roman, Ronald Schleifer, Henry Staten, Jon Thompson, Thomas Vogler, and Deborah Wilson. I have to single out Prabha Jha for his comments on an early version of Chapter 6. I am deeply indebted to his expertise in postcolonial literature and theory and eagerly await his work on the subject. Similarly, Deborah Wilson suggested ideas to me about Virginia Woolf that led me to write Chapter 4. I should also mention that Roland McHugh's *Annotations to "Finnegans Wake"* were an essential aid to my reading

Acknowledgments

of Joyce's "dark" book and not only where I have cited him. My special thanks go to the two readers of the manuscript, Gregory Jay and John T. Matthews. Their supportive and extremely useful comments have made this a better book. I would never have written this or any other book without the inspiration and guidance of the late Marcus W. Orr of Memphis State University. I remember him with affection. Finally, my greatest debt is to my wife, Joan Rey Lara Espey, and my son, Sean McGee. They never fail me.

I thank the National Endowment of the Humanities for the summer stipend that helped me to complete a preliminary phase of this project. Chapter 4 is a slightly revised version of "Woolf's Other: The University in Her Eye," *Novel* 23.3 (1990). Chapter 6 is a more substantially revised version of "Texts between Worlds: African Fiction as Political Allegory," in *Decolonizing Tradition: New Approaches to Twentieth-Century British Literary Canons*, ed. Karen Lawrence (University of Illinois Press, 1992). I am grateful to these publishers for their permission to use this material. Lines from "The Broken Tower" from *The Complete Poems and Selected Letters and Prose of Hart Crane*, edited by Brom Weber, are reprinted by permission of Liveright Publishing Corporation. Copyright 1933, © 1958, 1966 by Liveright Publishing Corporation. Material from *Absalom, Absalom!: The Corrected Text* by William Faulkner. Copyright © 1986 by Jill Faulkner Summers. Reprinted by permission of Random House, Inc., and Curtis Brown Ltd, London. Material from *Le corps lesbian* by Monique Wittig reprinted by permission of Editions de Minuit.

The translations in this text, unless otherwise noted, are my own.

This book is dedicated to the memory of my mother, Lillian McGee. She risked everything for me, and she continues to live in everything I write.

P. M.

Telling the Other

Introduction

There is no slogan or thesis that will explain the purpose of this book. For me, it started from the idea that it must be possible to destabilize the frames of value that mediate any approach I take toward a literary text. This idea arose out of my classroom experiences. Repeatedly, whether I was facing graduate students or undergraduates, I found that teaching literature made possible two ways of constructing a social relationship. The first way was to reinforce and virtually celebrate a preestablished value, a sense of the social good that was somehow embodied in the work of literature. This is not difficult to do. Students usually walk into a course on Milton or Joyce already convinced that the the work they are about to undertake is of value. Though they may be ignorant of the historical period, the biography of the author, the history of interpretation, and critical methodologies, they believe with a reasonable certainty that these things are worth knowing and, more important, that enhancing their knowledge and appreciation of an author's work increases their own personal value. This personal value, of course, is linked to the presence or absence of others. Completing a course on Milton or Joyce offers some objective evidence that one is able to read Milton or

Joyce; and this entitles one to membership in the community of those who know and understand the value of reading "great" authors. Interpretive communities, as Stanley Fish talks about them, not only preexist the classroom situation or the act of critical writing; they are constantly modified and reinforced by these critical practices.

For the truth is that an interpretive community is simply a social class, though "class" need not be taken as a reductive term. Reading Milton and Dante does not automatically make someone into a member of the "upper" class or the "ruling" class or even the class of the "culturally privileged." Class is not a fixed category but rather a form of relationship grounded in an assumption of value or what Pierre Bourdieu calls a "distinction." Class relationships operate everywhere in society, but they are not reducible to absolute divisions into homogeneous groups with stable interests. Class articulates relations of power between different social positions, but those positions are not univocal; and configurations of social power can be described only in terms of tendency. It may be that such-and-such a number of social distinctions can be translated into a specific quantity of social power; but the realization of that power by an individual is also dependent on the distribution of forces in the field to which he or she attempts to apply it. Finally, it is important to keep in mind that if distinctions constitute class relationships, they also presuppose class relationships. Professing literature, as Gerald Graff shows, has its own political and social history; and the construction of canons and literary preferences always responds to the ongoing struggle—I would call it a "class struggle"—between different social formations with different political tendencies.

So teaching literature involves, to some extent, constructing social relationships as a form of class identity. This observation doesn't strike me as terribly novel, nor does it point to an aspect of social reproduction that I would be willing to call evil. After all, it might be possible to use this dimension of pedagogy in ways that are subversive—to construct and inculcate new literary values for new class formations that may have the effect of destabilizing an "old" order of social relationships and of creating the practical possibility of social change toward a "new" or modified order. One should not underestimate the impact on general culture of new programs like Women's Studies, African-American Studies, or Cultural Studies. The effectiveness of these programs is testified to by the "hysterical" and frequently "paranoid" response of neoconservatives and other traditionalists in the fields of literary criticism and journalism who fancy themselves pitted against a neo-Marxist conspiracy to replace the giants of Western culture with the likes of Toni Morrison, Alice Walker, or Chinua Achebe. That such a debate can break out in the university and even get attention from such popular magazines as *Newsweek* shows that the idea of social change through cultural critique has become a legitimate concern within the public sphere. Those who want to maintain a Eurocentric tradition may try to crush the new curriculums; but ironically, in that very act, they cannot fail to recognize them.

My teaching experience also suggested to me, however, that there was another way of constructing a social relationship, one that seemed to undermine or at least question the teaching of literature as a form of value. Every teacher is aware that from time to time a sense of the uncanny can permeate a classroom when neither the student nor the teacher can speak with a finalized certainty about the purpose, meaning, or value of a literary work. This can happen with any text and at any level of instruction or discourse. It tends to happen more frequently, however, with such texts as Joyce's *Ulysses* and *Finnegans Wake*, the novels of Samuel Beckett, Ishmael Reed, Thomas Pynchon, or Kathy Acker, or the poetry of Hart Crane or the L-A-N-G-U-A-G-E poets, perhaps because these novels and poems self-consciously call into question their own "literariness" and the systems of value that implicitly support the division between literary and discursive writing, between genres, between high culture and popular or mass culture, and so forth. These texts possess one characteristic of what Peter Bürger calls the avant-gardiste work of art in tending to oppose themselves to art or literature as an institution. Bürger provides a historical explanation of the rise of the European avant-garde which may be subject to critical inquiry and revision. My own experience would indicate that these texts present a real challenge to students who enter the classroom with very traditional concepts of what literature is supposed to do or be. Professors and critics have worked vigilantly at identifying and classifying the indeterminacies or undecidables in these texts; and this work has given rise to the various theories of modernism, postmodernism, surrealism, and the avant-garde in general. Nevertheless, the experience of reading these texts can be immensely decentering and disturbing, especially for inexperienced readers who are not familiar with the complicated twists and turns of the modes of institutional authorization that make such works "safe" for traditional consumption.

It seems to me that deconstruction can be a model for reading or pedagogy which does not reduce the literary work to a fixed value (a value sometimes rooted in indeterminacy or unreadability) but rather opens it up to textuality as the condition of an interminable readability. I want to approach this subject through an example that will take the form of a parable. This parable is based on a real experience, but the parabolic form emphasizes the extent to which such an experience necessarily undergoes "imaginary" reshaping in the process of telling what is more than a personal anecdote.

I am going to use the example of a student named Paul (that is not his real name, of course). A few years ago I was trying to teach *Ulysses* to a group of undergraduates. There were no prerequisites and no limitations on the enrollment in this course because I felt an ethical obligation to do away with any notion that Joyce's text was for the privileged few. The result was a rather large body of students, who brought radically different backgrounds and literary experiences to the course. My approach, pedagogically, was simple. I would present the most radical reading of *Ulysses* I could; but I would do it in a language that was accessible as well as provocative so as to incite my students to dialogue, even on occasion to confrontation. This is easier said than done. My students and I went through the text (after some preliminary reading) episode by episode, paying careful attention to its language at those moments of the overturning and displacement of style, subjectivity, narrative form, politics, and sexual identity. The students were sometimes uncontrollably responsive, at other times dead silent. After a while, I began to read the class like a text, not as the transparent receivers of my message but as a complicated collection of "characters" whose readings of fiction were to some extent inseparable from the fictionality of their own lives. It is not that I forgot they were persons but that the transparency usually attributed to the concept of "person" was made somewhat opaque by those minimal revelations of how each person operates within a specific world of values and meanings that he or she takes for granted. I will not say that such a world is unreal, but there was more than one reality; and although these realities bore family resemblances to one another, they were not strictly identical. Obviously, I got only a glimpse of these fictions from time to time in the way they would inform a person's reading or resistance to reading. It was not my job, as I understood it, to write or to revise their different stories; but I did want to exploit the deconstructive turns of *Ulysses* to make them more critical and self-conscious about what they left unthought in their readings and perhaps in their lives.

Paul presented me with a response that forced me to question my own strategy. I began to notice that he was not keeping up with the reading assignments and could not respond to questions and discussion in class. This negligence bothered me because he seemed to be a capable and intelligent student; so we made an appointment to talk things over in my office. When we met, he explained to me what the problem was. He had decided that he was not going to move forward with the reading until he had come to some understanding of "Proteus," the third episode of *Ulysses*. He had been working on it for several weeks without the sense of getting anywhere. He was not immediately concerned about passing or not passing the course because he felt it was more important to stay exactly where he was and confront the wall of language that inhibited his progress. My first reaction was predictable. This sounded like the sort of rationalization that students, especially intelligent students, come up with to avoid the labor of reading. I pointed out to Paul that he was idealizing the act of reading. He aimed to achieve understanding as some sort of immediate experience or internal illumination; he expected the text to open itself to him, to make present its truth, its meaning, its purpose, its form—to produce a revelation as the fulfillment of his act of reading. He wanted closure, finality; then he would go on to the next episode of *Ulysses*, as if it were the next floor of a skyscraper—a single, unified, coherent structure. *Ulysses*, I suggested, resists just this sort of approach. Even the famous schemata illustrate the irreducibility of its form because they are never apparent within the text and yet can lend a tentative coherence to it. They are outside the text and yet somehow inside. The bridge between outside and inside turns out to be the interminable process of reading. Consequently, I said, you must go on.

Conscious that I was beginning to sound like a Beckett novel, I decided to leave it at that. Paul made it clear that he was committed to reading *Ulysses* and that, as far as he was concerned, he was going on. But he did say vaguely that he had never read anything like "Proteus" and he would not just pass it over. He wanted to read every word *critically*. His "seriousness" seemed proof enough that he would get back on the track. Still, I had the sense of something left undone by this interview. Somehow Paul's problem had become my own. I went back to "Proteus" looking for some clue as to why this episode could become such an impediment. After reading a few lines, I said to myself, "Of course! 'Proteus' is about reading—about reading the world as a phenomenal text, 'Signatures of all things I am here to read.' I know this." The density and reflexivity of "Proteus" make it difficult for any beginner because it illustrates in its subject matter precisely what the reader encounters in its style. It is about the opacity of the phenomenal world, the resistance of that world to any univocal reading, the very qualities that make experience into a text. So it was difficult but not impossible. If Paul could not deal with "Proteus," how was he going to work his way through "Sirens," "Cyclops," "Oxen of the Sun," and "Circe"? At least in "Proteus," there is some stability, some ground to the stylistic play, in Stephen Dedalus as the subject of a meditative stream of consciousness. But what about Stephen's subjectivity? How stable is it?

I remembered one of the most interesting passages in the episode, the one in which Stephen contemplates the Berkeleyan field of vision while writing a poem: "Who ever anywhere will read these written words? Signs on a white field. Somewhere to someone in your flutiest voice. The good bishop of Cloyne took the veil of the temple out of his shovel hat: veil of space with coloured emblems hatched on its field" (*Ulysses* 40). This passage almost begs for a deconstructive reading. Stephen confronts what Derrida, in his early work, calls *spacing*—the sense that between the word and the speaking or writing subject there is a necessary interval, the space that determines its iterability, that it can be repeated for another subject. This spacing is essential to the possibility of communication and yet it problematizes communication as an intentional act. Spacing gives ground to a certain slippage in the syntax of meaning, making inevitable the production of what Derrida calls an undecidable. For example, when Stephen writes his "signs on a white field," he writes for a reader who has no way of knowing whether the words convey a meaning that Stephen intended or whether they refer only to themselves. It is the difference between using a word and mentioning it. (As Don Gifford notes, Stephen's poem is not original but "a souped-up . . . version of the last stanza of 'My Grief on the Sea'" from Douglas Hyde's *Love Songs of Connacht* [62]. Is it a personal expression or pastiche? What criteria would enable the reader to decide whether it is one or the other? And how do we determine Joyce's exact intention for inserting it in this context? Is he suggesting that Stephen's mind lacks originality or that originality is itself an illusion? or an allusion?) Stephen thinks of projecting his words to someone in his "flutiest voice." Similarly, writing articulates a voice through its rhetorical style; and such a style lends an opacity to language which cannot be effaced before a pure intention, meaning, or truth. Experience itself must undergo spacing if it is to be articulate and communicable. Recalling Berkeley's philosophy, Stephen realizes that it is not just words that make a text but the whole field of perception. The "veil of space" that is our world is subject to the same displacement, the same slippage, as the words we write.

Still, there is more than one slippage in the passage quoted from "Proteus." For how do we govern our reading of these words? How do we limit the context? If we take one step back to the words immediately preceding my quotation, we find another of Stephen's questions: "Who watches me here?" Suddenly, Stephen appears to himself as one of the "coloured emblems hatched on its field." Stephen can be read. He is not just the subject who writes but the subject who is written by the gaze of another. He is "subject" to spacing. The reader of Joyce's *Ulysses* knows, of course, that Stephen is a sign on a white field, subject to the syntactical slippage I have already described. There is really no limit to the possible games we could play with context as long as we have not reached the end of textuality, and that end does not come within the boundaries of the book (nor outside those boundaries once we understand the idea of a general text). Even if we could imagine such an end, it would be impossible to express it without falling into spacing, into textuality. For deconstruction, no word ever exists apart from its context; but no context is ever saturated (see Derrida, "Living On"). Even the reader of *Ulysses* is another subject of spacing. That means Paul, of course; but it also means me.

After some thought, I began to reconsider my conversation with Paul and my dissatisfaction with its conclusion. Paul could be on to something. He had said that he would go on, that he wanted to read every word "critically." A week after the interview, I found out what he meant. He had gone on to read and reread "Proteus." He was trying to unpack every word by tracing out the different connections between words, including the words alluded to. Of course, this activity is exactly what I wanted from him, up to a point; but beyond that point it could become purposeless since in my experience it has no determinate end. But how could I know that? What context determined my own position as the subject of this knowledge? And did I assume that context to be stable? Of course, because I was Paul's teacher my context was the institution within which I worked and certain reading protocols that made sense within the framework of that institution. It made sense, for example, to require my students to begin at the beginning of *Ulysses* and work their way collectively to the end. I might work against that protocol, that sense of the natural or logical order of reading, by showing how the text contradicts such linearity. *Ulysses* requires us to read forward and backward as we progress through the various stylistic shifts that have the effect of reframing and calling into question our perception of earlier and later styles in the book. It might make more sense to begin *Ulysses* with "Oxen of the Sun" and then read all the other episodes as variations on the history of style. The whole of *Ulysses* would become pastiche. Or one could start with "Circe," which more than one critic has called the unconscious of the text, an episode that inverts and displaces the whole of the book. One could work through this unconsious, foregrounding the book's radical alterity, its difference from itself, toward the more fixed positions, the identities, of the linear narrative. Perhaps more practically, one could follow the strategy of Michael Groden in *"Ulysses" in Progress* and read the book through the process of its revision during and after the composition of "Circe." One could also follow Paul's strategy and start reading "seriously" wherever reading seems to become impossible, where the reading subject encounters the greatest density of resistance to the understanding. In principle, such a reading would be interminable and thus would entail a reading of the whole book, a reading of the author and the reader, and beyond—a reading of a specific culture and a multicultural world. As long as there is history, no context is saturated.

I can imagine one obvious response: there have to be protocols. Even if you don't begin at the beginning and end at the ending, you have to begin somewhere and there has to be some sort of temporal limit to the reading. The university must of necessity, by the nature of its evaluative procedures and in the interest of fairness, require uniformity. Paul cannot just do what he wants. He cannot live in his own world.

Nor can I, and so tacitly I must agree to the necessity of some methodological uniformity if I am to go on teaching. But deconstruction, it seems to me, challenges this form of tacit agreement. It brings under scrutiny not just any particular norm but the principle of normality itself. As a deconstructive text, *Ulysses* refuses any hierarchy of approaches, any reading authority that would set itself up as a standard rule. It deconstructs such authority by subjecting it to a method without a rule, a process without a determinate end or purpose. A deconstructive approach to *Ulysses*, therefore, cannot prescribe the rules for reading or even insist on heuristic protocols that command final authority in the classroom. On the contrary, the job of such an approach is to deconstruct the space of the classroom, to deconstruct the authority that has shaped itself around the body of the text. Derrida himself (in the interview with Imre Salusinszky) recognizes the problems inherent in deconstructive pedagogy: "You have to train people to become doctors or engineers or professors, and at the same time to train them in questioning all that— not only in a critical way, but I would say in a deconstructive way." He thinks of these as "two responsibilities which sometimes are not compatible" (17–18). *Ulysses* would seem to push such incompatibility to the point of contradiction. This pedagogical contradiction, however, does not preclude the possibility of historical resolution through social transformation. While deconstruction *in and of itself* cannot propose a unified pedagogy that would resolve the contradictions that arise in teaching a text like *Ulysses*, it can foreground the contradiction and thus stage a pedagogical crisis that can be worked through, perhaps interminably, as a symbolic act, a form of social affirmation. As Derrida further remarks to Salusinszky, "deconstruction is affirmation rather than questioning, in a sense which is not positive: I would distinguish between the positive, or positions, and affirmations" (20). A method without a rule, deconstruction works toward an affirmation that is not a position but a process, an opening.

The meaning of my parable helps to clarify the nature of this affirmation. Although Paul eventually submitted to university protocols and finished reading *Ulysses*, for a moment he had ruptured the stability of a set of institutional positions: those of the teacher, the student, and the text. The authority (or system of values) that governed these positions was momentarily suspended by a symbolic act that operated outside this normative structure of communicative exchange. *Ulysses* became something other, something different from the canonized object of high modernist tradition that usually goes by that name. It became incommensurable. The hierarchical relationship between student and teacher was dissolved by the interaction that permitted the student to evade the institutional authority of the teacher while the teacher confronted the undecidability of his difference from the student, of his social distinction. The two subjects confronted the text not as an object of exchange through which one subject confers value on, or transfers meaning to, the other. Rather, the text became an open process or event that gave the two subjects access to the space of the intersubject as the affirmative ground of any possible social position. The intersubject simultaneously posits and disrupts the subject as a distinct social identity and the object as a symbolic good. It articulates the social tie as the possibility of communication and value formation on the basis of a radical alterity that can neither precede nor succeed the mark of identity but must underwrite it as its nonidentity, as its trace. The intersubject affirms not the social positions through which communication takes place but the interminable displacement of positionality that the trace-structure of experience makes inevitable.

In this context, it may be useful to say what the intersubject is not. It is not the consensual ground of normal communication as Jürgen Habermas defines it in his criticism of deconstruction:

Under the pressure for decisions proper to the communicative practice of everyday life, participants are dependent upon agreements that coordinate their actions. The more removed interpretations are from the "seriousness of this type of situation," the more they can prescind from the idealizing supposition of an achievable consensus. But they can never be wholly absolved of the idea that wrong interpretations must in principle be criticizable in terms of consensus to be aimed for ideally. The interpreter does not impose this idea on his object; rather, with the performative attitude of a participant observer, he takes it over from the direct participants, *who can act communicatively only under the presupposition of intersubjectively identical ascriptions of meaning.* (198)

The problem with Habermas's way of reading the relation between supposedly marginal and normal modes of critical interpretation is that he cannot imagine that such uses of language have any function other than communication. No one—not even Derrida—would disagree that the idea of a wrong interpretation requires some form of consensus, some agreement between already positioned subjects about the ascriptions of meaning and value. Habermas assumes, in other words, that language operates only as a form of class relationship, through the mediation of interpretive communities, although he allows for the possibility of an ideal community, an ideal speech situation, that would aim—at least in principle—to embrace all class formations, indeed all humankind. For Habermas, intersubjectivity signifies the drive toward a universal consensus, which, though it can perhaps be realized only ideally, provides the necessary rational ground to any "serious" interpretation. Any reading that ignores consensus by refusing to heed the protocols and norms of "the communicative practice of everyday life" simply has nothing serious to say and cannot be a proper use of language. This thinking leaves the positionality of the subjects that constitute the intersubjective network completely unanalyzed. It makes it impossible to think or say anything that has not "ideally" already been thought.

Habermas seems to think that deconstruction has nothing to say about consensus or about value. Gregory S. Jay responds that the projects of deconstruction are undertaken "in the name of an other whose *value* is being posited." He continues: "And if the positing of the value of the other is inherent to the deconstruction of reason, an implicit normative claim of some kind haunts each of these texts" (43). Nevertheless, deconstruction does not aim at some ideal speech situation that leaves unanalyzed and unthought the positioning of communities of subjects with different relations to political and economic power. Deconstruction, according to Jay, "may assist in the *dissemination* of the subject, a process that includes the affirmation of those historical subject positions (marked by such categories as race, nationality, class, gender, et al.) previously marginalized by the Subject of History" (42). I would modify Jay's formulation in view of Derrida's remark to Imre Salusinszky. It is not subject positions or even value that deconstruction affirms by "positing" the value of the other. It is the alterity of "value" and "the subject." Positing the value of the other is the first step in the deconstruction of the authority of the Subject of History, the "overturning." What is overturned is nothing less than the inscription of Habermas's concept of intersubjectivity in an ideal speech situation, whose goal of universal consensus can lead only to imperialist knowledge by effacing the alterities that emerge from the construction of fixed subject positions. Beyond this overturning, however, lies the necessity of a "displacement" of any subject position as a stable value toward the intersubject that is neither a subject nor an other. The intersubject, as the rest of this book argues, bears a relation to what Lacan calls the "big Other," Baudrillard "symbolic exchange," and Derrida the "totally other." These terms are not equivalent but gesture toward a form of human relationship that disrupts the order of value and the class discourses derived from it.

My imaginary student and I approached the relationship of symbolic exchange through the deconstruction of a conventional act of reading. This occurs whenever the protocols of university procedure and the hierarchies of traditional values are momentarily suspended. I would never claim that such a "minor" gesture offers any sort of serious threat to the authority of institutions; but I would insist that incommensurable events like this one (which take place all the time, although they are usually attributed to ignorance or stupidity) reveal a social tie or form of exchange that is the repressed of the symbolic systems that make up institutional orders. These events usually take place in subtler ways, especially when subjects marked by differences of race, gender, nationality, sexual preference, and economic as well as other "class" distinctions confront forms of textual authority that implicitly negate their experiences and devalue their social identities. It is not my contention that a teacher must *precisely* anticipate the needs of students and the goals of social liberation by constructing courses along the lines of a predetermined "political correctness." This would only be another system of values that would indirectly support the repressive authority of the institution by blocking the expression of anomalous points of view and other forms of social resistance. Rather, it is necessary to be open to challenge and to listen to what others have to tell when their telling ceases to reproduce the order of value. Such a telling aims not at the teacher as the representative of cultural authority, nor is it the autonomous expression of the self-identical subject. It comes from the Other to the Other, the intersubject, the true subject. It *tells*—that is, gives an account of, divulges the truth or secret of, decides or determines the action of (the Other)—in the act of *telling*, speaking to, addressing (the Other).

It should be clear to the reader of this introduction that the example I chose to illustrate such an event is not innocent. Paul was not a member of any minority that I was aware of; he was white, male, and middle-class. Obviously, I have encountered more problematic and culturally compli-cated forms of social resistance in the classroom, particularly where I currently teach in the Deep South. Even the choice of *Ulysses* as an object of pedagogy points toward the limits of my own social situation, back-ground, and culturally determined predispositions. Perhaps a better ex-ample would have been the experience I had in Oklahoma of teaching John Ford's racist western *The Searchers* in a film and composition class that contained several Native American students. There I learned that, even though I recognized the film's racism and sexism and had made the exposure and analysis of these effects central to my pedagogy, I really could not control the impact of these social values on individual students. One Native American woman became very hostile, rejected my good pedagogical intentions altogether, and nearly left the course. It was only through a very lengthy dialogue during which I had to surrender some of my authority and rethink some of my good intentions that I was finally able to regain some legitimacy in this woman's eyes so that I could en-courage her to direct her anger toward an affirmative though critical writing experience. In teaching in the South, I have frequently chosen texts for basic courses that I thought would empower the voice of African-American students and enable them to challenge productively some of the symbolic violence that education almost inevitably inflicts upon them. This strategy is not without cost, however; and I am aware of students who feel alienated and even excluded by this opening to minor-ity voices that seem outside the mainstream of what they have been taught to believe is a self-evidently superior tradition. I may want to challenge the norms that support such a view and even the idea of normativity itself; but I still have to respect the integrity of the student's claim to truth. In other words, challenging the self-evident nature of normativity doesn't mean that I can do without norms. There is always a calculated risk in any pedagogical act that would do more than simply reproduce an already established version of reality; and regardless of whom I am trying to reach, it is always difficult to determine if I have enabled a student to articulate a "voice" that critically reflects or represents his or her social background and identity or if I have simply facilitated the effacement of that background by teaching the student to conform to the dominant system of values.

My own voice, of course, is no less problematic than that of my student. In the chapters that follow and in my teaching practices, I can hardly speak with any sort of universal authority for all the interests that have been articulated by the works in question—writings marked by historical differences of gender, race, nationality, and sexual orientation. I try to discuss this general issue more critically in Chapter 5 through a consideration of recent statements by Gayatri Spivak and Pierre Bourdieu. Here, I simply want to qualify my own authority as a speaking and writing subject by clarifying what I understand that category to be. For nearly twenty years the critique of the subject has been at the center of the debate over the nature and limits of literary criticism as well as of other forms of critical and social practice. Ironically, it seems to me, the one consistent recognition that has emerged from this debate is that the subject is a category we cannot do without. Monique Wittig, for example, who in some ways offers the most radical critique of the subject as the agent of cultural hegemony in language, nevertheless insists on the necessity of the subject as the potential agent of social change if it can be liberated from heterosexual domination. The apparent contradiction in this statement disappears, I think, if we think of the subject not as a category of formal identity but as the construction of an interest. It is the mark of a social interest that gives coherence and purposive direction to the body (not as a thing in itself but as the material ground of symbolic action). As the articulation of an interest, the subject is not the repository of unmediated will or natural desire; it is not original and it does not originate anything, since it is the effect of a network of social relations and histories that are not reducible to a linked and inevitable series of causal connections. The subject is not, strictly speaking, free. Since the interest that constitutes the subject is not reducible to a single cause or a unitary will, however—since it is the effect of a set of social relations that cannot be derived from a transcendental agency or a universal history—it possesses what Lacan would call a "little freedom," that is, a potentiality for becoming the ground of a socially symbolic act that contradicts or challenges another interest or system of interests. To me, this potentiality means that political intervention in the world of social interests is possible but severely limited; it is never simply a matter of the autonomous subject's arriving at a conception of what its "true" interests are and then acting on the basis of that knowledge. The subject is never pure but always already constituted by interests.

In practical terms, this notion of the subject as a constituted interest does not relieve the critic of responsibility. Rather it suggests to me that the responsibility of the critic must extend beyond his or her intention or conscious purpose toward the unconscious and not altogether predictable effects of her or his work. Intentionality is real enough and is certainly one parameter underlying any social act, but it is not the only dimension of truth. Stated differently, my freedom as a speaking subject is a fiction of social interests, but that fictionality is neither illusory nor imaginary. I have to act out of that fiction: I have to make decisions that are ethically responsible based on my "lived" relation to the world of interests. It would be irresponsible, however, to imagine that such a lived relation is the final limit of my responsibility or rather of the responsibility of criticism itself. Criticism must articulate and pursue its interests while it constructs the space of its own uncertainty, the undecidability of the ground of its authority. As Derrida has written, "Responsibility, if there is any, requires the experience of the undecidable as well as the irreducibility of the other" ("Like the Sound of the Sea" 639). Because teaching and writing are risky enterprises, I have to take responsibility for the effects they produce. I cannot simply address the other and convey my truth to it. Nor can I speak the truth of the other. I cannot address my students, my readers, or the objects of my criticism from outside the social conditions that determine our relationships to one another. I cannot unproblematically articulate or reproduce the voice and interests of those who are marked other by the hegemonic discourses of Western imperialist culture. I cannot speak as a woman or as a lesbian. It would be naïve, however, to think that, because I cannot speak from a social position I do not occupy, I necessarily speak from a reducible and fully transparent site of social power. My discourse is not univocal; the interests that constitute me are not transparent. As the form of interest, every subject is an other; that is, it is destabilized by the social system that constitutes it. It is subjected to and by the displacements of historical processes that are not fully readable and whose origins and directions are not strictly decidable. Thus, the other as something out there and fully external to me is an illusion of power and ideology. In practice, this illusion becomes apparent when I am confronted with a radical alterity that is not reducible to subject-object or master-slave relationships, when I am confronted with the fictionality, but not the illusion, of my own authority as a speaking subject. From this site of fictional authority, I cannot speak to the other as a sovereign subject or for the other as its representative. I can speak only *as an/other*. I can speak only as a material interest that should be subjected, on the one hand, to a deconstructive reversal and displacement but also, on the other hand, to negotiation and exchange.

In this book, I have tried to write in a way that would leave an opening. This is an appeal to the reader to assume the responsibility of going beyond what I say to what should be said in the present historical context. Such a responsibility necessarily takes the form of criticism, both negative and affirmative. Negatively, criticism will have the task of identifying the gaps in and limits of my project. Affirmatively, it must take responsibility for its own interest and negotiate the difference between it/self and its other in order to arrive at an affirmation of radical alterity. The purpose of such negotiation and affirmation lies in a commitment to the future and to the ongoing political effect of cultural work.

Telling the Other is not a book about pedagogy or a manual on how to teach. It is a series of readings and theoretical articulations that attempt to "defamiliarize" the terrain of literary study through various rhetorical strategies and logical arguments. Although the focus ranges widely over the field of modern literature and theory, it is not an attempt to construct a view of a cultural totality. Rather, it is an intervention at the level of critical interpretation and theories of reading in several distinct but related areas of modern literary study, areas that for convenience can be identified as "modern," "postmodern," and "postcolonial." I would not claim for this book any strict methodological kinship with Cultural Studies; but it does try to incorporate into the very shape and content of its analyses and interpretations what Raymond Williams identifies as the "central theoretical point" of Cultural Studies: "that you cannot understand an intellectual or artistic project without also understanding its formation; that the relation between a project and a formation is always decisive; and that the emphasis of Cultural Studies is precisely that it engages *both*, rather than specializing itself to one or the other" ("The Future of Cultural Studies" 151). It should also be clear from this introduction that I do not see any logical or historical contradiction between Cultural Studies and deconstruction. As I said before, the fundamental assumption behind any deconstructive reading is that every text is situated in a context but that no context is ever saturated. That is, ultimately, no text can ever be read in isolation from its historical context, but history is never complete, never the stable background of predetermined meanings against which one can situate and delimit the ambivalence of the text. To my mind, Derrida's concept of the general text (which, as Rodolphe Gasché stresses, makes textuality both possible and impossible, "since textuality as the essence of existing texts is structurally incapable of essentializing the plus or minus, the more or less of its margins" [289]) is the field of operations of a Cultural Studies methodology. As Williams emphasizes, the concepts "project" and "formation" address "not the relations between two separate entities, 'art' and 'society,' but processes which take these different material forms in social formations of a creative or a critical kind, or on the other hand the actual forms of artistic and intellectual work" ("The Future of Cultural Studies" 152). This book reads critical and literary texts as the articulations of social formations or processes that are also addressed and transformed—that is, virtually constituted—by the works to which they give rise.

Telling the Other means reading against the grain of value. This is what my students have taught me how to do in spite of themselves and in spite of me. So, in a sense, this book is addressed to them and to the truth that they sometimes imagine to be in me but which really seems to haunt the horizon of our relationship to one another. In this introduction, I have tried to draw a picture in parabolic form of the social context or formation from which this work is inseparable. This effort is never finished. But it is the political responsibility of the critic to continue the analysis until the Other has been affirmed and the true subject has been heard.

I

Criticism as Symbolic Exchange: Baudrillard, Hart Crane

In all domains, reversibility—cyclical reversal, annulment—
is the one encompassing form. It puts an end to the linearity
of time, language, economic exchange and accumulation,
and power. For us, it takes on the form of extermination and
death. It is the form of the symbolic, neither mystical nor
structural, but ineluctable.

> —JEAN BAUDRILLARD, "Symbolic Exchange
> and Death," *Selected Writings*

Questioning the value of Jean Baudrillard's critique of
value is possible only through the articulation of its
truth. This "truth," of course, is neither transcendental
nor abstractly universal but historical. It arises within
the determining space and time of contemporary history and cannot be generalized apart from that field of
forces. To speak of the value of any critique of value
requires the bracketing of the fundamental contradiction at the heart of this sort of critical gesture. The
question of value appears to have no outside and, consequently, no foundation on which to base an analysis.
Yet, the historical possibility of the transvaluation of
values implies that the realm of value can be disrupted
and disordered from the inside—indeed, that the bipo-
lar organization of value into an inside and an outside
is itself the object of a critique of value. In an excellent
reading of Baudrillard, Joseph Valente suggests that

contradiction recurs every time critical theories try "to delimit the fundamental structures of meaning and praxis": "Their systematic postulates,
the underlying laws or mechanisms they see as regulating thought, action,
and signification, tend to undercut the authority of the critique itself"
(54). It could be said that Baudrillard's style makes a virtue of the necessity of its internal contradictions; it always takes the risk of undercutting
itself. Any reading of Baudrillard must take another (same yet different)
risk (and this is true whether the reading is affirmative or negative). The
critique of value always implicitly questions its own authority and risks
becoming a parody (or, in Baudrillard's language, a simulation) of the
discourse it criticizes. Still, such a critique, as Gregory Jay stresses, is the
necessary first step that "makes historical criticism possible, because it
unbinds thought from the abstract universalism—the white mythology—
of humanist logocentrism. . . . Like truths, values are terms for which we
are responsible" (73–74). Baudrillard's discourse, whatever its errors, has
never stopped taking responsibility for the values of "our" world in its
formulations, has never failed to risk itself in the pursuit of its own
contradictions. It never stands above the object of analysis but succumbs
to the seductions of its own alterity. For this reason, it is the reader's
responsibility to pursue its truth not as the author's intention but as the
political effect of its textuality.

The truth of Baudrillard's theory of the symbolic does not emerge
from his reduction of it to the model of "primitive formations" as ex-
emplified in the work of Marcel Mauss on gift exchange. Nor is it dependent on the validity or invalidity of his critique of the Saussurian theory of
anagrams or the Marxist theory of value. The most complete criticism of
Baudrillard to date, that of Douglas Kellner, exposes the problems inherent in his rejection of Marxism by showing that many of the positions
advocated by Baudrillard against Marx are derived from Marx's own
thinking, including the critique of a *naturalist* conception of use values
and needs. Nevertheless, Kellner's demolition job on Baudrillard seems to
me far too dismissive of the theory of symbolic exchange which he sees as
nothing more than "a negative antithesis to 'productive' activity or to any
activity that follows the logic of capitalist societies." He suggests that
Baudrillard's critique of Marxist essentialism is discredited by "an essentialist anthropology" underlying the "celebration of symbolic exchange"
(45). Although I agree with Kellner that Baudrillard's Marx is practically
a straw man, I don't think Kellner makes any serious effort to grasp the
theory of symbolic exchange as a radical critique of value. In fact, he
largely ignores the question of value as a fundamental structure that
differently inhabits both cultural and economic systems without being

reducible to either. For Kellner it is possible to reject old "incorrect" values and create new "correct" ones, but it is not possible to question *value in itself*. The political interest of such a radical critique, from my perspective, is that it would make visible the historical finitude of value as a process and thus open it to the possibility of radical transformation.

My purpose here, however, is less to defend Baudrillard from his critics than to elaborate and possibly expand on his theory of symbolic exchange as a method of reading and social interaction that solicits and destabilizes transparent value. Baudrillard himself seems to identify his critical technique as a form of *symbolic exchange,* an attempt to reverse the irreversible, to disrupt the reproduction of value and meaning precisely in the discourses that are the foundation of his work: Marx, Freud, Saussure, Mauss, and others. In *L'échange symbolique et la mort,* Baudrillard describes his method as a form of "counterreference" ("une référence contrariée"): "Mauss must be turned against Mauss, Saussure against Saussure, Freud against Freud" ("Symbolic Exchange and Death," *Selected Writings* 120/*L'échange symbolique* 8). I want to read Baudrillard against Baudrillard—against the individual subject in the act of speculative writing—in order to foreground the question that his work poses even against itself. "The process of value," he writes, "is irreversible. Only reversibility then, and not release or drift, is fatal to the system. And this is exactly what is meant by the term symbolic 'exchange'" (*Selected Writings* 124). Kellner sees this concept of exchange as the binary opposite of value and suggests that it points toward the metaphysical tendency of Baudrillard's work (178). To my mind, he simply begs the question that Baudrillard raises by insisting that value is indeed irreversible. Such a position gets caught in its own metaphysical net.

Barbara Herrnstein Smith, when she tries to reopen this question for contemporary literary theory, makes visible the assumption underlying most bourgeois and some Marxist analyses of value. She notes that "for a responsive creature, to exist is to evaluate. We are always calculating how things 'figure' for us—always pricing them, so to speak, in relation to the total economy of our personal universe" (42). Although Smith offers an extremely subtle critique of value suggesting the impossibility for "individual or collective choices, practices, activities, or acts, 'economic' or otherwise, to be ultimately summed-up, compared, or evaluated: neither by the single-parameter hedonic calculus of classic utilitarianism, nor by the most elaborate multiple-character formulas of contemporary mathematical economics, nor by any mere inversion or presumptive transcendence of either" (149)—nevertheless, in her thought, "the total economy of our personal universe" seems to become the metaphysical ground of what constitutes the human; and although particular values are necessarily contingent, value in general reflects an irreversible social process. Again it is possible to substitute one value for another, but not to disrupt the process of evaluation itself. There is no place in such a restricted economy for the thought of the incommensurate as a transgression of value, as a disruption of the frame that mediates the perception of words and things. This is not to say that such a disruption will bring about a "pure" unmediated perception but that the process of perception can be disordered from within, decentered or reversed. The effect of such a reversal would be what Lyotard calls "the forgotten" or what Derrida calls "the blank part of the text"—some event (narrowly textual or real) that escapes every category of experience and perception, every protocol of interpretation, and that can never be known directly through a representation except as the site of a failure of representation. The thought of the incommensurate derives from the recognition that the construction of value necessarily produces an alterity or otherness. Any reading that would reverse fixed value must foreground this alterity and then destroy its binary opposition to value through a deconstructive strategy, not only overturning value to show its dependence on the excluded other but displacing the other toward a more general economy, an economy that is really not an economy since it is no longer reducible to a system of predetermined meanings. As Derrida summarizes Bataille, a restricted economy, like phenomenology, is "limited to the meaning and established value of objects, and to their *circulation*." The general economy is arrived at not through the erasure of meaning but through a deconstruction of the opposition between meaning and nonmeaning: "General economy folds these horizons [of knowledge] and figures [of meaning] so that they will be related not to a basis, but to the nonbasis of expenditure, not to the *telos* of meaning, but to the *indefinite* destruction of value" (*Writing and Difference* 271). The general economy transforms the other of value into the "totally other" of the nonbinary relation between value and nonvalue, meaning and nonmeaning, life and death. What unravels these binary oppositions is symbolic exchange.

Baudrillard's concept bears some comparison with Claude Lévi-Strauss's somewhat fantastic theory of the origin of language in his *Introduction to the Work of Marcel Mauss*. In analyzing Mauss's theory of exchange, Lévi-Strauss insists that, despite Mauss's striving "to reconstruct a whole out of parts," his work implies that exchange, as a symbolic thought, must precede the individual "obligations of giving, receiving and returning" (47, 58). The reciprocity of gift giving is not reducible to the individual acts in themselves or to the implicit equivalence between the things exchanged. Reciprocal exchange surmounts "the contradiction of perceiving things as elements of a dialogue, in respect of self and others simultaneously, and destined by nature to pass from one to the other." Indeed, those very positions, self and other, must be understood as "derivative from the initial relational aspect." The unity of exchange can be read not as the total effect of its parts but as the whole of a discontinuous relational process. This reading leads to one of Lévi-Strauss's most difficult insights, his celebrated, though rarely analyzed comment that "whatever may have been the moment and the circumstances of its appearance in the ascent of animal life, language can only have arisen all at once." Ironically, though everything could only have become significant all at once, "it was none the better known for being so" (58–60).

If I am reading Lévi-Strauss correctly, it is not language as a complete system which arose all at once but the relation to the world as signifiable. Language existed as soon as the possibility of organizing sounds and things into signifying relations emerged. Although this emergence "must have hastened the rhythm of the development of knowledge," "there is a fundamental opposition, in the history of the human mind, between symbolism, which is characteristically discontinuous, and knowledge, characterized by continuity." The signifier and the signified were "constituted simultaneously and interdependently, as complementary units; whereas knowledge, that is, the intellectual process which enables us to identify certain aspects of the signifier with certain aspects of the signified . . . only got started very slowly." Lévi-Strauss tries to illustrate what he means by comparing the relation between the signified and its signifier to that between a domain and its detailed plan or map. Humankind has inherited both, along with some notion of the reciprocal relationship between the two, but it has taken millennia to identify "specific symbols" with "different aspects of the domain." Because "the universe signified the totality of what humankind can expect to know about it" from the beginning, though only in a potential form, scientific knowledge "could only have been and can only ever be constituted out of processes of correcting and recutting of patterns, regrouping, defining relationships of belonging and discovering new resources, inside a totality which is closed and complementary to itself" (60–61).

It may make more sense to revise Lévi-Strauss's remark slightly and say that it is not language that happened all at once but the symbolic, of which language is the most evident form. And the symbolic not as the formal code of a cultural system but rather as a purely material signifying potential. This symbolic, which has no absolute value or meaning, though it points toward the possibility of meaning, is "closed and complementary to itself" in the sense not that its potential for signification can ever be exhausted but that the material ground of signification is always finite. Nothing can be known that is not potentially knowable in a signifying relation, but that does not mean that the progress of knowledge can ever exhaust that relation since it must always exclude some aspect of the symbolic in order to constitute knowledge as an identifiable continuity between signifier and signified. As Lévi-Strauss suggests, the symbolic as a totality contradicts knowledge founded on the principle of reason. In the former, the difference between signifier and signified remains undecidable; in the latter that relation must be fixed. But as the works of Lacan and Derrida have demonstrated from different perspectives, when the difference between signifier and signified is shown to be undecidable, then the distinction itself collapses and the structure of signification is reversed. In other words, what arose all at once was *the signifier itself* (or what Derrida would call the arché-trace or a general writing), and this contains in itself all the possibilities of relations between signifiers, including that of the rational structure of signification. I am suggesting that Baudrillard's concept of exchange identifies the symbolic as the realm of a purely signifying potential marked by indeterminacy or, in his vocabulary, ambivalence. Symbolic exchange reverses knowledge as positive, rational value by destroying the final authority of univocal signification, the unity-in-difference of the signifier and the signified.

Refusing to limit symbolic exchange to so-called primitive formations, Baudrillard insists that a "radical utopian version [of such a relation] is beginning to explode slowly at all levels of our society" ("Symbolic Exchange and Death," *Selected Writings* 119). Utopia, in this discourse, is never about the future per se but about the effort to break the linearity of historical time. Baudrillard distinguishes utopian thought from "historical materialism" with its supposed separation of the present and the future. He calls for the abolition of this separation and of the Marxian dialectic that determines it. For "the idealists of the dialectic," he says, "the revolution must be distilled in history; it must come on time; it must ripen in the sun of the contradictions. That it could be there immediately is unthinkable and *insufferable*" (*Mirror of Production* 164–65). He rejects Marxism as the law of social change or rather as a theory of social change by the law. Such a theory is idealistic in grounding itself on the principle of reason and thus underwriting a codified version of reality, a unitary reality that puts an end to the struggle for the definition and representation of the "real." Still, it seems to me that Marx the prophet of social change need not be rejected. Insofar as he speaks out against a particular historical closure, his word possesses precisely those characteristics of the utopian that Baudrillard identifies: "Utopia wants speech against power and against the reality principle which is only the phantasm of the system and its indefinite reproduction" (*Mirror of Production* 167). In order to attain this perspective on Marx, it is necessary to read him not as the scientist of capital but as a social revolutionary who wields theory in a struggle against hegemonic culture. His work must be read not as a finished system but as a process without a determinate end. The same is also true of Baudrillard whose critique of historical materialism must be situated in the struggle against a version of Marxism that allies itself with the order of "systematic value" and the pursuit of positive knowledge. For it is curious that what Baudrillard calls historical materialism and then rejects resembles what Walter Benjamin more properly calls historicism. Benjamin criticizes historicism in a language that resembles Baudrillard's and then posits a rather different notion of historical materialism, one possessing some of the characteristics of Baudrillard's utopia. In his "Theses on the Philosophy of History," Benjamin remarks,

> Historicism contents itself with establishing a causal connection between various moments in history. But no fact that is a cause is for that very reason historical. It became historical posthumously, as it were, through events that may be separated from it by thousands of years. A historian who takes this as his point of departure stops telling the sequence of events like the beads of a rosary. Instead, he grasps the constellation which his own era has formed with a definite earlier one. Thus he establishes a conception of the present as the "time of the now" which is shot through with chips of Messianic time. (*Illuminations* 263)

Messianic time is the time of utopia. It takes the "time of the now" and riddles it with the light of total history. It abolishes the temporal demarcations of reason and figures the past, present, and future in a single constellation. It explodes the linearity of rational time and subverts the process of social reproduction by calling into question the systems of value and finalities that constitute normative reality. "Total history," as I use it here, is neither the salvational history of Christianity nor the Hegelian or Marxist historical closures of absolute knowledge or communism. It is what, according to Baudrillard, poetry and utopian revolt have in common: "this actualization of desire no longer relegated to a future liberation, but demanded here, immediately, even in its death throes, in the extreme situation of life and death" (*Mirror of Production* 165). Thus, total history is not the completed form of history but the messianic form it takes in the moment of struggle. It is a question not of factual truth but of the lived relation to the present through some representation of the past. Significant social change would never take place without the lived sense of total history, the immediacy of past and future in the present, the reversal of the structure of value. In revolt, revolutionary subjects take back the value they have given or invested in the system, sacrifice themselves rather than submit to another exchange in the economic market, destroy what they have produced as a form of reappropriation, and aim at deriving a new life from the risk of death. Time is reversed when its value as progress is undone. (And for this reason, the eruption of messianic time never guarantees a desired political result or a necessarily progressive change. It always involves an absolute risk with the possibility of failure.)

Baudrillard links what he calls poetry to the utopian revolt. He correlates the system of social values with the system of linguistic values and then posits the extermination of value by utopian speech or poetry. This kind of thinking tends to idealize the poetic act as if it somehow transcended social determinations. It can become a form of nostalgia. The word "extermination," in addition to the connotations it carries in the post-Holocaust world, creates the temporal illusion of a time and place beyond value, which ironically assumes value as the end of value. This thought ultimately leads to a vicious circle. Nevertheless, it is possible to recognize in language a tendency toward the disruption of any simplified connection between the signifier and the signified (the paradigmatic level) or between signifiers (the syntagmatic level). Poetry could be said to feature such a disruptive tendency insofar as it explores what Paul de Man calls the rhetorical dimension of language. Such writing, however, is always subject to co-optation by aesthetic systems—precisely those systems of value that transform writing into literature. In the language of poetry, according to Baudrillard, nothing remains as value or meaning. For this reason, it "is opposed to linguistic discourse [the object contructed by linguistics—ordinary language or normal language use], which is a process of accumulation, production, and distribution of language as value" (*L'échange symbolique* 289). Again, this formula oversimplies, though it points in the right direction. Poetry could be considered the site of a contradiction between two tendencies within language, one aimed at the effacement of the material trace before the transparency of meaning, the other aimed at the destruction (or *deconstruction*) of transparent meaning through the foregrounding of language's irreducible play or suspended closure. This contradiction has assumed different forms in different critical discourses. For de Man, it appears as the difference between the rhetorical and cognitive dimensions of language; for Roman Jakobson, between the metaphoric and metonymic poles. One could speculate that literature as an institution had to be invented in order to contain these two poles. Literary autonomy, *as a European ideology*, aims at resolving the contradiction between form and content in discourse, a contradiction that emerged during the seventeenth century and was exacerbated thereafter by the rise of competing ideologies and class conflicts. It doesn't matter if literature is functional, referential, or formalist, as long as its effects are produced in a privileged domain, autonomous and separate from society, which it may mirror or criticize but never transform. Baudrillard may have a point, therefore, in casting suspicion on such linguists as Jakobson who have gone to great lengths to contain poetic language within the domain of linguistic description. Such work pinpoints, perhaps, the resistance of linguistics to the danger "in the simple formulation of another possible operation of language" (*L'échange symbolique* 289). Still, Baudrillard does not pay much attention to the institutional context of poetic production and consumption. What exactly is poetry when it is not framed by the institutions and hierarchies of culture? Does any linguistic act, poetic or otherwise, ever completely escape the determinations of value in a world as overdetermined as Baudrillard himself claims ours to be? His answers to and evasions of these questions help to elucidate the contradiction within language itself.

"The poetic," he writes, "is the insurrection of language against its own laws" (*L'échange symbolique* 289). This is well and good, but poetry has *its* laws, *its* hierarchies, and *its* values. Baudrillard suggests that poetic language "does not aim at the production of signifieds, but at the conscientious consumption, the cyclical resolution of a material signifier." It transforms the restricted economy of everyday language into the general economy of a language without reserve or remainder (the excluded other), without a structure of value that can govern the proliferation of meanings and avoid the excess that opens a relation to nonmeaning. The poetic signifier folds back on and doubles itself in an act of self-consumption, which, according to Baudrillard, "is the same movement as the gift and countergift, giving and rendering back, a reciprocity in which the exchange-value and the use-value of the object are abolished." Nevertheless, by unbinding the laws of equivalence and linearity on which "normal" language use is based, Baudrillard's "poetic signifier" destroys the opposition between literal and figurative language on which *poetry as an institution* is founded. It produces the effect "microscopically on the value/phoneme" which social revolution produces on the whole structural code of value (*L'échange symbolique* 297). Baudrillard's thinking here recalls Julia Kristeva's theorization of the revolution in poetic language. He remarks that her work comes close to a recognition of the form of the poetic, but he rejects what he calls "the superstition of a 'materialist production' of meaning" (*L'échange symbolique* 317). From this perspective, meaning is "the effect of infrastructural signification linked to the play of distinctive unities, of the minimal elements of discourse—but there again taken as positive valences (just as atoms and molecules have an elementary valence)" (*L'échange symbolique* 315). As soon as one defines it as a minimal substance, Baudrillard claims, the phoneme becomes a category of the ideal. Nevertheless, Kristeva articulates the fundamental *ambi-valence* of poetic language when she claims that it destabilizes value by dissolving the division between the concrete and the general, existence and nonexistence. Poetry calls into question the principle of reason on which every post-Enlightenment system of value bases itself. As Kristeva explains, "We know that what poetic language enunciates is *not* (in terms of the logic of the spoken word), but we accept the being of this non-being" (*Semeiotiké* 193). Baudrillard summarizes and draws out the implications of her thought:

> She poses the *ambivalence* of the poetic signified (and not the simple ambiguity). . . . Bivalent logic, that of discourse, reposes on the negation internal to the judgment, it founds the concept and its equivalence to itself (the signified is what it is). The negativity of the poetic is a radical negativity that *supersedes the logic of the judgment itself*. Something "is" and is not what it is: utopia (in the literal sense) of the signified. The equivalence of the thing to itself (and of the subject also, to be sure) is volatilized. (*L'échange symbolique* 317)

The ambivalence at the core of the poetic signified exceeds the common notion of ambiguity, which simply pluralizes an otherwise stable relation between the signifier and its signified. The signifier is linked to its multiple signifieds through the normal logic of linguistic value. Ambivalence, on the contrary, more closely resembles what Derrida calls dissemination, in which "there is no thematic unity or overall meaning to reappropriate beyond the textual instances, no total message located in some imaginary order, intentionality, or lived experience" (*Dissemination* 262). We can expand on this position by refusing to restrict *ambivalence* exclusively to poetic language (Derrida does not restrict *dissemination*, though his examples are usually from poetic and other literary texts). Rather, it destabilizes normal language, or what Baudrillard calls in his early work the political economy of the sign, and makes possible *a relation to language as open and indeterminate process*. In "normal" language, the logic of the commodity, which articulates the law of value as the reductive equivalence between the use and exchange values of an object, inscribes itself within the sign as the form of its rationality. The sign "structures itself through exclusion," shearing away "the virtualities of meaning," in order to proffer itself "as full value: positive, rational, exchangeable value." Ambivalence reverses this structure. It is the utopia of the sign—but only when it is understood as "a *rupture* of value, of another side or beyond of sign value, and as the *emergence of the symbolic*" (*Political Economy of the Sign* 149–50). This emergence involves a shift in the human relation to language and culture—a shift, as I will argue later, from the hegemony of reason and the sign toward what Lacan calls the big Other. Of course, the danger in Baudrillard's thought lies in its imagining this other side or beyond of value as a place, when it is only a figure for the disfigurative power of language, its tendency toward self-subversion. Baudrillard criticizes the topographical metaphors underpinning the Kristevan theory of intertextuality and specifically warns against reading the poetic effect as deriving from an "added erotic value, a play of additional phantasms, or from any metaphorical or metonymical value" (*L'échange symbolique* 317). Utopia is not another place or set of alternative values but the negation of place. It is not beyond the sign in the sense of preserving the sign as a position for which it is the op-position. Utopia is nowhere. It has no place in the order of things, in the hierarchies of value.

Ironically, Baudrillard's privileging of poetry as the site of symbolic exchange replicates the very structure he criticizes in Kristeva. If utopia is neither in nor out of the system, then how can it be situated exclusively in poetry? Such an effect of poetry is possible, and for historical reasons may even be inevitable, but it is important to remember that such terms as "poetry," "literature," and "art" carry heavy burdens of value in the tradition of Western aesthetics. In order to clarify the different tendencies in poetic language, it might be useful, in this context, to distinguish between poetry as an object and poetry as an irreducible set of effects. Any work of art—sculpture, painting, poetry, fiction, it doesn't matter— is imbued with value insofar as it is constituted as the object of an aesthetic judgment. It has been one of the traditional functions of criticism to make such judgments and to construct art objects through the authority of the aesthetic gaze. This is to say not that criticism creates art but that the aesthetic disposition fundamental to criticism and to artistic production reduces the ambivalence of the work, whose effects are indeterminate and interminable, to the "unique" value of the art object. Again, the object may be polyvalent or polysemic; but as long as it is reducible to a code of values, in this case the aesthetic code, it escapes the ambivalence of the work. Such a reduction is fundamental to the perception of art as "art," poetry as "poetry," literature as "literature." As Pierre Bourdieu remarks, "The 'pure' [aesthetic] gaze is a historical invention linked to the emergence of an autonomous field of artistic production, that is, a field capable of imposing its own norms on both the production and the consumption of its products" (3).

Bourdieu links the historical construction of the "aesthetic gaze" to the primary distinction between form and function. He says, "To assert the autonomy of production is to give primacy to that of which the artist is master, i.e., form, manner, style, rather than the 'subject,' the external referent, which involves subordination to functions—even if only the most elementary one, that of representing, signifying, saying something" (3). This statement implies that artistic value is rooted in the formalism of the artist, in the autonomy of his or her position as a creating subject who privileges the instruments of creativity—form, manner, style—over any particular reference or subject matter. Bourdieu takes for granted, it seems to me, the separation between subject and object on which any concept of the "unique" art object must be founded. If one accepts that separation as the necessary condition for perceiving art, it does not matter whether art or literature is functionalist or formalist as long as it is perceived through the aesthetic gaze, that is, as long as its value is rooted in the autonomy of the subject—that of either the artist or the critic. This subject expresses its value-making authority through its claim to the power of discrimination or "taste." According to Bourdieu, "Taste is the practical operator of the transmutation of things into distinct and distinctive signs, of continuous distributions into discontinuous oppositions; it raises the differences inscribed in the physical order of bodies to the symbolic order of significant distinctions" (174–75). The symbolic order in this context is not the symbolic as Baudrillard uses the term. It refers to the symbolic insofar as it has been sectioned off and organized into a system of values. Taste as a power of discrimination is usually ascribed to some natural gift even when it has been openly inculcated by programs of education. The historical origins of taste, however, must be related to the dynamics of class domination and class struggle: "'Distinction,' or better, 'class,' the transfigured, misrecognized, legitimate form of social class, only exists through the struggles for the exclusive appropriation of the distinctive signs which make 'natural distinction'" (Bourdieu 250). As the mystified form of the dominant system of values, taste transmutes incommensurable "things" into "distinct and distinctive signs," thus incorporating the incommensurate into the structure of value. In this context, it is perhaps misleading to speak of the "dominant" system of values, since the structure of value is inherently hegemonic and expands its empire every time one class or class fraction competes with another for the signs of distinction. In hegemony, all the classes play by the same rules and compete for the same values, although some are structurally (and economically) disabled from winning the game (see Gramsci 211–12).

A work of art can say something or nothing; or, more likely, if one thinks of a work such as *Finnegans Wake*, it can say something and nothing by radically exploiting the potential for ambivalence in language. In either case, its constitution as an art object, the repository of value, is determined not by its formal properties or the intrinsic nature of its language (although these can become factors in the struggle for artistic distinction) but by the structure of value expressed in the social judgment of taste. The work becomes an object for a subject. Just as science constitutes the object of its knowledge by reducing the multiple effects of phenomena to positive, rational values, criticism, in the traditional sense, constitutes the art object by shearing away the plurality of poetic effects in the construction of a "distinctive sign." Such a sign, as Bourdieu suggests, eradicates "continuous distributions," or what Baudrillard would call symbolic exchange, with "discontinuous oppositions." Even such a work as *Finnegans Wake*, despite its radical indeterminacy (which has persuaded some critics of its unreadability), becomes a distinctive sign of artistic power. As Joyce himself suggested, it signifies the power of the artist to do anything with language. Still, although the field of artistic production imposes its norms on both the production and consumption of objects, it can never fully master all the poetic effects; otherwise, art production itself would come to a standstill as the struggle for distinction collapsed in the absence of any new grounds for the construction of hierarchies.

By implication, a work of art can be analyzed in two ways: both as an object and as a process. As an object, it is the repository of aesthetic value; as a process, it is a series of effects which is not reducible to any global principle or law. Aesthetic criticism resembles what Baudrillard would call scientific analysis in that it accumulates value by subsuming the work of art within the traditional aesthetic systems. Through its strategies of classification, it reduces the plenitude of effects to a form of objectivity. Baudrillard, however, does not see this as the true form of analysis:

> Opposed to science as a process of accumulation, the true *analytical* operation is the one *which destroys its object*, which defeats it. The end of analysis—not its "constructive" finality, but its actual termination— is this volatilization of its object and of its own concepts, or even the displacement of the subject which, far from seeking to master its object, agrees in exchange to be analyzed by it, a gesture through which the respective positions of the one and the other are undone.

In this formulation, analysis destroys the separation between subject and object, while science "is bound to the construction of its object (and, at the same time, to the phantasmatic reproduction of the subject of knowledge)" (*L'échange symbolique* 297–98).

Criticism as a form of judgment is bound to the same phantasm of value. It reproduces value through the preservation of the canon and by propagating an understanding of literature and art grounded in selective tradition. As T. S. Eliot expressed it, "No poet, no artist of any art, has his complete meaning alone. His significance, his appreciation is the appreciation of his relation to the dead poets and artists. You cannot value him alone; you must set him, for contrast and comparison, among the dead" (4). From this perspective, every new work produces an effect (or, more accurately, a set of effects) that destabilizes the order or system of values; and it is the function of criticism to restore stability to the object—not just the individual work but the tradition itself—by translating the outlaw effect back into the code. Eliot understood perfectly well that what is at stake in the history of literature is not the value of this or that individual work, which may go up or down according to the pressures of the literary marketplace. It is the code (what Eliot calls the ideal order of existing monuments) that must be preserved with each new development in the field of artistic production. With the introduction of a new work of art into the system, "the relations, proportions, values of each work of art towards the whole are readjusted; and this is conformity between the old and the new" (5). From this perspective, the function of criticism is to expand the territory of the code—constantly to readjust the relations, proportions, and values of each work, so that the code remains stable and primary for the perception of art. The critic is a judge (the Greek root of the word *critic* means "a judge"). As Raymond Williams stresses, even though historically the critic's pretensions to authority have frequently been suspect, the "association between *criticism* and judgment as apparently general and natural processes" remains unchallenged (*Keywords* 76). Baudrillard's notion of the poetic as symbolic exchange is meant to call this assumption into question:

> The poetic is the restoration of symbolic exchange into the very heart of words. While, in the discourse of signification, words, all finalized as to meaning, do not respond to each other, do not speak to each other . . . , in the poetic, once the agency of sense is broken, all the constitutive elements start to exchange with one another and respond to one another. . . .
>
> The simple possibility of this is a revolution with respect to an order in which nothing and no one, neither words nor men, neither their bodies nor their gazes, are allowed to communicate directly, but rather must transit as values through the models which engender and reproduce them in total strangeness to one another... The revolution is everywhere where there emerges an exchange breaking the finality of models, the mediation of the code, and the consecutive cycle of value—whether this exchange is that infinitesimal one between phonemes and syllables in a poetic text, or that of thousands of men who speak to each other in an insurrectionary town. . . . [T]he revolution is symbolic, or it isn't. (*L'échange symbolique* 298–99)

Despite the nostalgia in Baudrillard's opposing "direct" communication to the "strangeness" of values and models, his analysis uncovers or foregrounds a necessary condition of any social change. For Baudrillard, all revolutions are cultural revolutions, since it is impossible to draw absolute lines between the social and the symbolic. Transforming an economic system necessarily requires transforming the symbolic order as constituted by the system of values that organizes every aspect of social life from the factory to the amusement park. It means transforming language as a social tie. Baudrillard's concept of the "poetic effect" directly opposes the poetic object; it blocks the agency of sense, or the law of value rooted in the production of meaning, so that, for a moment, tradition is ruptured, the code is silenced, and the word has no place in the system. This effect is utopia, nowhere. It takes place in the "time of the now," messianic time. And for this reason, because it takes place not outside the structure of value but through its annulment or reversal, it cannot be reduced to "poetry" in itself. Poetry may foreground symbolic exchange through its release of the signifier, but it is also constantly subjected to the institutional pressure of critical judgment. This pressure does not come to poetry only from the outside, from the writings of literary critics and university professors; it can emerge from within the poem, insofar as the poem becomes a criticism of itself and tries to subordinate or classify its own symbolic function. Yet a poem can also work self-consciously against critical judgment, against poetry's tendency toward aesthetic objectification.

Hart Crane's final poem, "The Broken Tower," illustrates both tendencies of human language in such a way that the tension between disruptive effect and determinate meaning is pushed as far as it will go without the one destroying the other. Consider stanza 3:

> The bells, I say, the bells break down their tower;
> And swing I know not where. Their tongues engrave
> Membrane through marrow, my long-scattered score
> Of broken intervals... And I, their sexton slave!
> (193, further references by line)

The bells break down their tower just as the poetic signifier breaks down or deconstructs formal signification, the structure of equivalence. The surface or rhetorical dimension of language swings or traces the path of ambivalence, "I know not where." From this point on, the logical connection between signifiers along the syntagmatic chain begins to loosen. The words "tongue," "engrave," "membrane," and "marrow" enter into a series of symbolic exchanges that cannot be subordinated to any unitary principle or rule, any order of value. It is not that these words cannot be shown to have semantic connections to one another but that those connections cannot be reduced to a hierarchy that would offer a definitive set of meanings. The shift from the assertive "I" to the possessive pronoun "my" before the phrase "long-scattered score / Of broken intervals" decenters the speaking subject, which merges with the object of its seeing and hearing. Ironically, this interpenetration of self and other is immediately broken by the ellipses, which lead to a reconstitution of self, only this time situated in a different relation to the object: "And I, their sexton slave!" The subject's authority is reversed: rather than the bells' being constituted by the eye and ear of the subject, it is the other way around; the subject is the effect of the other, of what is heard and seen. These rhetorical gestures decenter the subject just enough to call its autonomy into question. As Lee Edelman stresses, for Crane "the subject matter of a poem . . . frequently offers a displaced or allegorical interpretation of the rhetorical processes through which both the poem and the poet's subjectivity are constituted." However, he continues, "for Crane as for Lacan that identity is necessarily founded in division" (262–64).

The next stanza pushes the centrifugal force of the signifier even further:

> Oval encyclicals in canyons heaping
> The impasse high with choir. Banked voices slain!
> Pagodas, campaniles with reveilles outleaping—
> O terraced echoes prostrate on the plain!...
>
> (ll. 13–16)

Although it is always possible to translate the linguistic ambivalence of "oval encyclicals" back into some version of a naturalistic perception, this work of translation, the necessity for conscious reduction, paring away those effects that will not easily enter into another language, calls attention to the irreducibility of the poetic effect in question. Because the subject is only one effect among others in the "score of broken intervals," it cannot give absolute ground to the object of representation, making it not quite possible to draw equivalences between canyons and walls, impasse and dead-end street, "banked voices slain" and the echoing resonance of the bells. Are the "terraced echoes prostrate on the plain" the dying sounds of the bells, or just words in a tonal arrangement? The crucial figure here, as Edelman notes, is catachresis—a rhetorically suggestive imprecision of language. Ironically, "The bell-rope that gathers God at dawn / Dispatches" (ll. 1–2) Crane to a world in which words never quite reach their referents, though the suggestiveness of their relational play seems almost unlimited. Edelman argues that "the 'antiphonal carillons' [l. 7] that dismantle the tower also 'engrave' the poet's text; his own tongue thus shares the antithetical force that refuses to accept either transcendental claims of divinity or aspirations toward metaphysical unity" (268–69). For Edelman, Crane seems to anticipate Derrida's critique of the metaphysics of presence; but this may be too narrow or too abstract a description of the poem's intentional structure. Thomas Yingling offers a more effective analysis of Crane's work in general when he insists on a reading that takes into account Crane's formation as a homosexual subject. In an attempt to explain Crane's style, he notes that "a rhetoric of metonymic desire and misrecognition, of catachresis or misnaming, is relevant to the figuring of homosexual relation in a way that a more conventional poetics of metaphor, memory, and transcendental transformation would not be" (40–41). Yingling is not suggesting, however, that Crane's poetry is governed solely by the drive toward self-representation or by the resistance to a dominant ideology of art. On the contrary, his attitude toward art as an institution, like his attitude toward his own sexuality, is ambivalent and contradictory.

The fifth stanza of "The Broken Tower," for example, brings us back to a form of logical closure:

> And so it was I entered the broken world
> To trace the visionary company of love, its voice
> An instant in the wind (I know not whither hurled)
> But not for long to hold each desperate choice.
>
> (ll. 17–20)

The subject of the poem's opening returns, using the past tense to place or situate the ambivalence of stanzas 3 and 4 in a critically determining framework: "so it was I entered the broken world / To trace the visionary company of love." But is this the same subject or a reversal of the subject of the present tense which governs the first four stanzas of the poem? Is "the visionary company" the great tradition of romantic poetry or a mockery of tradition, an annulment of its authority, reducing it to an "instant in the wind" evading the "desperate choice" of critical judgment? In the seventh stanza, the past tense is transmuted back into the present as the poet fails to find in himself (in the "steep encroachments of my blood" [l. 25]) the answer to his question as to whether his word is "cognate" (l. 21) with the "crystal Word" (l. 24), the source of logocentric authority. (I will return to this point.) Out of this failure comes the hesitant thought that human limitations or "sweet mortality," which he genders as the feminine "she," may stir "latent power" (l. 27). A human vision is one rooted not in the transcendental but in the physical, material world. The speaker hears in his own pulse "The Angelus of wars my chest evokes: / What I hold healed, original now, and pure" (ll. 31–32). For Crane, the only originality, the only true value, must lie in the subject's reconciliation with its own mortality, in a symbolic exchange with death.

This subject in the "time of the now" transforms its own fragmented being into "a tower that is not stone / (Not stone can jacket heaven)—but slip / of pebbles" (ll. 33–35). He has, in effect, feminized the broken tower, remade the phallus into a womb or a vagina that can "jacket," that is, cover and contain without being subsumed by the heaven of phallocentric desire.

Perhaps, as Edelman stresses, "Crane chooses materiality and difference over metaphysical reconciliations," finding the origin of poetry in the "matrix of the heart" (270). But the words that frame the "matrix" figure suggest a more problematic reading: "visible wings of silence sown / In azure circles, widening as they dip / The matrix of the heart, lift down the eye / That shrines the quiet lake and swells a tower" (ll. 35–38). The power of dissemination in language is confronted as a form of "silence" (or nonmeaning), ultimately a signifier of death. If the word "eye" can be read as a pun, its being lifted down by the silence of the signifier entails a dismantling of the relationship between the subject and its world of objects, including nature and the human-made tower constructed or "shrined" by its gaze. This reversal of subjective authority and value, then, makes possible the final utopian figure of a "world without a self," in Woolf's phrase, or a world of difference: "The commodious, tall decorum of that sky / Unseals her earth, and lifts love in its shower" (ll. 39–40). Edelman reads the "disseminative ejaculation" of this last line as a "radical trope of originality":

> The ejaculatory scattering of this erotic 'shower' is performed under the aegis of the male and the female both. The 'tall' and apparently 'masculine' sky has been inverted here, opened and invaginated in order to render it 'commodious,' and its generative 'shower' rises from the feminine 'earth' that it 'unseals.' Such a 'shower' is more properly understood, then, as a fountain or spring, which is to say that it figures a 'literal' origin or source. (271)

Though I agree that the poem deconstructs its own quest for origins (including the origin of sexual difference), I am not sure that Edelman's reading does anything more than resituate or even mask the original subject behind the fountain of dissemination, which sounds suspiciously like Coleridge's fountain of imagination. At the same time, I cannot fully accept Yingling's reading, though I find it more appealing, that Crane is turning to "a healing female presence" (which would be based on his actual relationship with Peggy Baird at the time of writing) as a confession of the failure of his homosexual life (182–83). There is a another contradiction in this poem which would undermine any desire for a return to origins.

"The Broken Tower" subverts its own poetic ideology—that is, the implicit knowledge of its status as a poem or an object of literary value— through the revelation of its language *as language*, as the incomplete body of history. In stanza 6, which mirrors the "broken world" of stanza 5 without displacing it, Crane's "word" breaks down in the very act of totalizing its truth:

> My word I poured. But was it cognate, scored
> Of that tribunal monarch of the air
> Whose thigh embronzes earth, strikes crystal Word
> In wounds pledged once to hope—cleft to despair?
> (ll. 21–24)

Crane's poem calls into question its own derivation from a creative total- ity, the Word that engenders all words, or the logos. Implicitly, by failing to transcend the "broken world," since the logic of the question itself makes it impossible to do so, the poem criticizes the dominant ideology of poetic production since the Romantics. Joseph Riddel finally makes more sense than Edelman when he suggests that for Crane, "there is ultimately no resolution: neither the broken world nor the pure world he envisions is convincingly real for him, and hence no reconciliation of the two suffices, even were it possible" (495). The Derridean moment in Crane's poem lies not in the metaphor of the earth's shower but in the syntactical slippage that undermines the question it insists on posing. Is the word he pours cognate, he asks—that is, is it one with the paternal logos that gives foundation to language as value, that makes it legitimate and true, creative and eternal? Does it have a father? "Only a power of speech can have a father," as Derrida stresses in his reading of Plato; and so Crane's question is not just about whether his language is divinely or imaginatively inspired but about whether it is "living" speech or merely writing, a collection of dead letters. Derrida writes:

> Even though this hearth is the heart of all metaphoricity, "father of
> logos" is not a simple metaphor. To have simple metaphoricity, one
> would have to make the statement that some living creature incapable
> of language, if anyone still wished to believe in such a thing, has a
> father. One must thus proceed to undertake a general reversal of all

metaphorical directions, no longer asking whether *logos* can have a father but understanding that what the father claims to be the father of cannot go without the essential possibility of *logos*. (*Dissemination* 81)

Derrida's reading of Plato bridges the gap between his own postromantic and late capitalist historical position *and* the foundations of Western culture in Greek philosophy. To the extent that Plato still authorizes our discourses by representing a tradition without which we could not determine the value of our culture (both in its concepts of the good and in its cultural goods), no discourse can be produced that does not take into account, or as Derrida would say, has not invested in or is not indebted to, Plato's discourse. By reading Plato anachronistically, that is to say, by reading his word, his logos, not only as embedded in its own historical context but as a function of our historical present, Derrida subjects the past itself, the historical tradition, to a reversal. Only in the world of capitalist rationalization, where even Plato is just one more commodity, does it become possible to overturn his authority, to annul the logic of the logos, by disclosing the incommensurate within the logos, in the household, so to speak. Derrida defamiliarizes the familiarity of Plato's word, destroys the separation between metaphor and literal meaning, and discloses the incommensurable relation of the logos to itself. Plato's word, his writing of the logos, *insofar as it is writing*, has no father because it contains the father in its internal structure of signification. As soon as the bar separating truth and metaphor is removed, it becomes impossible to determine the value of the logos, to save it from ambivalence. It is both the father and the parricide, speech and writing, truth and metaphor, life and death, and so forth.

In a similar gesture, Crane's poem questions the authority of his word, asking if it was "scored / Of that tribunal monarch of the air." The question, of course, cannot be answered because it is overtaken by its own ambivalence. The verb "strikes," predicated of the "tribunal monarch," bears all the force of this ambivalence, at once signifying violation and harmony, rupture and creative participation; and this ambivalence carries over into the next line, where the object of this striking, the "crystal Word," or logos, is linked to the "Word made flesh" through the "wounds pledged once to hope—cleft to despair." The creative word is both the faithful son and the parricide, both our salvation and our despair. In other words, Crane's poetry cannot assure itself of its own paternity, of its sexual identity, of the truth of its origins, or of its value within the system of poetic values, which includes the ideology of poetic genius and the literary imagination. The effect of Crane's poem, and of his poetry in general, is not to create visionary *objects* of perception but to deconstruct the object, to deconstruct the order of value by disclosing the contradiction at the heart of the romantic project. Riddel's notion of the "poetics of failure" comes close to what I want to say, though perhaps for completely different reasons. In Crane's poetry, he remarks, "not only is the self betrayed, the poetic method is betrayed; or better, it betrays itself at every turn." For Riddel, this betrayal means that Crane, with his longing to transcend the "broken world," must constantly repurify language, that is, renew it; and the fatality of this process, its perpetual failure, "finally becomes the poet's onus" (495) But as Yingling would insist, it also becomes the poet's challenge to a traditional aesthetic—in this case, the transcendental heritage of American poetry. "If the heterosexual discourse of Thoreau and Emerson," writes Yingling, "is an *in*semination of the father's word, Crane's discourse and the homosexual discourse it more generally indicates is a *dis*semination; Crane replaces the clear syntax of insight with one that is opaque" (151–52). Crane's failure is a challenge to the traditional concept of the poetic object, to Eliot's ideal order of existing monuments, and to the normative concept of artistic value that links the production of art to a specific sexual identity. The disseminated text is "unruly": "It shoots its mouth off, so to speak, as well as shooting off from other parts of its body, so (in order) to speak" (Yingling 152). Irreducible to the code of poetic values, the only effect Crane's poem can have is incommensurable.

In overturning the structure of poetic value, Crane's poem is constituted as an event and articulates what Jerome McGann calls "knowledge through the incommensurate." As McGann speculates, "at the dawning of the incommensurate we come to understand that the human world is not made up of 'facts' and/or 'interpretations,' it is made up of *events*—specific and worlded engagements in which meaning is rendered and used. Poetic work locates one type of event. Its special function is to display the eventuality of meaning through representations of the incommensurable." McGann's insight needs to be qualified when it refers to the "structure of knowledge through incommensurability" (72). The word "structure" carries the presupposition of a position for the knowing subject which I believe goes against the grain of event as the incommensurate. Where there is structure, the subject still has a stable place, a view from the outside. The word I have been using, "effect," bears a similar burden of contradiction, since it is usually thought of as bound to a cause or to a structure of causality. I am suggesting, however, that what we call an effect resembles what Freud called a symptom, and that before we can speak of its structure of causality or determination we have to take a step backward through a process of secondary revision. In this process a structure of causality is elaborated and the effect inserted into it. Before that act of construction, the effect is nowhere: it is an event. The world is not made up of facts or interpretations, because these are the products of secondary revision, that is, *systems* of meaning and value. It is made up of events, through which "meaning is rendered and used." I would draw out the implications of this statement by saying that meaning is rendered *back* and used *up*: it is brought back to its status as an event or one more irreducible effect. This brings us to what McGann calls

> the context in which we are to understand the idea of the "incommensurate" in poetry and art—the "irrelevant detail," the "accidentalities," all those arresting particulars of fact, language, text, and event which seem to escape both the ideologies of the works themselves as well as the ideologies of criticism. . . . Accidentalities and incommensurates in art localize this permanent discontinuity between "the consciousness" of the poetical work and its complete if unrealized self-understanding.

McGann, like Baudrillard, still idealizes poetry as a genre by implicitly identifying it as the privileged place of the incommensurate. Nevertheless, poetry has this effect whenever it suggests a relation to language and art which ruptures critical ideologies, whether they are embodied in the work itself or in the critical reading. The incommensurate raises the specter of messianic time, which it cannot simply represent. In the passage just quoted, McGann defines the aim of poetry as establishing "a holistic and totalizing act of representation." Since representation belongs to the order of value, however, in that it gives determinate form to irreducible differences, it seems to contradict the incommensurate as event. The incommensurate actually manifests total history as the "time of the now," and its value is indeterminate because it calls all systems of value (and of representation) into question. McGann suggests as much himself in saying that the "project or purpose [of poetry] can be achieved only in the dynamic condition of the work itself—which is to say that it must look to have, like the human life it reflects, an *actual* rather than a conceptual fulfillment, a completion in the continuous deed and event which is the poetic work" (129). As the reflection metaphor implies, McGann has difficulty thinking beyond the concept of representation. Perhaps it makes more sense to say, after Wittgenstein, that poetry is not a reflection but a *form of life*, a language game. It is not a closed system but an open process that can always generate new rules through practice. The "continuous deed and event" of poetry as a symbolic act subverts the longing for totality as a closed form by bringing history and all its determining forces into the present. History becomes a process without a telos, as Louis Althusser would say (162). The knowledge poetry conveys through its effects—not through its status as an art object—is not scientific or objective knowledge but rather knowledge as revelation, as event.

Hart Crane's "Broken Tower" conveys this sort of knowledge—not of totality in a completed form but of totality as the interminable process of completion. It emerges not out of the "mind of the artist" (that stable entity) but out of the contradiction between the poem's consciousness of itself as poetry and "its complete if unrealized self-understanding," that is, its implicit understanding of itself as a finite process, a "broken world." It is the difference between its self-conception as value and its self-analysis as symbolic exchange. Beyond value the poem articulates the paradoxical knowledge that it is not about a tower or about Crane—that it is not *about* anything. (Though, I do not mean that it is an autonomous object completely detached from the historical and sexual formation of the subject who writes it.) It accentuates this effect through its failure to control it—to codify it. Still, one could argue that this kind of effect could also emerge from the reading of a poem such as Yeats's "Tower," which clearly is about a tower. Such a reading would constitute not a critical judgment but the reversal of such judgment, attempting to open the objectivity of the work to the process of symbolic exchange. It deconstructs judgment through an analysis that destroys the hierarchy or metaphysical gap between subject and object. Crane's poetry performs this analysis for itself and thus bridges the separation between criticism and poetry, between poetry and writing. In Riddel's words, methodologically, "it betrays itself at every turn." Crane's poetry ceases to be "poetry" precisely where the poetic effect overtakes and destroys the aesthetic laws that would delimit the poem's meaning or meanings and determine its value. It becomes criticism not as judgment but as analysis—*criticism as symbolic exchange.*

2

Faulkner's Letter

There are some things which happen to us which the intelligence and the senses refuse just as the stomach sometimes refuses what the palate has accepted but which digestion cannot compass—occurrences which stop us dead as though by some impalpable intervention, like a sheet of glass through which we watch all subsequent events transpire as though in a soundless vacuum, and fade, vanish; are gone, leaving us immobile, impotent, helpless; fixed, until we can die.

—WILLIAM FAULKNER, *Absalom, Absalom!*

Writing sometimes has the force to "stop us dead as though by some impalpable intervention." As the words of Rosa Coldfield in Faulkner's *Absalom, Absalom!* suggest, in such a moment we see the world as through a glass, as something other. When language becomes an end in itself beyond the aesthetic dimension (we are not talking here about beautiful style), it ceases to support reality as a stable entity, an object of representation. Reality gives way to the "broken world," to what Lacan calls *the real*. Curiously, in refusing the completion of signification, language gives rise to desire and the longing for totality, even if that totality must take the form of death. Such desire, for both death and utopia, animates the modernist narrative.

Fredric Jameson, in rethinking the Lukácsian concept of totality, paraphrases Sartre's *What Is Literature?* on the subject of what constitutes the ordinary reader's sense of completeness in narrative: "Social class provides a readership with boundaries of *familiarity*, with a ready tolerance for all the things and realities which do not have to be said (and which can therefore be ignored), with some properly ideological sense of when a given act or experience grasped within our own class perspective is felt to be 'complete' and to 'need no further explanation.'" He then posits in opposition to this ideological sense of completeness the *"aspiration to totality,"* which

> would then in the narrative realm involve a refusal of these habitual limits and boundaries and even a defamiliarization of our habitual sense of the recognition and the understanding of human acts and passions. It projects *interrelationship* as an aesthetic by way of the tendential sense that in order to show what a given event is in reality, the novelist must somehow overcome the presentational constraints of the immediate, and *somehow* suggest the active influence and effects of that whole range of social and historical forces without which this unique event is finally inconceivable. The word "somehow" here marks the status of this expanded and "totalizing" conception of realism as an ideal, and indeed, as an aesthetic form or language as yet unrealized (and realizable, as well, in a great variety of unpredictable and as yet unimaginable ways). (*"History and Class Consciousness* as an 'Unfinished Project'"* 55)

I would lay even greater emphasis on the word "somehow." For once the mold of familiarity has been broken, once the objectivity of the work has been blurred, there can be no determinate boundaries to the process of its eventuality. Ironically, only through this fragmentation, this destruction of the work as a finished whole, does the aspiration to totality take hold of it. But to my mind, it is not necessary to see this conception as an ideal or even as an "aesthetic form." It breaks away from the aesthetic through its articulation of the incommensurate, which must always seem "unpredictable" and even "unimaginable." The work as fragment aspires to totality through perpetual and indeterminate interrelationship. It connects to everything and nothing in unbinding the hierarchies of relationship through its constant movement *between* (*inter-*) the poles of social difference. The work becomes nothing in itself as it connects to everything. It is only an effect of interrelationality. This is not the same thing as structure, for nothing is excluded. Differences of class, race, and gender may still exist, but the determinate values assigned to them by the system are momentarily ruptured. The work becomes the site of total history not simply in suggesting the "social and historical forces" that have determined it. On the contrary, it reveals the ultimate ground of historicity in the indeterminacy (precisely through its overdetermination) of the event itself. Just as the true event ruptures the linearity of historical time—that is, the time of historicism—by revealing the "time of the now," so the work of art as an event becomes the instrument of revelation. It constructs a passage to messianic time: "For every second of time was the strait gate through which the Messiah might enter" (Benjamin, *Illuminations* 264).

The Messiah who enters is neither a person nor a thing but an effect. After Baudrillard, I have called this effect "poetic," though I have expressed reservations about that adjective because poetry as an art form operates within a historically specific aesthetic system. Pierre Bourdieu, in terms reminiscent of Aristotle's in the *Poetics*, addresses this issue when he speaks of "the very logic of literary language, whose whole value lies in an *écart*, i.e., a distance from simple, common ways of speaking" (226). This perspective, however, does not account for every effect that poetry is capable of. More important, it does not account for language *as language*, which always has one effect beyond meaning, that is, the effect of the social tie, the material link between human beings as symbolic creatures or creations. As a social tie, language aspires to its own historical totality, which is never one or whole, except in the imaginary register (Eden against Babel), but is always in the process of becoming. The more thoroughly the illusion of semantic closure is destroyed—in other words, the more fragmentary any particular linguistic event—the more language aspires to totality.

The prison house of language is the structure of value. Meaning as a fixed unity of signifier and signified always establishes the bar, a rigid division or separation that then shapes meaning effects according to an equational structure. One could say that such a structure is an inevitable tendency of meaning production under the law of value. This tendency may even be necessary to communication; but as Raymond Williams notes in summarizing V. N. Volosinov, this does not tell the whole story: "The quality of the sign . . . is that it is effective in communication, a genuine fusion of a formal element and a meaning . . . ; but also that as a function of continuing social activity it is capable of modification and development: the real processes that may be observed in the history of a language." A sign (or what Williams, in the same passage, prefers to call "a signifying element of a language") can always be drawn away from fixed meaning and back into the social process where meanings are made. Any linguistic act that ruptures a fixed meaning makes the reader aware of signification as such a "practical material activity." Williams calls it "a means of production" (*Marxism and Literature* 38–39). If language is thought of as a "means," however, it must be subordinated to the end or value of production. Meaning becomes its purpose. Thus, a practical material activity must necessarily end in the production of value, and any linguistic effect outside of value and meaning is either negligible or secondary. Implicitly, both Williams and Bourdieu maintain such a position (and this is close to the position of Habermas). Baudrillard, on the contrary, has taken the strongest stand against the production model: "Production merely accumulates and is never diverted from its end. It replaces all illusions with just one: its own, which has become the reality principle" ("On Seduction," *Selected Writings* 162–63).

Faulkner's *Absalom, Absalom!* analyzes a language that has been diverted from its end in the letter Judith Sutpen receives from her fiancé, Charles Bon. This letter seems significant to Mr Compson, the teller of this section of the novel, because he imagines it to embody the thing he looks for by narrating, the missing explanation. He comments repeatedly that "he [Bon] and Judith saw one another three times in two years, for a total period of twelve days," and even then a good deal of Bon's time was taken up by Judith's mother, Ellen. What is the mystery behind their relationship and behind her brother's violent reaction to it? Why is she "bent on marrying him to the extent of forcing her brother [Henry] to the last resort of homicide, even if not murder to prevent it" (*Absalom, Absalom!* 78–79)? Mr Compson speculates on the motives behind these characters: Henry's fear that Bon is a bigamist and Thomas Sutpen's suspicion and final denunciation of Bon to Henry, though Mr Compson does not know what Sutpen's denunciation was really about. Mr Compson's lack of knowledge captures Quentin's (and the reader's) desire to know, to figure out what lies beyond the inexplicable bits of detail available to the isolated historical subject:

> It's just incredible. It just does not explain. Or perhaps that's it: they don't explain and we are not supposed to know. We have a few old mouth-to-mouth tales; we exhume from old trunks and boxes and drawers letters without salutation or signature, in which men and women who once lived and breathed are now merely initials or nicknames out of some now incomprehensible affection which sound to us like Sanskrit or Chocktaw . . . —Yes, Judith, Bon, Henry, Sutpen: all of them. They are there, yet something is missing; they are like a chemical formula exhumed along with the letters from that forgotten chest, . . . the writing faded, almost indecipherable, yet meaningful . . . ; you bring them together in the proportions called for, but

nothing happens; you re-read, tedious and intent, poring, making sure
that you have forgotten nothing, made no miscalculation; you bring
them together again and again nothing happens; just the words, the
symbols, the shapes themselves, shadowy inscrutable and serene,
against the turgid background of a horrid and bloody mischancing of
human affairs. (*Absalom, Absalom!* 80)

More than the other narrators of this novel, except perhaps Rosa
Coldfield, Mr Compson's method of narration aims at producing truth as
a function of poetic form. Thomas Sutpen acts out his life in the belief
that he can impose his own will on things; but "while he was still playing
the scene to the audience, behind him Fate, destiny, retribution, irony—
the stage manager, call him what you will—was already striking the set
and dragging on the synthetic and spurious shadows and shapes of the
next one" (*Absalom, Absalom!* 57). Mr Compson would like to force the
history of the Sutpen family into the form of ancient Greek tragedy and
govern his representation of them with the figure of irony (Moreland 23–
78), but something resists his making Thomas Sutpen into another
Oedipus. The resistance comes from the letter, that is, from history as the
letter. Whether the historical record survives orally or textually, it never
survives without ambivalence; and to the mind set on tradition, determined to see history as a system of values, this ambivalence of the letter
presents a block to the understanding, so that even a familiar language
becomes something alien—like Sanskrit or Choctaw to the ethnocentric Western patriarchal subject. What is missing from the chemical
formula—or rather those historical proper names that can be reduced to
something like a chemical formula—are the valences, their specific values
and proper significations. The letters are "without salutation or signature" because the synchrony of the proper name has been destabilized by
the diachrony of the letter, which reveals the *proper* itself as the effect of a
code. When history is read *to the letter*, against the grain of the master
code, it becomes "indecipherable, yet meaningful." It becomes a gateway
to the messianic, to the possibility of historical rupture, so that the past
ceases to be "past" and enters the present as the material of social practice. In and of itself, outside the structure of value, the past is nothing. Its
words, symbols, and shapes resist the code that would pin them down *as
a whole* to a specific purpose or end. For the master, such emptiness of
meaning, which defines totality as the nonexclusion of meaning, is the
cause of ultimate despair; but for the materialist, it represents, says Walter
Benjamin, "a Messianic cessation of happening, or, put differently, a

revolutionary chance in the fight for the oppressed past" (*Illuminations* 263). Such a fight may and should eventually lead to the construction of new values, but it would be a profound error to subordinate the historical letter to this end. The letter necessarily resists every interpretation, every new construction of value; or it loses its effect as a concrete social tie, the incommensurable ground of intersubjectivity. Mr Compson fetishizes the past by subordinating it to the law of aesthetic value, though he realizes his own failure to impose that law. This insistence on the law puts him into the same category with Thomas and Henry Sutpen, as well as with his own son Quentin, who all three insist that history has a formal design, emanating either from the *human* will or from some *universal* will or Fate. In choosing Greek tragic form over the historical letter, Mr Compson also resembles Isaac McCaslin in "The Bear," who chooses the Bible over the commissary ledgers, transtextual revelation over the material traces of "real" history. Judith Sutpen, by sending the letter in a different direction, shows that true revelation leads not to God but to symbolic exchange.

Although Judith received several letters from Charles Bon while he was at college in north Mississippi, she received only one letter after he left with the university company for the Civil War. It came four years later, "written on a sheet of paper salvaged from a gutted house in Carolina, with stove polish found in some captured Yankee stores" (*Absalom, Absalom!* 85). While she may have destroyed the others, Mr Compson speculates, the last one survived because she gave it to the grandmother of Quentin Compson. As Mr Compson tells Quentin, a week after Judith buried Charles Bon, that is, after her brother Henry killed him, she went to town and gave the letter "to your grandmother, who (Judith) never called on anyone now, had no friends now, doubtless knowing no more why she chose your grandmother to give the letter to than your grandmother knew" (*Absalom, Absalom!* 100). The particulars in this scene—the paper once owned by a Southern aristocrat, the stove polish manufactured in New England, and the Mississippi grandmother—may be the accidental effects of historical process; but they are not irrelevant details. Charles Bon, lacking his own means, uses captured stove polish and salvaged paper to write a letter, thus destroying commodity values by diverting these things from their original owners and their original use. As Wesley Morris comments, "The writing of this letter is a transgression, a misappropriation and misuse of materials" (174). He also stresses that the letter is presented to Quentin "without date or salutation or signature" (*Absalom, Absalom!* 129). The misappropriated materials themselves manifest the signature of history and imply what is missing by representing "the very conditions of the letter's composition, its occasion. They not only date its composition but personalize the act of composing." They graphically illustrate that "like the text, the signature is contextualized in the sense that personal expression cannot exist outside of collective discursive practice" (Morris 174–75). The ambivalence of signature as the expression of personal identity is reflected in the ambivalence of the letter as a whole toward its own historical emplacement:

> Because I cannot say when to expect me. Because what WAS is one thing, and now it is not because it is dead, it died in 1861. . . . Because what IS is something else again because it was not even alive then. And since because within this sheet of paper you now hold the best of the old South which is dead, and the words you read were written upon it with the best (each box said, the very best) of the new North which has conquered and which therefore, whether it likes it or not, will have to survive, I now believe that you and I are, strangely enough, included among those who are doomed to live. (*Absalom, Absalom!* 104–5)

For Bon, IS and WAS are in permanent contradiction. In the South after the Civil War, *what is* must cancel out *what was* because there is no longer any *meaningful* (i.e., meaning-producing) relation between the present and the past. Hypothetically, the value of the past should lie in its power to determine the validity of human experience in the present. But if history reverses that power, if the present defeats the past and traditional order is cast aside or bypassed, then that present which was once determined by the past was already an illusion, was already WAS before it entered the present. The past in the sense of WAS *is no longer* because it never was: WAS was already an effect of IS. But Bon cannot express this ambivalence, this indeterminacy of value, with words. The paper and the stove polish, construed as symbolic effects, say it. They say it through their incommensurable materiality—material not because they are things with a function but because they are also things, symbolic things, without a function. They say, "You and I live through this connection, we survive in this impossible present through this indecipherable and unexpected social tie." This effect takes place beyond any fixed meaning Bon may have intended to produce and in spite of his suffering and fate. It is not dependent on any understanding or purpose on his part. It simply binds him to another subject in the time of the now. It dooms him to life even in the midst of death. It manifests the literal truth of history.

Judith's response to the letter differs radically from Mr Compson's. She takes it *literally*. She does not seek to discover Bon's final intention or to situate the letter within the closure of a personal tragedy. On the contrary, she gives the letter to Quentin's grandmother about whom the reader knows nothing. She gives it to one of the few characters in this novel who appears to stand outside the circuits of the narrative, outside Thomas Sutpen's historical designs, outside the history of domination and possession that the Sutpen family seems to represent. As such, indeed *as a woman*, the grandmother represents the incommensurate inscribed within the patriarchal order of Sutpen and the other men of Jefferson county. I don't mean, of course, that she opposes or even resists the patriarchy but that in this instance, as the receiver of the letter, she occupies an unmarked position in the system, a break in the structure, beyond the code. In receiving the letter, she says, "Me? You want me to keep it?" And Judith replies,

"Yes. . . . Or destroy it. As you like. Read it if you like or dont read it if you like. Because you make so little impression, you see. You get born and you try this and you dont know why only you keep on trying it and you are born at the same time with a lot of other people, all mixed up with them, like trying to, having to, move your arms and legs with strings only the same strings are hitched to all the other arms and legs and the others all trying and they dont know why either except that the strings are all in one another's way like five or six people all trying to make a rug on the same loom only each one wants to weave his own pattern into the rug; and it cant matter, you know that, or the Ones that set up the loom would have arranged things a little better, and yet it must matter because you keep on trying or having to keep on trying and then all of a sudden it's all over and all you have left is a block of stone with scratches on it provided there was someone to remember to have the marble scratched and set up or had time to, and it rains on it and the sun shines on it and after a while they dont even remember the name and what the scratches were trying to tell, and it doesn't matter. And so maybe if you could go to someone, the stranger the better, and give them something—a scrap of paper—something, anything, it not to mean anything in itself and them not even to read it or keep it, not even bother to throw it away or destroy it, at least it would be something just because it would have happened, be remembered even if only from passing from one hand to another, one mind to another, and it would be at least a scratch, something, something that might make a mark on something that *was* once for the reason that it can die someday, while the block of stone cant be *is* because it never can become *was* because it cant ever die or perish... " (*Absalom, Absalom!* 100–101)

According to Carolyn Porter, these words come from Judith Sutpen's "single recorded speech" in the novel (265); but there are disagreements about the provenance of her speech. David Krause insists that the "context, construction, length, style, and tone all mark it as fundamentally the (re-)invention of Compson" in moment of self-reflexivity, a calling into question of his own authority. Mr Compson's "Fate" as a transcendent meaning is rendered dubious by the symbolic gesture of handing the letter to a stranger, which "activates new and unstable contexts, intentions, and audiences, inevitably smudging, erasing, any recoverable original meaning" (Krause 231–32). Richard Moreland argues that Quentin hears two voices in the speech: first, "something of the same blind obedience to an inscrutable cosmic irony on Judith's part which Compson wants to emphasize"; and then, the sense "of other different human designs; of victims . . . of other human's cross-purposes; of humans as both authors and victims of one another's fates" (71). It seems to me that the exchange of the letter as a social act breaks down Compson's ironic discourse and forces it to turn against itself in a moment of self-criticism, the verbosity of which may point as much to Compson's resistance to the letter's disruption of his monologue as to the resistance of the letter to interpretation. The letter can be read or not read, destroyed or preserved, in its literality as symbolic material. The impression that Charles Bon chose to make in writing the letter, the meaning he sought to impose on the historical situation from which it derives, the message he weaves with words—these are superseded by the act of exchange. Judith may know what Addie Bundren knew in *As I Lay Dying* where she says that a word, even a word like "love," is "just a shape to fill a lack" (172). But Judith also knows something more than Addie. She recognizes implicitly that the lack is only a function of the desire for meaning, the futile desire for a transcendent design or purpose to human life. The strings that attach one human being to another are the common languages they speak. I say languages because words are only one modality of the symbolic; and anything that can function like a language and enter the circuits of social exchange, like the stove polish, has a symbolic effect. Judith's act suggests that, if there is a Fate, it is purposeless and disorganized: the strings are not linked to anything beyond the human material condition. The ones who made the loom did not make it to correspond to human desires.

Judith distinguishes the letter from a tombstone, such as the one her mother is buried under, one of the two tombstones Thomas Sutpen dragged home from the war in 1864 to mark the family grave. These represent the desire for transcendence. They separate Sutpen and his family—in other words, his design—from the human collective. They virtually cut the strings of connection to other human beings by insisting that if one is a Sutpen, the wife or child of Thomas Sutpen, one has a place in the order of things, fixed for eternity. Though nothing is permanent, the tombstone embodies the desire for permanence; the writing on a tombstone tries to transcend its own condition as a social practice whose meaning is perishable. Just as Mr Compson believes in Fate, the mythic Thomas Sutpen believes in himself as the master of his own fate—believes in his capacity to impose a personal order on human history. The price of this order and the transcendental subjectivity to which it gives expression is the exclusion of the other son, Charles Bon, and of the other race (of which Bon becomes the signifier). Racism and transcendence are interconnected. There can be no social transcendence (or "white mythology") without the construction-through-exclusion of the racial other. Ultimately, the retelling of Sutpen's story by Quentin and Shreve shows that the same rule applies to gender and class. Sutpen seems incapable of love and merely uses women as the necessary means to the fulfillment of his design—a point driven home when he suggests to Rosa Coldfield that she bear him a son before they formalize their proposed marriage. Eventually the daughter of Wash Jones becomes his human brood mare, and his rejection of her after she fails to produce the desired son awakens a belated sense of class consciousness in Wash. His murder of Sutpen mirrors Sutpen's own violence against Charles Bon through Henry, and this derives from the self-alienated consciousness imposed on him as a child by the antebellum Southern class structure. By violating the boundaries of class with Wash's daughter, even as he insists on the recognition of class difference, Sutpen dispels the illusion of his natural superiority and brings about his own destruction by the *class other* he has created. With both Rosa and Wash, Sutpen betrays his own truth in a scene reminiscent of Hegel's master-slave dialectic.

Judith Sutpen evades this violent circularity through a simple gesture. For her, as Carolyn Porter points out, Bon's "letter functions like the 'churinga,' which Claude Lévi-Strauss describes as an object passed on from one generation to the next in certain tribes, to furnish 'the tangible proof that the ancestor and his living descendants are of one flesh'" (265). This comparison should be qualified, however. In passing Bon's letter to Quentin's grandmother, Judith ties herself not so much to the past as to the future, to the descendants of the entire human community. By passing it out of her family, she passes it to the radical alterity of an indeterminate history where its trajectory and purpose cannot be governed or predicted. She reaches out for totality in that sense. Ideally, the person to whom she gives the letter should be a stranger, someone who could not begin to grasp what the letter means to Bon and Judith. By passing the letter to her, Judith chooses to privilege the letter as symbol— more precisely, as *sumbolon*, a part or fragment—over its meaning in the closed structure of signification. She refuses to impose her own design and thus fall victim to the imaginary, to the belief in transparent meaning—particularly, when it attempts to incorporate totality, as do Mr Compson's Fate and Sutpen's design. Totality for Judith is a never-completed process. The letter, when it is passed on, enters into that process. Hypothetically, it could be passed on by Quentin's grandmother or it could be laid aside; but in either case it remains a fragment of an indeterminate whole. Judith's act directs the letter away from its end, purpose, value, or meaning. What remains is a trace or, as she puts it, a scratch. In itself, the scratch is nothing. Either it can be invested with meaning and value in the imaginary register or it enters into the process of symbolic exchange. Through exchange, the letter as event (re)con-stitutes the human collective. There are still meanings; but they have become moments within an open process. Meaning is neither the begin-ning nor the end of language. It is an effect of language.

Through symbolic exchange, *the word is made flesh* in a way that defeats the logocentric understanding of that phrase. The word is made flesh when it is recognized as a practical material activity, when it is understood that the loom of human culture is made by human beings, who unmake and remake it constantly. The word is flesh when it enters the time of the now and carries the burden of its own death within it. The *was* is implicated in *is*. When Judith Sutpen hands Charles Bon's letter to Quentin's grandmother, she enters the time of the now. She refuses to worship at the altar of death, either Charles Bon's or her own. At the suggestion that she might be thinking of suicide, she says, "Women dont do that for love. I dont even believe that men do. And not now, anyway" (*Absalom, Absalom!* 101). As Moreland notes, her fictive presence in Mr Compson's monologue responds to and perhaps overturns his irony with its "grim humor" (72–73). The emphasis should be on the word *now*. This *now*, of course, is not an escape from history but an immersion in it. Even if it isn't by Judith, Bon's letter becomes her trace and rejects the choice of Charles Bon to seek out death as the resolution of the social contradictions he cannot *not* face. It rejects Thomas Sutpen's design, his attempt to erect a monument to his own will to power. It rejects Comp-son's Fate. It rejects, in other words, the death drive animating all these characters, not to mention Quentin Compson, and transforming her brother Henry into its instrument. Her act of exchanging the letter shows the truth underlying all the events of this novel which none of the characters, with the possible exception of Judith, can see. Even Judith, who demonstrates her implicit knowledge of it, cannot say it; she can only *show* it. Carolyn Porter summarizes what her speech shows about the whole of *Absalom, Absalom!*: "All speaking and hearing, dominated as it is by a single narrative voice, represents an ongoing social act which, though it cannot found a dynasty, can create a community among the living as well as between the living and the dead" (266).

It could be said that Mr Compson's voice, which is perhaps the most logocentric in the novel (if we keep in mind that Sutpen really has no voice since he must signify the others and be "signified upon" by the others), articulates its own alterity through Judith's speech and Bon's letter. Mr Compson's quest for the truth, the missing explanation, operates through an economy of presence and absence that presupposes the autonomy of the subject who speaks. Unlike Quentin and Shreve later in the novel, who embroider Sutpen's story so shamelessly as to make apparent the force of desire underlying their own versions of the truth, Mr Compson rigorously insists upon the absence of explanation, which finally opens the door to the ultimate and most univocal of explanations— Fate itself. This becomes the god term of his narrative, the projection of his own subjectivity into a metaphysical principle of final authority. Fate is the stage manager that finally recuperates the blindness of individuals like Sutpen or even like Mr Compson. It justifies their lives by incorporating them into the master narrative of some universal history. Like God's, its presence is traced through its absence: the tragic form of Sutpen's life constitutes its meaning through the very absence of an explanation. Ironically, as the transcendental subject, Fate gives a ground to the individual subjects, who would never otherwise escape from the realm of fictionality that *Absalom, Absalom!* so powerfully dramatizes. It is essential to Mr Compson's narrative that we can never grasp or fully understand the mystery of Sutpen or, most particularly, of Charles Bon. They are the pawns of Fate; but because they are, their subjective lives are given autonomy as expressions of the highest authority, that unnameable and incomprehensible power beyond which there can be no appeal. In effect, Fate makes these men real. Women, however, seem to be outside this economy. As Mr Compson says later in the novel, "They lead such beautiful lives— women. Lives not only divorced from, but irrevocably excommunicated from, all reality" (*Absalom, Absalom!* 156).

With these words, Mr Compson unknowingly aligns himself with another celebrated literary voice, that of Marlow in Conrad's *Heart of Darkness*, which says: "It's queer how out of touch with truth women are! They live in a world of their own and there had never been anything like it and never can be. It is too beautiful altogether" (16). This exclusion of women from truth and reality is not the only thing Mr Compson and Marlow have in common. As Edward Said has remarked of Conrad's novella, it is "not only a work about imperialism, it is a work of imperialism itself." The latter enterprise "is presented by Conrad . . . as, (a)— inevitable, given the relevant historical forces, and (b)—inevitable as understood by a certain kind of personal mythology held by the adventurer, whom he [Conrad] profoundly admired" ("Intellectuals in the Postcolonial World" 74). Said's attribution of this sense of the inevitable to Conrad depends on an identification of Marlow's narrative style with Conrad's point of view. Certainly, it is difficult to separate the two since there is no other character in the book, not even the frame narrator, who offers anything like an alternative perspective. In a passage where he contemplates his own kinship with native Africans, with their "wild and passionate uproar," Marlow concludes, "I have a voice too, and for good or evil mine is the speech that cannot be silenced" (*Heart of Darkness* 38). Mr Compson's discourse is also imperialist in bestowing inevitability on the historical violence of slavery and Southern racism. He identifies with what he takes to be the personal mythology of Southern men like Thomas Sutpen and Charles Bon, a mythology that occludes the real social contradictions their lives express. Sutpen is a southern Kurtz who embodies the inevitable force of paternal law. Bon is his romantic opposition, his mysterious counterpart, his double—the one who epitomizes everything Sutpen has had to repress in order to achieve his empire: pleasure, manners, love. But Bon also reveals and exploits the violence at the root of Sutpen's power, the homoerotic truth underlying male patriarchal authority. Just as Marlow expresses his loyalty to Kurtz by lying to his Intended and denying her access to the truth, Bon expresses his love for Sutpen's son (and indirectly for Sutpen) by capturing the love of the sister and daughter. Yet, as Mr Compson notes,

> it was not Judith who was the object of Bon's love or of Henry's solicitude. She was just the blank shape, the empty vessel in which each of them strove to preserve, not the illusion of himself nor his illusion of the other but what each conceived the other to believe him to be—the man and the youth, seducer and seduced, who had known one another, seduced and been seduced, victimized in turn each by the other, con-

querer vanquished by his own strength, vanquished conquering by his own weakness, before Judith came into their joint lives even by so much as a girlname. (*Absalom, Absalom!* 95)

Judith is the vessel, the blank shape (just as Africa, according to Marlow, was a "blank space" on the Eurocentric map of the world before it became the object of imperialist enterprise), the mirror, through which men express their love for one another, their self-identity in the game of conqueror and conquered. From a Lacanian perspective, such "masculine" identity is a function of the imaginary register, the interplay of aggressivity and narcissism. This kind of relationship repeats itself in the struggle of Quentin Compson to define his own identity through storytelling in the face of his father's imperialistic discourse, "the speech that cannot be silenced." He wants to find his own voice and his own version of history, but everywhere he turns he encounters the authority of the father. Shreve, when he takes over the storytelling process, sounds "almost exactly like Father" (*Absalom, Absalom!* 168). Quentin finally takes over by telling the story that he claims Sutpen told his grandfather, the history of Sutpen's design. Since it is never entirely clear how Quentin could have learned everything he knows, it makes sense to see this segment of the novel as Quentin's struggle for self-authorization, his struggle to define his own historicity and his own voice. At first the effort seems futile, for Shreve insists that he and Quentin both sound "like your old man." Indeed, Quentin thinks to himself, "Yes, we are both Father. Or Maybe Father and I are both Shreve, maybe it took Father and me both to make Shreve or Shreve and me both to make Father or maybe Thomas Sutpen to make all of us" (*Absalom, Absalom!* 210). Quentin cannot escape the law of the father as long as he needs to reproduce its authority as the condition for his own speech. He has been seduced by the father who remains the conqueror even when Quentin conquers him, since he defines himself through his ability or inability to assume the paternal function in narrative. He authorizes the father who authorizes him. In this act, he repeats the fundamental assertion of patriarchal power that is virtually chronicled by this novel. As the symbolic father of all those who tell his story, Sutpen spent his entire life authorizing himself by authorizing those very forces that excluded him in the first place. This act is repeated by every character who tries to make narrative sense out of Sutpen's historical existence. Whether he is a tragic figure (according to Mr Compson) or a godlike brute (according to Rosa) or even a sort of historical victim ("Sutpen's trouble was innocence," as Quentin and

Shreve suggest [*Absalom, Absalom!* 220]), he becomes the focus of the desire for truth and authority. His life explains and justifies the present.

John T. Matthews has argued that "Sutpen's notorious design rests on a naïve use of language," an innocence that "directly confounds Sutpen's efforts to articulate himself" (153). As a boy, he experiences a "metaphysical concussion" when he finds himself reduced to inferior status by the planter aristocracy that uses a slave to send him to the back door for his business (154). From that moment on, he tries to transform his life into "a simple statement," which would "restore the aura of total coherence that marks Sutpen's childhood." His design "honors a phallic, paternal model of meaning" and produces a "statement of dynastic sense" that "disregards the complexities of language" (156–57). Within the framework of Matthews's larger thesis, the language of Sutpen's design betrays the disseminating free play of language that Faulkner foregrounds in *Absalom, Absalom!* Wesley Morris, on the other hand, calls this a "Derridean misconstruction," which reads "Sutpen's design as a metaphysical project." For Morris, "Sutpen is no metaphysicican; he repeats what he hears and thinks he sees: the phallic, paternal model of meaning. That model deconstructs under the force of translation into propositional action, into performance" (188–89). In other words, the flaw in Sutpen's design has less to do with a "naïve use of language" than with the contradiction between phallocentric desire and reality. In its original formulation, the design is a response to lack of social power, to the realization that by himself the boy Sutpen cannot harm the aristocracy that reduces him to social marginality. This knowledge comes to him "like an explosion—a bright glare that vanished and left nothing, no ashes nor refuse; just a limitless flat plain with the severe shape of his intact innocence rising from it like a monument." Sutpen loses his innocence when he understands that "to combat them you got to have what they have that made them do what he did" (*Absalom, Absalom!* 192). As Morris stresses, there is a shift here from "a remote world of romanticized personal combat, to a depersonalized and paranoic '*them*,' to a realm where things become symbols of prestige, power, and economic exchange, where 'land and niggers and a fine house' are signs of abstract value, signs that 'do' things" (190). Sutpen is inducted into the world of reification when he discovers that his own value as a human commodity depends on how much abstract value, how many commodities, he can accumulate (read Carolyn Porter for whom Sutpen is "the virtual reincarnation of reification" [208]). But Sutpen's identity as an effect of this system is not pure: it remains contaminated by innocence in its monumental form.

Morris sees this form as a "repression of the imaginary, of the personal, of that which represents the body, of the effect of words on the body" (191). This repression is also a form of idealization. From this perspective, Sutpen is haunted not by innocence so much as by the ongoing repression of innocence. He idealizes his origin by projecting it onto a place outside of history; then, ironically, he reduces his whole being to the status of a machine—one completely in the service of progress.

Ironically, Sutpen may have been the very machine Rosa Coldfield wishes for as she remembers once seeing the photograph of Charles Bon: "If I were God I would invent out of this seething turmoil we call progress something (a machine perhaps) which would adorn the barren mirror altars of every plain girl who breathes with such as this . . . —this pictured face" (*Absalom, Absalom!* 118). Sutpen is the machine of progress who supplies her with the dream of Charles Bon as his by-product, his own romantic other. Bon, with his longing for recognition, embodies that imaginary realm of personal identity which Sutpen so vehemently represses. Morris argues that Sutpen's refusal to recognize Bon is a blindness to reality (191). But it strikes me as a blindness to the social construction of reality, a blindness to the personal desire animating his own quest for recognition. Sutpen has made himself identical with the law of value by shearing away every effect, every social element, that does not fit into the Southern aristocratic code as he understands it. If he were to recognize Bon and allow him into the design, he would open it to the possibility of displacement. He would lose the sense of himself as the embodiment of inevitable progress, a master narrative whose truth depends on its exclusivity. They are not origins that Sutpen rejects, for he insists upon the monumental version of his origins insofar as he idealizes a world before his recognition of social difference and hierarchy. He rejects, as Matthews suggests, "a world in which origin and priority have lost their privilege, in which rival sons claim the same father, differing signs the same signified" (157). In effect, he refuses to recognize the possibity of more than one narrative, more than one purpose to human history.

Morris, it seems to me, misreads Matthews, who never really claims that "Bon must have some sort of prior claim on entail, which would disenfranchise Sutpen's legitimate son, Henry" (192). Matthews says something more subtle—that Bon "erases the distinction between legitimacy and illegitimacy" (93). Bon makes manifest the undecidability of the master narrative and its legitimation function. He is, as Morris suggests, "a shocking return of the repressed image of the body"—but a body marked by racial, sexual, and class ambivalence (192). Bon's presence is not an unmitigated reality that threatens to destroy the system of illusions that constitutes Sutpen's ideology of progress and the self-made man. Rather, Bon suggests the possibility of another story, an unwritten history, which cannot present itself as the truth pure and simple but insists on the incompleteness of any narrative. In his desire for recognition by the father, Bon only repeats the same pattern of history that Sutpen's whole life epitomizes. But by introducing into that pattern the principle of alterity, by showing that no version of reality truly masters the "real" since it must encounter its own difference from itself, Bon's story displaces the law of the father, with its patriarchal values (female virginity, racial purity, and class distinction), toward a representation of reality without law or center or exclusivity—a reality marked by differentiation and process, that is, the incommensurate. Finally, both Matthews and Morris are right. Sutpen's design is an evasion not of reality but of the "real." "The true real," says Lacan, "implies the absence of law. The real has no order" ("Le sinthome" 11). Insofar as Sutpen sees his design as univocally corresponding with the "real," it is metaphysical; and such a metaphysics must be understood as an evasion of the "real," or of that which lies beyond symbolization as irreducible, indeterminate process. It is not simply Sutpen's use of language that is naïve but his relation to the symbolic itself. Resisting his own social marginalization, he plays by the same rules that alienated him in the first place. He legitimates cultural hegemony and becomes a monument to his own innocence, his imaginary relation to the body as self-identity. As the inflexible instrument of patriarchal law, he values his own children, legitimate and illegitimate alike, according to their conformity to the design, to its metaphysical authority. In this context the metaphysical is "imaginary" insofar as it posits reality as a thing-in-itself rather than a social construction. Identifying himself as "natural" authority, Sutpen uses Henry to kill Bon and brings about Henry's banishment to the margins of society. He reduces Judith to permanent widowhood. He remains faithful to the authority of his design but fails to see the inevitable self-destruction inscribed within it. Monumental authority—more metaphysical than historical—is only a sublimated or misrecognized form of the death wish. To the historical subject that would banish all difference, including its own difference—that would reduce human history to a univocal text— life can have only one goal: death. In *Absalom, Absalom!* Sutpen becomes a walking death principle; and like Kurtz in *Heart of Darkness*, he both attracts and repels.

In fact, Sutpen also resembles Kurtz in his function as a signifier. As Lacan suggests, "a signifier is that which represents the subject for another signifier" (*"Ecrits": A Selection* 316). Sutpen's function as signifier differs according to the subject represented (Rosa, Mr Compson, Quentin, Shreve) and the other signifier for which it is represented: the different links in the syntagmatic chain of signifiers constituting the text of Southern history. Just as "All Europe contributed to the making of Kurtz" (*Heart of Darkness* 50), Sutpen embodies not only the history of the South for those subjects who identify that history as their own but also the history of the United States. He is the typical American hero and thus bears a resemblance to the greatest hero of American history. As Eric Sundquist stresses, "there is an analogy between Lincoln and Sutpen, each of whom labors heroically to build or preserve a magnificent 'house' of his national and personal dream, and both of whom, at about the same time, face a crisis in the house and try desperately to postpone it" (105). Emblematically, Sutpen's historical legacy finds its text in the letter sent by Mr Compson to Quentin at Harvard, which literally creates a symbolic link between North and South. (This letter frames the second half of the novel since the first part appears on page 141 and the last part nearly at the end.) It is possible to read Quentin and Shreve's efforts at contructing Sutpen's history as an attempt to fill the blank space opened up by this announcement of Rosa Coldfield's death. In explaining Rosa's life through that of Sutpen and his family, they give meaning and purpose to her death and, by implication, to the history of the antebellum and the reconstructed South that produced her. In sharing the letter with Shreve, Quentin repeats Judith Sutpen's act of symbolic exchange in transferring her letter from Charles Bon to Quentin's grandmother. Again, this act seems to displace the logocentric desire animating Sutpen's design and the design of those who would make final sense of it: Rosa, Mr Compson, and Quentin. Although Quentin struggles to master Sutpen's story and to gain its paternal authority for himself, he also succumbs to the dialogue between himself and Shreve, which reimagines the dialogue of the human community:

> Some happy marriage of speaking and hearing wherein each before the demand, the requirement, forgave condoned and forgot the faulting of the other—faultings both in the creating of this shade whom they discussed (rather, existed in) and in the hearing and sifting and discarding the false and conserving what seemed true, or fit the preconceived—in order to overpass to love, where there might be paradox and inconsistency but nothing fault nor false. (*Absalom, Absalom!* 253)

The "happy marriage of speaking and hearing" has nothing to do with the conveying of information. The history recreated by Quentin and Shreve has no value in the marketplace of knowledge. It is an exchange of words constituting a social tie, and the effect of that tie is not to reproduce the law of the father but to reduce it to alterity. As alterity, the law becomes a fiction, a form of desire without finality. Quentin and Shreve subject the law to the possibility of displacement away from the master narrative which rationalizes total history by excluding different histories, including different versions of the same history. They try to articulate their own desire through a rewriting of history that can justify the hope suggested by Mr Compson's letter. For Rosa Coldfield, Mr Compson writes, "it will do no harm to hope—You see I have written hope, not think. So let it be hope.—that the one [Thomas Sutpen] cannot escape the censure which no doubt he deserves, that the other no longer lack the commiseration which let us hope (while we are hoping) that they have longed for." The ambivalence of this sentence marks the operation of desire in any relation to the past. Mr Compson hopes for an order to human life—hopes that the unjust are punished and that their victims receive the commiseration they deserve. Even more important, he hopes that those shadows of the past—Rosa, Judith, Henry, Bon—shared the same hope for justice and commiseration because, as the sentence concludes, "they are about to receive it [commiseration, at least] whether they will or no" (*Absalom, Absalom!* 302). They are about to receive it, one assumes, from Mr Compson; but there is no guarantee that this commiseration is what they hoped for. History, even the official version written by professional historians, is always marked by alterity, by its difference from itself. The past is a letter that can be marked, stamped, and delivered to the future only through the mediation of an unknown third person such as Quentin's grandmother or Mr Compson or Quentin himself—by someone who cannot know the truth as an immediate experience. Historical truth in this context can only be an investment of desire in the letter of the past; and just as there is more than one desire, there has to be more than one history. Shreve, the stranger from Canada, finally identifies the promise of a different history in the figure of Jim Bond, Charles Bon's black grandson: "The Jim Bonds are going to conquer the western hemisphere" (*Absalom, Absalom!* 302). This prophecy, however, is based on a history that *Absalom, Absalom!* fails to record. As myth, fantasy, or fact, the history of Jim Bond's white genealogy is covered; but the history of African-Americans remains a blank space. Shreve identifies this blankness as the gap in Jim Bond's mind. If he had known who his father was, "it would have touched and then vanished from what you (not he) would have had to call his mind long before it could have set up any reaction at all, either of pride or pleasure, anger or grief" (*Absalom, Absalom!* 174). After the immolation of Sutpen's mansion, Jim Bond becomes the "last of his race" (*Absalom, Absalom!* 300). He is the last Sutpen, but the only speech he can make is a howling. Denied a voice and a history, Jim Bond marks the limit of the novel's linguistic play and its reinscription of racist ideology.

Absalom, Absalom! is itself Faulkner's letter to the unknown reader. It is a historical narrative and a critique of historical narrative, an analysis that destroys the simplicity of the object it analyzes through its own self-analysis. The effect on the reader is notoriously decentering and calls into question those codes of reading that govern any normative or traditional understanding of the past. Nearly everything written about *Absalom, Absalom!* focuses on its linguistic and structural ambivalence and its destabilization of the historical referent. This involves, on one level, a political critique of the sign as a structure of equivalence, and on another, a critique of the sign system. Raymond Williams distinguishes between "sign" and "system" in a way that pinpoints what lies beyond both:

> "Sign" itself—the mark or token; the formal element—has to be re-valued to emphasize its variability and internally active elements, indi-cating not only an internal structure but an internal dynamic. Similarly, "system" has to be revalued to emphasize social process rather than fixed sociality. . . . Here [in social process], as a matter of absolute priority, men relate and continue to relate before any system which is their product can as a matter of practical rather than abstract con-sciousness be grasped and exercise its determination. (*Marxism and Literature* 42)

Williams suggests that social process has priority over social system or structure. Despite Williams's language of evaluation (even the word "pri-ority" operates in that framework), the point is not to transfer value from system to process. Value is the product of system: the production of value—whether exchange value or use value, aesthetic value or ethical value—requires system and structure. Historically, however, system is only an effect of social process. It is not that social process precedes and hierarchically stands over system as its opposite; rather, the social process operates through the production and the destruction of systems of value. For example, in *Absalom, Absalom!* Thomas Sutpen mistakenly assumes the antebellum Southern class system to be the end of social process, a finalized self-contained structure that can be mastered and possessed. Only Judith seems to realize that every social system leaves a trace—in her case, Bon's letter—as the material on which social process continues to operate. Such a process is fundamentally *deconstructive*: it constructs social positions through overturning and displacement. These positions are never stable, however; for the process of displacement has no end.

Sutpen's design articulates order through the use of a production metaphor. According to Baudrillard, this figure attempts to reduce and delimit the totality of the social process: "Everywhere productivist discourse reigns and, whether this productivity has objective ends or is deployed for itself, it is itself the form of value." Production as the form of value permeates everyday life insofar as men (Sutpen could be their model) try to identify themselves with social positions, goals, and titles. In all these productive designs, Baudrillard sees

> something of what Lacan describes in the mirror stage: through this scheme of production, this *mirror* of production, the human species comes to consciousness [*la prise de conscience*] *in the imaginary*. Production, labor, value, everything through which an objective world emerges and through which man recognizes himself objectively—this is the imaginary. Here man is embarked on a continual deciphering of himself through his works, finalized by his shadow (his own end), reflected by this operational mirror, this sort of ideal of a productivist ego. (*Mirror of Production* 18–19)

One could almost describe the modernist text as such a mirror for the production of human consciousness. The modernist hero continually deciphers him- or herself in the quest for personal value or meaning, in the production of a unified ego that withstands the violence of historical fragmentation. Even when this quest fails, and it usually does, the production metaphor still rules as long as the human subject is measured against his or her potentiality for unity. James, Hardy, Conrad, Forster, Joyce, Lawrence, Woolf, and Faulkner have all written works in which this production of the autonomous self occupies a central place. It also underlies the Eliotic quest and the Yeatsian mask. But a few modernist works—*Absalom, Absalom!* would be one, as well as *Ulysses*, *Finnegans Wake*, and *The Waves*—push the mirror of production to the point at which, to use a Joycean metaphor, it cracks. It is not that the mirror of production does not operate on these works but that their effects exceed the production model. Not even the author's intention can control and delimit their ambivalence. Insofar, of course, as we grasp *Ulysses* as the production of Leopold Bloom or *Absalom, Absalom!* as the saga of Thomas Sutpen's self-creation and self-destruction, then these novels seem to conform to the mirror of production. We can go a step further and posit their objectivity as the creations of authorial subjects—Joyce and Faulkner. Through the act of canonization these works are invested with the value of universal truth, the interest of which accrues to the consciousness of the author. She or he enters a great tradition and becomes a signifier of authority and aesthetic value. Any new or rediscovered author can quickly be measured against the Joycean or Faulknerian or any other established model; and nothing is allowed to stand outside this system of values, except that which has been consigned to silence and oblivion. In other words, the production metaphor governs not only the content of modernist works but the the mode of their reception. It both articulates and silences the text in question. *Ulysses* and *Absalom, Absalom!* can be read through this metaphor, and that may be the tendency reinforced by the university. But it is also possible to read them against the grain: to foreground the "decolonizing" tendencies of Joyce's language or the implicit critique of American (and Southern) ideology in Faulkner's historical narrative.

For although these texts have been *instituted*, which is to say transformed into symbolic capital, it is also possible to de-institute them, to challenge their emplacement within a system of values. If we look at the origins of the word "institute" in Latin (*instituere*), it yields a meaning that clarifies my point: to set up in a position—to establish, arrange, teach. To institute a text is to teach it, and thereby to establish its position in the arrangement of all "instituted" works as a system. Teaching cannot be limited to this function, however, since it is always possible to displace any given arrangement, to move things around in a way that calls the "natural" order—or canon—into question. It is no coincidence that high modernist literature has always had to be taught, almost as if it had been written for the university. Joyce, Woolf, and even Faulkner did write with the university in mind, though it is possible to say that their relation to the university from different perspectives was *critical*. Nevertheless, it should not be forgotten that if the modernist text has a closer affinity with the university than, for example, the Victorian novel, the reason may lie not in its conformity but in its resistance to the institution and reproduction of value. This resistance would arise from the modernist foregrounding of language as a social process. This is not a universal characteristic of modernism but a tendency that can be situated in some modernist texts.

Such a foregrounding is what I will call the *pedagogical effect*. The compelling force of the production metaphor is felt as soon as I try to discuss this term, for it seems *natural* to argue that modernist works *produce* such an effect. Still, it is essential to understand that the effect I speak of takes place outside of production. Like the poetic effect that Baudrillard discusses, it ruptures production as the form of value. I prefer the term *pedagogical effect* to *poetic effect*, nevertheless, because it strips away the illusion of value that the privileging of poetry as a special discourse inevitably harbors. The pedagogical effect can emerge at any moment in any kind of language; in fact, it is always operative in language even when it is overlaid and repressed by systems of value. Whenever language is recognized as a social tie, whenever men and women "relate and continue to relate" through symbolic exchange beyond the necessity of communication, the pedagogical effect reveals itself. I use the word "reveal" because it is a revelation and not a production. The "true" pedagogical effect must be distinguished from didacticism which is always *produced by a code*. If a text has didactic value, then it can be decoded: it has a message so to speak. The pedagogical effect ruptures the code and reverses the message. Conventional meaning is annulled. But something else happens.

In *Absalom, Absalom!* Thomas Sutpen could be read as one version of the "ideal of a productivist ego" (Baudrillard 103). He is not just a signifier for other subjects but an *image* of the integrated self to which these subjects aspire. In deciphering Sutpen's life, they are projecting themselves into the saga of the self-made man, a social allegory which has bearing on more than the southern part of the United States. Sutpen's relation to Native Americans, African-Americans, and women epitomizes the forms of exploitation on which the American empire and its ideological representations were founded. He reduces land and people to elements of production in a global scheme of self-aggrandizement. He makes a world of objects until he is destroyed by the objects he has made. If his world collapses, the ideal he represents does not. But this ideal or law of value is challenged by the forms of social interaction that escape the system and its various designs. The incommensurate that value destroys may seem to have its own value when viewed through the lenses of hegemonic culture. But the truth of the incommensurate—Faulkner's "letter" or the pedagogical effect of his work—does not lie in the projection of a utopia but in the rupture of a tradition and an imposed order. Beyond the shadow of every authority lies the possibility of symbolic exchange.

3

Writing as a Forbidden Pleasure: Irigaray, Lacan, Joyce

If it should happen that I leave, you may say that it is only in order to be at last Other. One can be happy being Other like everybody else after a life spent, in spite of the Law, trying to be Other.
—JACQUES LACAN, Jan. 15, 1980 (cited by de Certeau 48)

And if, by chance, you were to have the impression of not having yet understood everything, then perhaps you would do well to leave your ears half-open for what is in such close touch with itself that it confounds your discretion.
—LUCE IRIGARAY, *This Sex Which Is Not One*

And each was wrought with his other.
—JAMES JOYCE, *Finnegans Wake*

These quotations from Lacan, Irigaray, and Joyce are meant to articulate a space for writing that is not identical to itself or, to use Lacan's phrase from *Encore*, that is *pas tout*, not-everything. Lacan's words, of course, constitute a sort of epitaph by which the "master" consigns himself to the alterity of death. His life is defined quite plainly as a quest for such alterity, so that in a sense it was already there—and I want to emphasize that the place where it already was is his writing. Even in his speech, the record of which is his seminar, the will to writing, to disclosing the alterity within speech, governs its performative dimension. This will to writing must also be linked to an attempted subversion of the will to knowledge (in the conventional sense); and this is the point of Irigaray's remark (which actually resonates with a number of statements by Lacan himself to which I will return). In a context that is at once critical and interpretive of Lacan's text, her statement reminds us that the objective of her critique is not knowledge as a whole or of the whole (even Lacan's system taken as a whole) but knowledge of what is not-all. To read Lacan or to read Irigaray's reading of Lacan is to have the sense of not having understood everything. Many, it seems, have read Irigaray in the opposite direction and claim she has understood everything of Lacan and dismissed it as phallocentric. But this reading misses the multiple directions of her critique, which does not aim simply at rectifying a Lacanian error—in this case, the error of situating women exclusively in the place of alterity where they become impossible as beings-who-exist and thus give univocal expression to the not-all: "Their exclusion is *internal* to an order from which nothing escapes: the order of (man's) discourse. To the objection that this discourse is perhaps not all there is, the response will be that it is women who are 'not-all'" (Irigaray 88). For Lacan, it seems, women are not-all, that is, Other. But if Lacan wanted to be Other, does that mean that he wanted to be a woman? And did he have to die in order to undergo this sex change and escape the law of that which is One and the Same? I don't think so. It seems to me that Irigaray's reading tries to make Lacan's statements, the semblance of his program, true to his style. If she is "wroth" with Lacan, it is because Lacan is "wrought" with his other. And it works the other way around. Here emerges a symbolic exchange between Lacan and Irigaray through the *jouissance* of language, through a pleasure that is, in Baudrillard's words, "the hemorrhaging of value, the disintegration of the code, of the repressive logos" ("Beyond the Unconscious" 70–71). And this brings us back to the Joyce of *Finnegans Wake* and to the problem of reading a book that can only be read as not-all by a fractured and incomplete subject.

What is it that confounds our discretion and requires us to leave our ears half open? For Irigaray, this something "in such close touch with itself" would seem to be feminine. The masculine is different: its "auto-affection needs instruments—unlike woman, man needs instruments in order to touch himself: woman's hand, woman's sex and body, language—hasn't that syntax necessarily, according to an economic logic, exploited everything in order to caress itself?" (132). Patriarchal culture can be thought of as an enormous desiring machine at the service of masculine auto-affection. Women are different because they don't need all this. A woman "touches herself in and of herself without any need for mediation, and before there is any way to distinguish activity from passivity. Woman 'touches herself' all the time, and moreover no one can forbid her to do so, for her genitals are formed of two lips in continuous contact. Thus, within herself, she is already two—but not divisible into one(s)—that caress each other" (24). This passage has been read, of course, as a version of biological essentialism. Despite the historical idealization of masculine sexuality in the phallus, which defines masculinity as the positive term, the One sex, in the binary relation masculine-feminine, the individual male is physically bound to his other who must be the instrument of his pleasure if he is to have any. Even touching himself requires manipulation, which reduces his self, his body, to being the instrument of its own pleasure. A woman, on the other hand, doesn't have to do a thing, change a thing, or manipulate anything in order to experience sexual touch. In fact, she feels it all the time, continuously, as the sexual caress of her biological form. Ironically, it turns out that man, *and not woman*, is genuinely lacking something, which he projects onto woman by making her the privileged instrument of masculine pleasure. In this capacity, she is then ridiculed for and circumscribed by her difference. She is the one who lacks, for she is only the instrument of the One sex—the sex that cannot have sex without the *other*. She becomes what Lacan calls the *object a* or the little other—literally a function, in the mathematical sense, of masculine desire.

This is not really a question of biology. After all, it isn't just a woman's sexual pleasure that is repressed; for how would you repress what is continuous and unmediated? It is the feminine imaginary. As Irigaray suggests, "The more or less exclusive—and highly anxious—attention paid to erection in Western sexuality proves to what extent *the imaginary that governs it* is foreign to the feminine" (24, my emphasis). What reads like an appeal to biological destiny is the way we talk about sexuality within the framework of patriarchal culture. Irigaray cannot be refuted simply by asserting, with Ellie Ragland-Sullivan, that she has failed "to accept the structural effect and symbolic nature of the Lacanian phallic signifier—*neutral in its own right*" (273, my emphasis). Even Lacan explodes this myth of neutrality in this remark from "The Meaning of the Phallus":

The phallus is the privileged signifier of that mark where the share of the logos is wedded to the advent of desire. One might say that this signifier is chosen as what stands out as most easily seized upon in the real of sexual copulation, and also as the most symbolic in the literal (typographical) sense of the term, since it is the equivalent in that relation of the (logical) copula. One might also say that by virtue of its turgidity, it is the image of the vital flow as it is transmitted in genera- tion. (*Feminine Sexuality* 82)

Ragland-Sullivan faults Irigaray with a poor understanding of Lacan's mirror phase but fails to see the extent to which the Lacanian symbolic order borrows its terms from an imaginary register that already marks the penis as the phallic signifier, as the typographical and logical representa- tion of sexual difference. According to Ragland-Sullivan, Irigaray con- fuses "the fixing of a species-specific *Gestalt* during the mirror stage with the phallic fixing of sexual identity that occurs *after* the mirror stage" (276–77). Ragland-Sullivan takes Lacan's gestures toward a develop- mental psychology very seriously, but she never offers any explanation of the actual relationship between the phallus and the penis. As David Mac- ey has shown, Lacanians and Lacan himself, despite the cry "the phallus, not the penis," have had the greatest difficulty separating the two terms in their own writings and clinical practice (187–92).

There might be more than one way to read a penis or the body of a man if we could think beyond phallocentrism. The first step in that direction would be to think and write the feminine imaginary, the very possibility of which seems to have been repressed by the dominant sexual imaginary. To the "masculine" notion that a woman "does not have a sex organ," Irigaray responds, "She has at least two of them, but they are not identifiable as ones. Indeed, she has many more. Her sexuality, always at least double, goes even further: it is *plural*." A woman can be said to feel pleasure all over her body; she "*has sex organs more or less everywhere*" (28). Irigaray is not simply describing the female body; she is constructing the feminine. (This is what I believe Naomi Schor is suggesting by identi- fying two levels of mimesis in Irigaray's critical strategy beyond simple masquerade, which would aim at "parrotting the master's discourse": "At a second level, parrotting becomes parody, and mimesis signifies not a deluded masquerade, but a canny mimicry. And, finally, . . . mimesis comes to signify difference as positivity, a joyful reappropriation of the attributes of the other that is not in any way to be confused with a mere reversal of the existing phallocentric distribution of power" [48].) In effect, she transforms the Lacanian *pas tout* into something other. The not-all is grounded not in lack but in diversity: it is not-all because it is not One and cannot be reduced to the economy of one thing. The feminine imaginary throws the phallic economy into disequilibrium. The thought of a sexuality that is *not* One but that *is* one makes the *pas tout* a ground for radical difference. Woman is no longer a function of man. In addition, the feminine imaginary opens up the possibility of an-other man, of a masculine sexuality other than the One. The feminine imaginary makes it possible to rewrite the masculine imaginary in such a way as to make it not one. Not one what? Not the "masculine" as that term has come to signify the privileged position in the binary opposition man-woman. Not one sexuality that would be normative for either or any sex. If sexuality is something that is written, then it can be rewritten. Historical psychoanalysis, which "takes *discourse itself* as the object of its investigations" (Irigaray 87), recognizes the condition but misses the implied conclusion:

> Psychoanalytic theory thus utters the truth about the status of female sexuality, and about the sexual relation. But it stops there. Refusing to interpret the historical determinants of its discourse—" ...that thing I detest for the best of reasons, that is, History"—and in particular what is implied by the up to now exclusively masculine sexualization of the application of its laws, it remains caught up in phallocentrism, which it claims to make into a universal and eternal value. (Irigaray 102)

Value appears where rewriting becomes impossible. For Irigaray, such value takes the form in Lacan's discourse of a rejection of history—"that thing I detest for the best of reasons." He spells this History with a capital *H* and says that it "is made precisely in order to give us the idea that it has some sort of meaning." The truth is different. History simply presents us with the words of another, "who recounts for us his stupidities, his embarrassments, his obstacles, his anxieties, and what do we read there?—nothing other than the effects of his words." Lacan blurs the distinction between the individual who recounts his case history and the professional historian, though there is a difference suggested when he asks whether it would be possible that "language should have other effects than leading people by the nose to reproduce themselves." Writing (*l'écrit*) would represent the possibility of this other effect (*Encore* 45). Hayden White speaks of historical writing as "the discourse of the real"; and though he does not wish to push the Lacanian aspects of this phrase too far, he speculates that "we can comprehend the appeal of historical discourse by recognizing the extent to which it makes the real desirable, makes the real into an object of desire, and does so by its imposition, upon events that are represented as real, of the formal coherency that stories possess" (20–21). But for White, history as a narrative form derives from "the impulse to moralize reality, that is, to identify it with the social system" (14). Such a history aims at transparent meaning, the immediate understanding that resides in the imaginary register. Lacan, on the other hand, posits a writing that "is not to be understood. For this reason you are not compelled to understand my own [writings]. If you don't understand them, all the better, it will justifiably give you the occasion to explicate them" (*Encore* 35). Lacan seizes this occasion himself for reading an ancient philosopher: "If Aristotle is not so easily comprehended by reason of the distance separating us from him, this expressly justifies my telling you that reading does not oblige us to understand anything. It is necessary to read first" (*Encore* 61); and presumably the same rule would apply to the reading of Freud. Reading without understanding—this is what writing requires if we are to go beyond the imaginary to the "real" of history. A textual explication does not simply fill the gap in objective knowledge but extends the process of learning—which means that no writing (*écrit*) can simply produce the final truth (though, as Irigaray stresses, "psychoanalytic discourse on female sexuality is the discourse of truth," a "discourse that tells the truth about the logic of truth" [86]). The truth of writing, of psychoanalysis as writing, is something different, something that evades the logic of truth as the traditions of Western philosophy have defined it: "Truth [as writing] is what cannot be said. It is what can be said only on condition that it not be pushed to the end, that it manages to be only half-said [*mi-dire*]" (Lacan, *Encore* 85). This truth that can be only half said may require us to keep our ears only half open; for *mi-dire* runs the risk of *médire*, slandering—in fact, slandering women.

Lacan says it himself: "There is only one way to be able to write *la femme* [woman] without having to cross out the *la*—it is at that level where woman is the truth. And for this reason one can only half-speak [*mi-dire*] of her" (*Encore* 94). Lacan argues in *Encore* that *la femme* does not exist: "There is no such thing as '*la' femme* [woman], where the definite article stands for the universal. There is no such thing as '*la' femme* [woman] since of her essence . . . she is not all" ("God and the *Jouissance* of ~~The~~ Woman," *Feminine Sexuality* 144/*Encore* 68, translation modified). The full force of Irigaray's critique would have to fall on the word "essence," which implies that the language of sexual difference is rooted in some transcendental order of things, whether that order is natural or symbolic (on the problem of Irigaray's own essentialism, see Diana Fuss 55–72 and again Naomi Schor). There is no question that the universal, as Monique Wittig insists, "is what the so-called masculine gender means, for the class of men have appropriated the universal for themselves" ("Mark of Gender" 66). This category has nothing to do with essence, however, but with historical actions subject to reversal. Lacan's slandering of woman articulates what is half true: in the first place, that the universal as a category defines the masculine, and in the second, that the feminine identifies the masculine as a fiction, calls into question the universal with the force of what is not-all. For a woman is not-all not only in the sense that she is marked as incomplete by her relation to the phallic function but in the sense that there is something for her outside that function. "Her being not all in the phallic function does not mean that she is not in it at all. . . . She is right in it. But there is something more." The phallic function does not fully describe female sexuality because "there is a *jouissance . . . beyond the phallus*" ("God and the *Jouissance* of The Woman," *Feminine Sexuality* 147/*Encore* 69). Woman does not exist as a universal category within the patriarchal allegory that defines her as the instrument of masculine pleasure. Still, there is a way of writing "woman" as a universal category, and that is to half speak her as the truth. The truth of what? The answer has to be the Other, with a capital O. This half-spoken truth situates a feminine *jouissance* at the site of a different relation to language and culture, a different relation to thought. In order to explicate this relation, it is first necessary to grapple with what is meant by radical alterity or the Other.

Jacques Lacan introduced the "big Other" in his seminar on the ego. There he insists that the ego is an imaginary construction, which "doesn't take anything away from it. . . . If it weren't imaginary, we wouldn't be men, we would be moons" (*The Ego* 243). What distinguishes human consciousness from a thing is that it is constituted in contradiction. The human subject perceives "its fellow being, in the form of the specular other. This form of the other has a very close relation to the ego, which can be superimposed on it, and we write it as *a'*." Lacan further suggests that human communication takes place through a process of identification with the other: "When the subject talks to his fellow beings, he uses ordinary language, which holds the imaginary egos to be [real] things. . . . In so far as the subject brings them into relation with his own image, those with whom he speaks are also those with whom he identifies" (*The Ego* 244). Lacan says something here that rhetoricians such as Kenneth Burke have long understood: "You persuade a man only insofar as you can talk his language by speech, gesture, tonality, order, image, attitude, idea, *identifying* your ways with his" (Burke 55). One could apply this theory of persuasion to communication in general. A linguistic act that conveys an understanding from one human subject to another, that conveys information in a way that makes immediate sense, operates in the imaginary register of specular identification. It creates the illusion that language, at least for the given moment of communication, is a transparent entity, beyond the slippages of history and the instability of the subject. In such a communication, the subject claims to know itself, to know its own intention and what it wants to convey. It assumes that the other, to whom the subject wishes to convey a message, is *like the subject,* like *me* (the word in Lacan's French translated by "ego" is *moi*). In effect, the other is a metaphor of the self, while the *self* (ego/*moi*) is a figuration of the subject: *I* am the One in the mirror. Lacan's mirror phase is not some eternal truth about human nature but the necessarily ideological representation of the formation of the modern bourgeois subject. As Baudrillard might suggest, in the mirror phase the human subject produces itself or rather posits itself as the effect or end of production. It takes itself for an object or a thing—the *object a.*

The human subject *knows* itself and others *objectively* in the imaginary register. Still, any use of language, regardless of whether it communicates effectively, implies something that Lacan, speaking as an analyst for the community of analysts, regards as "our basic assumption—we think there are subjects other than us, that authentically intersubjective relations exist." The proof of such intersubjectivity is that "the subject can lie to us" (Lacan, *The Ego* 244). One could add to this proof the subject's ability to lie to itself. In a sense, meaning as the mirror of production is always historically false, and truth is the absence of meaning. Truth is what our speech seeks beyond meaning, beyond the transparencies of the ego—"those we do not know, true Others, true subjects": "They are on the other side of the wall of language, there where in principle I never reach them. Fundamentally, it is them I'm aiming at every time I utter true speech, but I always attain *a'*, *a''*, through reflection. I always aim at true subjects, and I have to be content with shadows. The subject is separated from the Others, the true ones, by the wall of language." The wall of language is a figure for the alterity within language. The symbolic truth lies there, while the objective content of communication may be conventionally true or false, that is, verifiable. The possibility of falsehood is present in every conventional truth. The "real" truth cannot be false because it cannot be known objectively; it cannot be communicated, though perhaps it can be shown or suggested. It cannot be verified or falsified because it is not an objective fact but a relation, an effect:

If speech is founded in the existence of the Other, the true one, language is so made as to return us to the objectified other, to the other whom we can make what we want of, including thinking that he is an object, that is to say that he doesn't know what he's saying. When we use language, our relation with the other always plays on this ambiguity. In other words, *language is as much there to found us in the Other as to drastically prevent us from understanding him.* (Lacan, *The Ego* 244, my emphasis)

Only the subject speaks; but this speaking subject must be distinguished from the ego: it is neither autonomous nor whole. The subject is a symbolic effect and, as such, is rooted in the Other, where it marks the possibility of speech as a social tie or event—in other words, the intersubjective relation itself. Lévi-Strauss speculated that we could think the origin of language only as something that happened all at once. This formula is imaginary, but it points to what is true. *Language as an event happens all at once.* It cannot, however, be reduced simply to a system or a structure. On the one hand, language as a structure is a function of the imaginary; it is what language becomes when it is objectified, a system of differential values. Such a system presupposes a stable subject or ego and makes possible the acts of encoding and decoding on which communication is founded. But on the other hand, language beyond the system—or the relation to language from the Other side—is an interminable process of differentiation, the moments or instances of which are incommensurable with one another. The subject in this process is unstable or sliding. It is an impermanent effect. This speaking subject is a point of articulation for the discourse of the Other. Rooted in the alterity of language, the subject directs its speech back to the Other through the act of symbolic exchange. With respect to the structural law of value, however, such speech is alienated and can be answered only by the objectified other that it anticipates. From the side of the true Other, the situation looks rather different. The big Other has no other. The true subject has no object. Language as symbolic exchange is intersubjective, reciprocal—that is, without return. In this social act, no response is necessary because meaning has lost its value. As Shoshana Felman writes,

Lacan's analysis of the signifier opens up a radically new assumption, an assumption that is an insightful logical and methodological consequence of Freud's discovery: that what *can* be read (and perhaps what *should* be read) is not just meaning but the lack of meaning; that significance lies not just in consciousness but, specifically, in its disruption; that the signifier can be analyzed in its effects without its signified being known; that the lack of meaning—the discontinuity in conscious understanding—can and should be interpreted as such, without necessarily being transformed into meaning. (45)

Juliet Flower McCannell qualifies what she sees as Felman's celebration of form with the warning that for Lacan the preponderance of form is also the "*source* of our ills." It is what prevents the analysis that aims at meaning from ever arriving at it, since the process is always mediated by alterity. "The inter-human is always given over to a medium which will shape and (re)direct it: language, culture" (McCannell 40). It is possible, however, that the insistence on fixed meaning—even the meaning of the phallus—is what blocks or breaks down the interhuman relationship. For language as a communication system separates the subject from the true Others, and from itself as an effect of the Other. This system makes it impossible for the subject to know itself except through the imaginary constructions of the ego. This impossibility does not mean, of course, that beyond the system lies the possibility for true self-knowledge, knowledge of the individual self as the true subject. All that lies beyond the system of language as a mirror of production is intersubjectivity, or the social tie. The true subject *is* the Other.

In the *Encore* seminar, nearly twenty years after the seminar on the ego, Lacan remarked, "Hence the Other, in my language, can only be the Other sex" (*Encore* 40). This "Other sex," I would argue, does not refer to Woman as the polar opposite of Man. Again, the universal Woman—in the sense of a transcendent or essential Woman (as we will see later, Wittig provides us with a different way of reading the universal)—cannot exist since she is constructed from within the phallic relation that makes her the instrument of the One sex. Lacan's "Other sex"—and not the universal Woman—opposes the One sex by subverting its unity. The reason that woman as man's sexual partner, the object of his love, does not exist is that the ground of sexual pleasure does not lie in the body of the woman but in the Other. Irigaray quotes this crucial passage from *Encore*:

> The sexualized being of these not-all women is not channeled through the body, but through what results from a logical requirement in speech. Indeed, the logic, the coherence inscribed in the fact that language exists and that it is external to the bodies that are agitated by it, in short the Other that is becoming incarnate, so to speak, as a sexualized being, requires the one-by-one procedure. (88–89; see *Encore* 15)

In this formulation—according to Irigaray—language as the Other "is transcendent with respect to bodies, which would necessitate, in order to become incarnate, 'so to speak,' taking women one by one." She takes this conception to mean that "woman does not exist, but that language exists" (89). As Lacan states it, "the signifier is the cause of *jouissance*" (*Encore* 27). The Other takes on the body of a woman as the form of its sexualized being. The sexual relation is not between the body of man and the body of woman but between the signifier man and the signifier woman, between the human subject and the big Other. For the masculine subject, the body of a woman is the semblance or fantasy of the Other, the *object a*. A woman participates in this fantasy by submitting to the phallic function, but this is not all she is. There is a *jouissance* of the Other beyond the phallus to which she relates: "The Other is not only this place where truth falters. . . . By her being in the sexual relation radically Other, in relation to what can be said of the unconscious, the woman is that which relates to this Other" ("A Love Letter," *Feminine Sexuality* 151/*Encore* 75). The truth falters over the not-all where it can no longer claim fullness or self-presence but must be only half spoken. But once the truth has faltered it is also revealed in its alterity or difference from itself. The truth of the One is shown to be a fiction so that only the half-truth is true. The phallic function becomes a dimension of alterity. From this perspective, woman, as she relates to the Other, articulates the radical contingency of the phallic function as it represents her "sexualized being." Lacan's formula for the impossibility of the sexual relation—it *"never ceases* not to be written"—leads to this conclusion: "The apparent necessity of the phallic function is discovered to be only a contingency. As the mode of the contingent, it *ceases* not to be written" (*Encore* 87, my emphases). The phallus is a contingent representation of what cannot be represented universally—that is, sexual difference. It is a historically limited representation.

Irigaray takes the greatest exception to these words from Lacan's discourse: "There is woman only as excluded by the nature of things which is the nature of words, and it has to be said that if there is one thing they themselves are complaining about enough at the moment, it is well and truly that [*c'est bien de ça*]—only they don't know what they are saying, which is all the difference between them and me [*entre elles et moi*]" ("God and the *Jouissance* of ~~The~~ Woman," *Feminine Sexuality* 144/*Encore* 68). Irigaray's analysis suggests that Lacan the *moi* knows what women are saying only to the extent that he does not know what he is saying. But does he know that he does not know? He presents a formula that is meant, I think, to qualify his teaching: "I ask you to refuse what I offer you because that's not it" (*Encore* 101). He stresses that the *it* (*ça*) which his discourse is not is the *object a*. His discourse is not the knowledge of an object, which it would be if Lacan were speaking "truly" as the subject of an absolute knowledge. It could, nevertheless, be taken as such which makes this paradoxical formula performative in a way not easy to grasp. In asking us to refuse what he offers, in submitting his own message to the excesses of a style that makes it almost impossible for a reader to accept his words, Lacan makes a statement that undoes itself by transforming its cause into its effect: *That's not it (my discourse is not the "object a") because I ask you to refuse what I offer you.* For example, he offers the truth about women, which is that he knows what they are saying when they don't know, when they complain about having "been excluded by the nature of things which is the nature of words." But this truth, taken as a whole, as the *tout*, must be refused because it is not the *object a* that it would be if it were not refused. Whatever Lacan says, if we are to hear the truth, which is only half true, we must close our ears halfway. We must evade the message in order to arrive at the alterity of his style.

Lacan's style has always been the problem; and, as Michel de Certeau points out, his awareness of this problem can be traced back to the beginning of his career: "In 1933, Lacan's thesis opens onto 'the problem of style,' that is, onto a group of questions 'forever unresolvable for an anthropology which is not freed from the naïve realism of the object'" (de Certeau 52). Derrida identifies Lacan's style as an obstacle, which he describes in *Positions* as "an art of evasion" (110). Later, in "Le facteur de la vérité," he produces this more rigorous formulation: "Lacan's 'style' was constructed so as to check almost permanently any access to an isolatable content, to an unequivocal, determinable meaning beyond writing" (*The Post Card* 420). In *Encore*, Lacan gives his own version of Derrida's observation: "A discourse such as analytic discourse aims at meaning. Clearly I can only deliver to each of you that part of meaning you are already on the way to absorbing. This has a limit, given by the meaning in which you are living. . . . What analytic discourse brings out is precisely the idea that this meaning is mere semblance" ("A Love Letter," *Feminine Sexuality* 149–50/*Encore* 74). Meaning is semblance, including the meaning at which analytic discourse aims. The only meaning Lacan delivers is the image of what is already there, operative in the individual history of the subject. Consequently, psychoanalysis must implement an "ethics of speech," to use de Certeau's phrase, which evades the very meaning at which it aims: "In the field of research, [Lacan] violates the rule which bases the salability of knowledge upon the readability of its statements. What he sets forth he will not allow to be understood" (47–48). He posits his not being understood as an ethical imperative; for he refuses to substitute one semblance for another, one speech for another, since to do so would result in a hegemony of speech through which the analyst would become the policeman of truth. Analytic discourse aims at meaning but delivers only "a style" (Lacan, *Ecrits* 458).

Lacan suggests that those who read him well need not read him faithfully—out of love, so to speak. If they hate him, however, it only means they "de-suppose" him of knowledge: "And why not indeed? Why not, if it transpires that this is the precondition of what I call a reading?" ("God and the *Jouissance* of ~~The~~ Woman," *Feminine Sexuality* 139–40/*Encore* 64). Still, as we discover in the section of *Encore* titled "A Love Letter," "there is no love without hate" (*Feminine Sexuality* 160/*Encore* 82). Just as women have a special relation to the Other, so they have a special relation to the symbolic as "the support of that which was made into God." For Lacan, God embodies the relation of alterity: "The Supreme Being, which is manifestly mythical in Aristotle, the immobile sphere from which originate all movements . . . is situated in the place, the opaque place of the *jouissance* of the Other—the Other which, if she existed, the woman might be" ("A Love Letter," *Feminine Sexuality* 153–54/*Encore* 77). The woman becomes Other (and thus comes closer to God) when she experiences the symbolic as Other without knowing it, when she feels the *jouissance* about which she can say nothing. Saying something, in this context, would mean producing a meaning. The woman cannot produce the meaning of her experience of what is beyond the phallus, but man is always willing to produce it for her. Which leads Lacan to conclude: "The more man may ascribe to the woman in confusion with God, that is, in confusion with what it is she comes from, the less he hates, the lesser he is, . . . the less he loves" ("A Love Letter," *Feminine Sexuality* 160/*Encore* 82). The more completely she is effaced by the law of the father (embodied in God the father), the less is man capable of loving or hating her. And vice versa, the more authority we attribute to Lacan, the less we are able to read him, to write about him, to derive unspeakable pleasure from his writing. There is a phallic *jouissance*, the sexual pleasure that has been coded and overcoded by patriarchal society and thus is speakable; and there is the *jouissance* of the Other about which we can know nothing, which means we cannot reduce it to a function, the *object a*. Lacan's style works to prevent this reduction of his own text; but nothing is perfect, not even Lacan's evasion of authority. He calls his discourse, or the writing within his speech, a love letter, "the only thing one can do with a measure of seriousness." A few paragraphs earlier, he remarks, "speaking of love is in itself a *jouissance*" ("A Love Letter," *Feminine Sexuality* 154/*Encore* 77–78). And even earlier: "Thought is *jouissance*" ("God and the *Jouissance* of ~~The~~ Woman," *Feminine Sexuality* 142/*Encore* 66). It is implied that Lacan's own writing is a *jouissance*, a way of experiencing the Other without knowing anything about it. This *jouissance* of the Other is what lies beyond the phallus. He identifies such writing with the "essential testimony of the mystics" when he insists that "their mystical ejaculations are neither idle gossip nor mere verbiage, in fact they are the best thing you can read— note right at the bottom of the page, *Add the* Ecrits *of Jacques Lacan*, which is of the same order" ("God and the *Jouissance* of ~~The~~ Woman," *Feminine Sexuality* 147/*Encore* 71).

According to de Certeau, Lacan "belongs to no one. . . . He is Other" (48). His style suggests that he would like to be Other, but the messages he sends out are not always so ambivalent. (For example, the same Jacques Lacan who tells us to refuse what he offers also appointed in 1974 the commission of three members at the University of Vincennes which rejected Irigaray's teaching project, leading to her suspension [Irigaray 167n].) Still, there is no reason to confuse Lacan's style with his authority any more than we should confuse real women with the *object a* or their pleasure with God. Lacan's system, that is, his message, would seem to reduce women to the status of what Irigaray calls "awoman"—the woman who is not-all and whose pleasure has no law. But this message remains operative solely within the patriarchal economy of writing that imagines the phallus to be a necessary rather than a contingent representation. To say that patriarchal language, or phallogocentrism, is not-all, to say that woman as defined by this discourse is not-all, also points toward a different economy of writing, a style in excess and irreducible to what is the same. When the not-all defines the general economy of the symbolic rather than a supplementary relation to the One, it destroys the binary concept of sexual difference and articulates a radical difference. As Irigaray states it, it is no longer necessary for women to answer the question "What is woman?" Rather, "they should signify that with respect to this [logocentric] logic a *disruptive excess* is possible on the feminine side" (78). This excess constitutes a style that is not a style in the traditional sense: "This 'style,' or 'writing,' of women . . . resists and explodes every firmly established form, figure, idea or concept." Such a style "cannot be upheld as a thesis, cannot be the object of a position" (79). Though it does not make sense to say that such a style is the exclusive property of women (for it reverses the masculine logic of property), there are obviously historical reasons why women would find a voice in such a style. Lacan's voice is also marked by this style of excess—but not exclusively. There is a contradiction in his teaching between the voice of patriarchal authority and the style of the Other, between the desire for meaning and the *jouissance* of writing. Michel de Certeau argues that "Lacan is first of all an exercise of literature (a literature which would know what it is)" (51). A literature that would know what it is, is one reduced to self-identity as value. I would argue that Lacan's style does not know what it is, though it is always seeking that knowledge. It seeks knowledge of itself as Other but comes up only with the *object a*, about which all that can be said is, *that's not it*. This style that does not know what it is, like the writings of the mystics, nevertheless represents the "experience" of something. This something Other helps to explain Lacan's fascination with the other way of writing *jouissance*—Joyce.

At the Fifth International James Joyce Symposium at the Sorbonne on June 16, 1975, Lacan said of Joyce to an audience of Joyceans, "No one had ever made literature like this" ("Joyce le symptome I" 26). He was thinking of *Finnegans Wake*, about which he had already said a few things in *Encore*. Because "the signifiers are boxed in by one another, composed of one another, telescoped into one another . . . something is produced which, as signified, can appear enigmatic, but which clearly is nearest to what we other analysts, thanks to the analytic discourse, have to read—the *lapsus*" (37). Literature as the lapsus is a writing that does not know itself. At the Sorbonne, Lacan specified the application of the word *literature* to Joyce's writing by repeating "the equivocation on which Joyce frequently plays—*letter, litter*. The letter is waste" ("Joyce le symptome I" 26). The letter is litter: specifically, in *Finnegans Wake* it is the litter of the mother, the *jouissance* of the Other. As Lacan says in *Encore*, "*Jouissance* is that which has no use" (10), suggesting that, in writing, the play of language cannot be reduced to the meaning or functional value of a whole. *Finnegans Wake*—"the letter selfpenned to one's other, the neverperfect everplanned" (*Finnegans Wake* 489.33–34, citing page and lines)—operates on the general economy of the not-all so that in practice reading it is never simply a question of mastery. Despite the illusion of wholeness (this book formally closes in on itself, beginning and ending at the same structural point), nothing is ever the same from one sentence to the next. The same is always new, different (see Hart 31). John Bishop explains his technique of reading *Finnegans Wake* by lifting "quotations from all over the book, ripping single words out of context and attributing to the *Wake*'s sleeping hero phrases that ostensibly bear on other characters." As a critic, he abandons "sequential progression" and "has cultivated sense by a broad-ranging and digressive association whose only limits have been the covers of the book and the terms contained in it" (305). But Bishop finally rationalizes this process of reading by appealing to the traditional interpretation of *Finnegans Wake* as the representation of sleep and dreaming. With this sleight of hand, he can overthrow the economy of the not-all and regain a position for his reading that at least approaches the mastery of the whole. Derek Attridge has recently exposed and analyzed this strategy and concludes that the dream is "one among a number of such [interpretive] contexts which, though incompatible with one another, all have some potential value" (26). Though the use of the word "value" may seem innocent or innocuous in this context, I want to argue that it can never be so. To insist on critical pluralism in approaching *Finnegans Wake* leaves the phallogocentric economy intact. From this perspective, although there are as many readings as there are critics who can find different ways into the text, each approach must have its own integrity, must be One. David Hayman's genetic approach to the text through the analysis of the manuscripts and notebooks leads to the more radical concept of "an endlessly unfolding and self-enfolding process text, a Penelope's web that includes the reader in its perpetual elaboration and unmaking" (7). Does any reading that seeks the systematic answer to a question ever escape the desire for structural closure? For example, how do we analyze the representation of sexual difference in the *Finnegans Wake*?

Since an answer requires my own reading, I want to state plainly my assumptions about what animates such an activity. It is the desire of and for the Other. *Finnegans Wake* is a book of letters. It is the *litteral* truth of the letter. Though words can be constructed from these letters by both the eye and the ear, the word itself is not the medium of the book. Even when letters assume the "conventional" form of words, the letter takes priority over the word; for the word requires a stable syntax for the production of its identity as a meaningful whole. And this syntax is what *Finnegans Wake* continually dissolves. The ninth question in the "Riddles" chapter both states and illustrates what I mean: If a human being could have an "earsighted view of old hopeinhaven with all the ingredient and egregiunt whights and ways to which . . . the course of his tory will had been having recourses," including "the redissolusingness of mind-mouldered ease and the thereby hang of the Hoel of it, could such a none . . . byhold at ones what is main and why tis twain, how one once meet melts in tother wants poingnings, . . . then *what* would that fargazer seem to seemself to seem seeming of, dimm it all?" The answer is "A collideorscape!" (143.9–28). If I use these letters as a formula for reading *Finnegans Wake*, I have to keep in mind Attridge's observation: "The trouble with appealing to such a description to explain what the book is about is that it poses exactly the same problems as those which, on a wider canvas, it is being used to solve" (15). In my case, I have to read this text in order to devise a theory about how it is to be read. I can approach its truth as radical alterity only by situating it as the *object a* in relation to my desire as a subject. That is, I start out from the assumption that this writing knows what it is and that it can be made to speak of what it knows. But this assumption is contradicted by the fact that in order to make it speak I have to cut away part of it and reduce it to an equational structure. Therefore, the first rule of this reading is that I cannot read everything, I can read only the *not-everything*.

The "earsighted view of old hopeinhaven" implies a view of the Other—the Other world, perhaps, but also the view of this world seen as Other, a utopia beyond the hegemony of the eye. It is the world seen through the ear and, therefore, seen as near, in proximity. The object of this "nearsighted" view is not-all, but it is close. It touches us with the comings and goings ("ingredient and egregiunt") of humans and cultures that have dominated history, the tory or aristocratic story,—that is, history from the viewpoint of the victors. That this his-story "will had been" is the hope for a future *Other than the past*. As the *Wake* children learn at their studies, "Pastimes is past times" (263.17). History always was a pastime, or a children's game, for those who succumb to what Stephen Dedalus in *Ulysses* calls a "dull ease of the mind" (*Ulysses* 20), which harbors the illusion that it has grasped the "whole." The whole is a hole. But the word "hole" contains the proper name Hoel. He was the father of Isolde of the White Hands, the one Tristram married in lieu of the one he loved. As she was the proper daughter, Hoel is the proper father or the Law of the Father, which dissolves, disintegrates, or becomes dissolute in the process of time. Can a human who is constituted as "none," that is, not-One, behold or look at the Ones and see that what appears as central or "main" is in fact double? Can the not-One see how the One that was once proper or "meet" melts into its other, how One meets different "ones," or heterogeneity, and wants points or purposes or laws to rationalize and limit difference? (According to Adaline Glasheen, "poingnings" alludes to Sir Edward Poyning, who "in 1459 [more accurately, 1494] induced the Irish parliament to pass 'Poyning's Law,' which said all acts of the English parliament were in force in Ireland, and the Irish parliament could pass no laws without the king's approval" [238]). From these perspectives what would the "fargazer" (who is in fact near- or earsighted) seem to his seeming-self (Lacan's *moi*) to seem to see the appearances of, damn it all and dim the all? The answer is: collide or escape. That is, the gazer *either* enters the process of culture and collides with the chain of signifiers that makes it up *or* escapes into the ideal, the *all*, the view from the outside. In either case, what is seen or experienced is the kaleidoscope, a world of differences. The human either enters into "experience" (i.e, the margin between the symbolic and the "real") or observes it from the outside. Attridge reformulates the question: "Is our 'human being' looking at something real out there—a landscape of collisions (history, myth, family life, politics, religion, a changing rainbow)—or at something that he has created himself by shaking the kaleidoscope, a projection of his own interpretive activity?" (17). My conclusion is that the one who thinks he or she sees the "real" as a whole from a detached position escapes into the supreme fiction or delusion. The other who collides with the world comes to see or hear or feel or touch the world as the not-all. The self becomes an *it*, a link in the chain, a metonymic point of proximity and not a self-contained whole.

This reading, of course, is not all. It lacks "integrity." It tells us that we either collide with the text, in which case we cannot see it as a whole; or we withdraw from it and so see it at the price of not reading its letters (the fate of the nearsighted). The only authentic response to the reading I have produced is to say with Lacan, *that's not it*. The reading of the text does not produce an object that is identical to itself. It only opens the space for further reading in the interminable process of symbolization. Nevertheless, such a reading, while it fails to give us knowledge of the text by reducing it to an integral meaning essential to the whole, brings us face to face with the alterity of writing, with the wall of language, with the letter as litter.

It is probably not a coincidence that the riddle immediately following the one I have been reading occasions as its answer the first of Issy's three hypothetical letters (excluding her practice letter) in *Finnegans Wake*: "What bitter's love but yurning, what' sour lovemutch but a bref burning till shee that drawes dothe smoake retourne?" (143.29–30). According to Roland McHugh, the riddle parodies these lines from a song by Rosseter:

"What then is love but mourning, / What Desire but a self-burning, / Till she that hates doth love return." In Joyce's rewriting, the "mourning" becomes the bitterness of desire; and the "self-burning" is the brief burning of love's letter (German *der Brief*) which sours the love match. The letter burns until the "shee" who draws desire to her as a fireplace draws air burns out and sends up smoke. The suggestion is that love and hate are the smoke screens of each other. But what is the letter? In the answer to the riddle, Issy supposedly writes a letter to her other—both her lover and her reflection in the mirror. Since Danis Rose and John O'Hanlon identify Shaun as "the answerer *par excellence*" in this section as well as in the rest of *Finnegans Wake*, it could be argued that Joyce wants to represent the co-optation of the feminine voice by the masculine subject (88). This reading, however, ignores the undecidability of the subject position in this text. In any case, it is always the voice of Joyce's symptom that we are reading and to which we must ascribe a language of *jouissance*: "Now open, pet, your lips, pepette, like I used my sweet parted lipsabuss with Dan Holohan of facetious memory taught me after the flannel dance, with the proof of love, up Smock Alley the first night he smelled pouder and I coloured beneath my fan, *pipetta mia*, when you learned me the linguo to melt" (147.29–34).

Mimicking Swift's "little language" in *The Journal to Stella*, these words could be read as Issy's address to her mirror image while she puts on lipstick. Or they could be a message to the lover who taught her how to use the tongue (Latin *lingua*) in order to melt or come. Shari Benstock observes that the lips could also be labia since "lips and labia are opened and silenced (momentarily) by the sexual act" ("Apostrophizing the Feminine" 595). In any case, Issy's lover also taught her how to use language (lingo) in order to come. Since readers can never be completely certain as to the sexual identity of this speaker (unless they accept one interpretive framework), they can also insert themselves into the position of addressee. Then the passage becomes an invitation to open your lips and speak the language of melting. *Finnegans Wake* is sometimes thought of as a book that should be read aloud if one is to experience its language and take pleasure in it:

> Whowham would have ears like ours, the blackhaired! Do you like that, *silenzioso*? Are you enjoying, this same little me, my life, my love? Why do you like my whisping? Is it not divinely deluscious? But in't bafforyou? *Misi, misi!* Tell me till my thrillme comes! I will not break the seal. I am enjoying it still, I swear I am! Why do you prefer its in these dark nets, if why may ask, my sweetykins? (147.34–148.4)

Who or what blackguard would have ears like ours? The answer is everyone. We the readers, the others, have to be silent (*silenzioso*) in order to listen. Issy is associated with listening just as Shaun is with seeing and Shem with hearing (Rose and O'Hanlon 93n). If seeing is identified with masculine aggression and activity and hearing with passivity, Issy's "listening" is active-passive. It dissolves the boundaries separating subject and object. She says, "Are you enjoying . . . I am enjoying it still," because there is no self-other boundary to this *jouissance*. The "whisping" that we like, Issy's lisping, is the discourse of the big Other, the lapsus, the word that does not know itself. The seal must not be broken or the meaning revealed if we are to experience the alterity of the letter. *Why do you* (reader, other, lover, self) *prefer its* (the *jouissance* of the Other, the it) *in these dark nets,* (the discourse of the Other), *if why* (the unconscious or barred subject) *may ask, my sweetykins?* There is no answer to this question, for the subject of this discourse does not know what it is saying, and says so: "I thought ye knew all and more, ye aucthor, to explique to ones the significat of their exsystems with your nieu nivulon lead" (148.16–18). Issy would seem to be addressing the author as actor and complaining that he ought to be able to use his new lead role as a cloudy sky (Provençal *nivoulan*) or his new lead pencil to explain to the "ones"—to men who see themselves each one as One—the significance of their existences, that is, their lives as constructed from systems (of value and meaning). The author's new lead role is that of Nuvoletta ("little cloud") or Issy herself as she appears in the tale of the Mookse and the Gripes "in her lightdress, spun of sisteen shimmers" (157.8). The author would seem to be resisting the forbidden pleasure of his own writing: "Did you really never in all our cantalang [sorrowful? from Irish *canntal,* "sorrow"] lives speak clothse to a girl's before" (148.22–24). Did he never speak close to a girl? Or did his speech as clothing never come close to a girl's?

As John Gordon remarks, "If Issy is the dreamer's dream-girl, then it seems natural for her to be identified with his dream, which is to say, with the *Wake* itself" (79). This statement presupposes that *Finnegans Wake* is the *representation* of a dream; but if Issy were able to represent the *Wake,* it would be by manifesting in language the unspeakable *jouissance* that dislocates the subject-object dyad on which any representation is founded. David Macey has written that in Lacan's discourse *jouissance* "can . . . signify the ecstatic or orgasmic enjoyment of something or someone, and the expression *jouissance de la femme* can simultaneously mean 'the female orgasm' and the 'enjoyment of the woman'" (202). Still, these categories of *jouissance* both operate within the phallic economy as

Lacan understands it. He says early in *Encore*, "The analytic experience shows that everything [*tout*] turns around phallic *jouissance*, and, through this, that woman is defined positionally . . . as the *not-everything* [*pas-tout*] with respect to phallic *jouissance*" (13). But phallic *jouissance* is not the experience of orgasm in itself, male or female, but the representation of sexual pleasure within the phallocentric system of meaning. The "experience" of orgasm and other sexual pleasures are in the "real" and thus resist symbolization. Phallocentrism determines and represents male and female pleasure as a function of the phallus, of what can be seen and visually represented. Any pleasure outside the determinations of this representation is transgressive, that is, outside the law of patriarchy. As Irigaray observes, "the predominance of the visual, and of the discrimination and individualization of form, is particularly foreign to female eroticism." Within the scopic economy, the woman's "sexual organ represents *the horror of nothing to see.*" Consequently, "if woman takes pleasure precisely from this incompleteness of form which allows her organ to touch itself over and over again, indefinitely, by itself, that pleasure is denied by a civilization that privileges phallomorphism" (26). Such a feminine pleasure, beyond the phallus, cannot be expressed in language without threatening "the underpinnings of logical operations" (77). I take this to be not a dismissal of logic per se but a refusal to submit to the universal logic of patriarchy, which limits language to the functions of representation and communication. The *jouissance* underlying patriarchal language is clearly phallic. It reduces language to a univocal value as the means of transferral of information. Every other linguistic function is set aside or downgraded as fiction or nonsense. Still, this phallocentric economy of language can be challenged by a different economy in which "there would no longer be either a right side or a wrong side of discourse, or even of texts, but each passing from one to the other would make audible and comprehensible even what resists the recto-verso structure that shores up common sense" (Irigaray 80). Such a linguistic economy, or style, would articulate the *jouissance* beyond the phallus and, therefore, one that could be written as "feminine." But the word "feminine" would no longer operate within the "recto-verso structure" of patriarchal discourse. The *jouissance* of the Other, beyond the phallus, could be written as feminine but not exclusively as feminine in the sense that the feminine would be the only one. The *jouissance* of the Other is not-One not only in the sense that it is incomplete (that would be its definition within the phallic economy) but in the sense that it negates the One and makes possible the play (and pleasure) of radical alterity.

At the end of her first letter, Issy admits to her inexperienced lover/self the truth of her own desire: "As I'd live to, O, I'd love to! Liss, liss! I muss whiss! . . . Or ever for bitter be the frucht of this hour!" (148.26–29). (Translating roughly, to be alive is to desire, and love is the form desire takes. But listen, listen, I must know [German *muss wissen*] this experience or ever forbidden and bitter be the fruit of this hour!) For Issy, the pleasures of love are bitter precisely to the extent they are forbidden, or outside the law. But that bitterness is also a form of ecstasy before the unbearable face of death/God/the Other. It involves the drive "to be at last Other" which Lacan described as the goal of his life. David Macey remarks that "*Jouissance* . . . comprises an element of horror, a highly eroticized death drive that makes terrible promises, which goes far beyond the pleasure principle and which can imply possession in both an active and a passive sense." He then cites Serge Leclaire's description of *jouissance* as signaling "immediacy of access to that 'pure difference' which the erotic seeks to find at the extreme point where it borders on death, and sometimes even in the annulment of the border itself" (204). Issy longs for the Other sex, not the masculine sex or its opposite, but the pure difference constitutive of her own being. There is some horror or bitterness in this longing because patriarchal law defines anything outside its norms as a monstrosity. But there is also sweetness: "Pipette. I can almost feed their sweetness with my lisplips" (276, n. 6). Issy's lisp and lips as figures of the "experience" of *jouissance* beyond the phallus almost anticipate Irigaray's attempt to construct a sexual imaginary based on the form of the female body: "Her genitals are formed of two lips in continuous contact" (24). Even if cultural norms have alienated women from the pleasure of their own bodies, the result may be a pleasure that is bittersweet, beyond the order of representation, though it may take the form of the mystical as the only *legal* way to articulate itself in patriarchal language.

In her second letter, the long footnote in the "Night Lessons" section, Issy writes that, with all the "gelded ewes" about, that is, her female others who sheepishly conform to the patriarchy that defines them as gelded or incomplete, "I was thinking fairly killing times of putting an end to myself and my malody, when I remembered all your pupil-teacher's erringnesses in perfection class. You sh'undn't write you can't if you w'udn't pass for undevelopmented" (279n, lines 3–6). Issy's letter signifies what Julia Kristeva would call the abject, a writing that emerges from the borderline between subject and object, life and death. What causes abjection, says Kristeva, is "what disturbs identity, system, order.

What does not respect borders, positions, rules. The in-between, the ambiguous, the composite" (*Powers of Horror* 4). Issy writes her abjection as a letter in order to go on living, but in a class on perfection every abject writing is really an erring or wandering away from the point. As a figure in the margins, writing the footnotes to the logocentric text of patriarchal culture, she feels that her writing lacks authorization—that she shouldn't write, since she can't, if she wouldn't pass for undeveloped. Still, she can reverse the conventions that confine her: "This is the propper [writing "proper" improperly, with two p's, recalling the "Ppt" of Swift's little language] way to say that, Sr. If it's me chews to swallow all you saidn't you can eat my words for it as sure as there's a key in my kiss" (279n, lines 6–8). Having swallowed the forbidden fruit (all that the teacher did not say), Issy passes it to the master as the discourse of forbidden pleasure, the key in her kiss. She is Arrah-na-Pogue or Nora of the Kiss (from Dion Boucicault's play), who gets her heroic brother out of jail by hiding a message in her mouth and conveying it with a kiss. Her kiss takes the form of a style, "all the runes of the gamest game ever" learned "from my old nourse Asa" (279n, lines 19–20). Ironically, her old nurse is also her old Nordic father, Odin or Asa. She implies that she can use the letters or "runes" of the father's language for her own purposes, to write her bittersweet pleasure. As she boasts, "This isabella I'm on knows the ruelles of the rut [the rules of the road] and she don't fear andy mandy [any man]" (279n, lines 30–31). She also knows the rules of the rut, the passageways to sexual ecstasy.

In her third letter, Issy writes the "little language" of love to Shaun (her "male corrispondee" [457.28]), though once again it is difficult to distinguish subject from object, self from other. As Shari Benstock comments, "There lurks too the suspicion that Issy like Swift may be playing both the male and female parts, a hint at sex reversal as well as narcissism" ("The Genuine Christine" 188). (In this connection, William Atherton notes, "It is from this idea of a Swift divided in himself that Joyce quotes the remark about 'That letter selfpenned to one's other,' for it was Swift who was accused of writing letters to himself—owing to the similarity of Stella's handwriting to his own" [116].) Issy prays for Shaun with "Madge, my linkingclass girl"; and it may be that this looking-glass other is the real object of Issy's desire. This "Sosy" (or twin), who is her "sosiety," "would kiss my white arms for me so gratefully but apart from that she's terribly nice really, my sister, . . . and I'll be strictly forbidden always and true in my own way and private where I will long long to betrue you along with one who will so betrue you that not once while I betreu him not once well he be betray himself." What is forbidden and made private (as in private property) are her privates where she longs to betray "you" (Shaun or her imaginary other?) and be "true" to the Other. This big Other is the truth that cannot betray (or reveal) itself or "him"; for both self and other, masculine and feminine, are grounded in the alterity of this social text. "He fell for my lips, for my lisp, for my lewd speaker. I felt for his strength, his manhood, his do you mind?" (459.4–29). He falls for her lisping language of unrepresentable pleasure, while she feels for his strength and his phallic masculine mind. But Issy is not a vampire and says, "You can trust me though I change thy name though not the letter never. . . . I will give your lovely face of mine away, my boyish bob, . . . to my second mate, with the twirlers the engineer of the passioflower (O the wicked untruth! whot a tell! that he has bought me in his wellingtons what you haven't got!), in one of those pure clean lupstucks of yours thankfully, Arrah of the passkeys, no matter what" (459.31–460.3). Issy may change the name of the father, the phallus, the masculine subject, but not the letter as the material substance of the social tie. She will give the image of herself that she sees in her "boyish bob" to her second mate, her other self in the mirror. I don't know who or what the "twirlers" are, but they seem to engineer the flower of passion when lips get stuck together. Parenthetically, Issy comments to her other self about the "wicked untruth" of this man's imagining that he has bought her with his phallus (the duke of Wellington's memorial resembled one), which her specular image seemed to lack. On the contrary, Issy holds the key to her sexual pleasure in her own mouth. The passkey is her tongue or her ability to speak, which enables her to articulate her own *jouissance*. Her love may seem narcissistic, but in loving her neighbor as herself (especially the neighbor locked in the mirror next to her: "Lock my mearest next myself" [460.4]), she experiences the Other that has no other. She speaks as the collective subject ("We. We. Issy done that, I confesh!" [459.6–7]) and begs our trust: "We say. Trust us. Our game" (460.14–15). She promises to write down all the names of her other (not just Shaun but all the others including HCE, ALP, Shem, and the looking-glass girl). She empties the property out of the *proper* name by reducing it to the letter. "Everyday, precious, while m'm'ry's leaves are falling deeply on my Jungfraud's Messongebook I will dream telepath posts dulcets on this isingglass stream (but don't tell him or I'll be the mort of him)" (460.19–22). The letters are written in her memory; and, as the leaves fall on Freud and Jung's fraudulent book of lies (French *mensonges*) or book of my dreams (*mes songes*), she sends her boy sweet messages telepathically in her dreams, through her looking-glass (Issy-is-in-[the]-glass) stream. Her letters constitute an unconscious discourse, a lapsus or lisp, that should not be told, or it will confront the subject with the radical alterity of death.

(Issy's discourse could be said to anticipate Lacan's break with Freud in the way it conceptualizes the unconscious. Though the unconscious is structured *like* a language, it should not be construed to be identical with language; for as the discourse of the Other, it refers not to an objective system but to a relation. It resembles Baudrillard's *symbolic* discourse, which can be radically distinguished from the object of classical psycho-analysis:

> In poetic (symbolic) discourse, the signifier is absolutely dissolved—whereas in psychoanalytic discourse it is only altered under the effect of primary processes, distorted by the crumpling action of repressed values—but whether it [the psychoanalytic signifier] is distorted, trans-versal, or "padded," it remains a surface indexed on the heaving reality of the unconscious. On the other hand, in poetic discourse, it [the signifier] is diffracted and irradiated in the anagrammatic process, it no longer falls under the sway of the law which sets it up, nor under the influence of the repressed content which binds it, it no longer has anything to designate, not even the ambivalence of a repressed signified. It is no longer anything other than dissemination, absolution from value—and this is experienced without a trace of anguish, in total and non-perverse pleasure. The illumination of the work of art, or of the symbolic act, is in that point of non-repression, of no residue, of no return—that illumination which suspends repression and the endless repetiton of inhibition and value—and unhesitatingly plays the card of its own death in the dissolution of meaning. ("Beyond the Unconscious" 66)

Similarly, for Lacan there is only the signifier to articulate the uncon-scious as a concrete relation, or symbolic exchange, between life and death. Freud's dream book is a book of lies when it sets up an economy of equivalences between manifest and latent content. Lacan theorizes the unconscious "beyond the Unconscious," as that which is read in the disfigurations or dislocutions of style.)

Issy's looking glass does not simply reflect. It is a stream like the one Nuvoletta falls into after the Mookse and the Gripes, or Shaun and Shem, ignore her to death. After this fall, "her muddied name was Missisliffi" (159.12–13). Through her writing, her reduction of the proper names to the letter as litter, the discourse of the Other, which patriarchal man in his dual (that is, imaginary) relation to himself will not hear, Issy becomes her mother. Irigaray, in reading the Lacan of *Encore*, is particularly critical of his suggestion that, in her words, "there is, *for women*, no possible law for their pleasure. No more than there is any possible discourse" (95). But if there is an/Other *jouissance* beyond the phallus, to what law does it appeal? Julia Kristeva tries to define this Other authority: "Writing causes the subject who ventures in it to confront an archaic authority, on the nether side of the proper Name. The maternal connotations of this authority never escaped great writers, no more than the coming face to face with what we have called abjection" (*Powers of Horror* 75). I don't think this is just another idealization of the mother; it is a recognition that the mother's body signifies for the human subject a relation to language beyond the closed structures of patriarchal ideology. Kristeva specifies her position at the end of *Powers of Horror*:

> If "something maternal" happens to bear upon the uncertainty that I call abjection, it illuminates the literary scription of the essential struggle that a writer (man or woman) has to engage in with what he calls demonic only to call attention to it as the inseparable obverse of his very being, of the other (sex), that torments and possesses him. Does one write under any other condition than being possessed by abjection, in an indefinite catharsis? (208)

If ALP embodies in *Finnegans Wake* this "something maternal," it is nevertheless Issy's function to mark the site of a struggle with the demonic by writing the *jouissance* of the Other. It is her indefinite catharsis, her abjection, her bitter litter, that cracks the mirror of identity (and production) in order to get at the "pure difference," that is, the difference irreducible to any system of values, any privileging of one term (or one sex) over the other.

Issy cracks her mirror and undoes the imaginary world of representation: "Though Wonderlawn's lost us for ever. Alis, alas, she broke the glass! Liddell lokker through the leafery, ours is a mistery of pain" (270.19–22). Like the Alice modeled on Charles Dodgson's little friend Alice Liddell, Issy goes through the looking glass only to discover the mystery of pain. Her footnote to this passage of "Night Lessons" reads: "Dear and I trust in all frivolity I may be pardoned for trespassing but I think I may add hell" (270 n. 3). Issy's transgressions lead her to "hell," the place for everything escaping the codifications of patriarchal law. It is also the place of a bitter burning desire. But she speaks of it "in all frivolity," reminding us that behind the mist of pain lies the ecstasy of Eucharistic transubstantiation (the French *pain*, or bread), the mystery of becoming Other. As "lokker" (that is, looker or, in Dutch, tempter), Issy tempts or seduces patriarchal language away from its meaning functions toward truth (not verification). To quote Baudrillard again, her style manifests "the original way in which [a discourse] absorbs meaning and empties itself of meaning in order better to fascinate others: the primitive seduction of language" ("On Seduction," *Selected Writings* 150).

In "The Mime of Mick, Nick, and the Maggies," Issy tries to teach Shem how to read the letters on the surface of language as the key to her desire. She demonstrates the problem in her first clue: "I am (twintomine) all these thing. Up tighty in the front, down again on the loose, drim and drumming on her back and a pop from her whistle. What is that, O holytroopers? Isot givin yoe?" (223.9–11). This is a lesson on how to read *Finnegans Wake*. Although Issy's color, heliotrope, is rewritten in the word "holytroopers," what Shem really needs to guess is her sexual identity as his "twintomine," his imaginary other. This masculine imaginary creates the illusion of depth, beyond which lies the surface, the pantomine or sexual masquerade that Shem has to learn how to spell out if he is ever to experience the *jouissance* that his sister's language game articulates. She sends him a message "on herzian waves," "a butterfly from her zipclasped handbag, a wounded dove astarted from, escaping out her forecotes. Isle wail for yews, O doherlynt!" (232.10–13). The message that Issy's linguistic heart broadcasts recalls what Stephen Dedalus describes in *A Portrait of the Artist as a Young Man* as "the silent stasis of esthetic pleasure, a spiritual state very like to that cardiac condition . . . called an enchantment of the heart" (203), with the exception that this pleasure is no longer static or merely aesthetic. It emerges on the borderline between the symbolic and the physical (that is, the "real")— the place of the letter. Issy's body is her "house of breathings" of which we can say: "There lies her word, you reder!" (249.6–14). Eventually, Issy gives up on Shem, who can't see the letters for the words, the fantasy of *whole* words. He does better in the next episode, "Night Lessons," where it is Shaun who cannot spell. In the Mime, Shem is Glugg, the "duvlin sulph" or Devil himself (222.25), that is, in Kristeva's terms, the demonic other sex that Issy would like to seduce away from the phallic economy (she says, "For I see through your weapon" [248.15]) toward the economy of the big Other, the not-all. He is the obverse of her being. When she turns to Shaun with the words, "And Sunny, my gander, he's coming to land her. The boy which she now adores" (249.18–19), she is really turning away from the Other sex to her self as the other. Shaun is her "gander" because he defines her gender *heliotropically* within the visual economy of phallocentrism. If she has gone as far as "she could shake him" with Shem, who is "An oaf, no more," she still has enough hope to think he might make a good tutor, "and she be waxen in his hands. Turning up and fingering over the most dantellising peaches in the lingerous longerous book of the dark." Dante's most tantalizing peaches are the fruits of his writing beyond the message of his Christianity, the letters that can be incorporated into that "lingerous longerous book of the dark," *Finnegans Wake*. It is Issy's turn to take the risks and confront the particularity of her own relation to language: "Let his be exasperated, letters be blowed! I is a femaline person. O, of provocative gender. U unisingular case" (251.21–32). As Bonnie Kime Scott comments,

> While these last lines could be interpreted as Issy's renunciation of "letters," and more evidence of her mindlessness, there is more to them. "Femaline" shows the same concern with her own shape or "line" as do many of the mirror passages—a desire to know herself. "Provocative" can make Issy a confirmed "temptress" if that is what one is looking for. Or she can be reviewed as a protester. "Unisingular case" insists on her oneness, her separation. The IOU links Issy's musings to Stephen's in the library scene of *Ulysses*, where he states "A.E.I.O.U." Both have a debt to the establishment, which they resent even as they acknowledge it, and insist on their separateness. (*Joyce and Feminism* 191–92)

I would suggest that Issy's debt is ambivalent. Though she recognizes her inscription within the established patriarchal culture that writes her as female, provocative, and alone, she also draws attention to the letters that signify her debt. She does not say, "IOU"; rather, she decomposes the letters in order to rewrite her debt as the pure difference that constitutes her social tie. Let the letters be blowed—that is, blown apart and separated. Language is not a prison house of identities but a collection of letters that can be rearranged and rewritten. Issy's style, like Lacan's style, contradicts its own message. If she wants to know herself and to see herself, her "I", as one and universal (which is to see herself in the imaginary as if the mirror were not broken), she is deflected from such self-knowledge by the opacity of her style (the broken mirror). Who is Issy? "What will be is. Is is" (620.32). Issy is *is*—not what is, the object of being, but the being of being, the *jouissance* of being. "What analytic discourse brings out," says Lacan, "is this fact, which was already intimated in the philosophy of being—that there is a *jouissance* of being" ("God and the *Jouissance* of ~~The~~ Woman," *Feminine Sexuality* 142/*Encore* 66). Since, as Adaline Glasheen comments, "every 'is' [in the *Wake*] indicates Issy" (138), her name has no unity or identity but rather disseminates or doubles itself. This double copula articulates a being beyond the objects of being or the objectivity of being: it divides being from itself. Lacan says that in the symbolic the phallus is "the equivalent . . . of the (logical) copula" ("The Meaning of the Phallus," *Feminine Sexuality* 82). In this connection, the phallus as representation erases irreducible difference through the construction of the One sex. The double copula reverses that effect by subverting the logical function of identity and articulating a being in difference, a writing of being as difference, a *jouissance* of being beyond the dichotomy between subject and object. The object of being can be represented as One, but the being of being is not-One (and calls into question the ontological difference of Being written with a capital *B*).

Issy is the *Wake* itself, but not because she is somebody's dream girl. She is Joyce's language, the joyce of language, Joyce's *jouissance*. On the page following Issy's IOU, we read that "each was wrought with his other" (252.14). The brothers and their "siss" are wrought with one another; and each is wrought with the big Other. In "Night Lessons," the line reappears with different letters: "And Key was wreathed with his pother" (303.15). "Key" could be she or he; "pother" could be brother or other. The other with the *p* is associated with Issy's use of Swift's little language, "pepette." The key is the message hidden in her kiss. From the last to the first page of *Finnegans Wake*, her lips are the keys, the gift of her mother: "Lps. The keys to. Given! A way a lone a last a loved a long the" (628.15–16)—the?—the "riverrun" (3.1) of *jouissance*.

Lacan states rather plainly what should be the effect of psychoanalysis: "The analysis must aim at the passage of true speech, joining the subject to an other subject, on the other side of the wall of language. That is the final relation of the subject to a genuine Other, to the Other who gives the answer one doesn't expect, which defines the terminal point of the analysis" (*The Ego* 246). The termination of *Finnegans Wake* is the beginning, the arrival of the unexpected answer to the question the book never ceases to pose. The answer is never finished, the book never complete. Like psychoanalysis, it is not-all. The termination of analysis comes about not through psychic resolution or the reconstruction of the "whole subject" (ego) or the whole text. It happens when the imaginary system has been ruptured and the symbolic social tie reestablished. It happens when communication fails, the mirror cracks, and the "genuine Other" gives the unexpected answer. Communication always falters on the unexpected. In a literary work, this effect is not reducible to the intention of the artist or, deterministically, to a single dimension of the social context. It demonstrates or reveals the process of overdetermination through its resistance to any single determination, any simple cause. In *Finnegans Wake*, "riverrun" marks the unexpected, language as excess and overflow, a *jouissance* beyond the phallus. It induces the "experience" of alterity in the ecstasy of a style.

4
Woolf's Other

All for a moment wavered and bent in uncertainty and ambiguity, as if a great moth sailing through the room had shadowed the immense solidity of chairs and tables with floating wings.

—VIRGINIA WOOLF, *The Waves*

Virginia Woolf called *The Waves* "my first work in my own style" (*Diary* 4:53). She considered it a beginning, achieved only after she had passed through a crisis of style in trying to write what she called at first "The Moths." In 1928 she thought the latter "was to be an abstract mystical eyeless book." She wanted to get beyond the style of *To the Lighthouse*: "so fluent and fluid that it runs through the mind like water." She thought of writing "books that relieve other books: a variety of styles & subjects: for after all, that is my temperament, I think: to be very little persuaded of the truth of anything—what I say, what people say—always to follow, blindly instinctively with a sense of leaping over a precipice—the call of—the call of—now, if I write The Moths I must come to terms with these mystical feelings" (*Diary* 3:203). It seems to me that these mystical feelings have little to do with the call of some other world or God but with the alterity of the symbolic dimension. After reading a negative review, Woolf came almost to distrust the "fluent and fluid" style of *To the Lighthouse* as an experience or *jouissance* that leaves no trace as it passes "through the mind like water." Or perhaps the trace it leaves insinuates an experience of excess that points to another economy beyond that of pleasure and pain. It was such ambivalence after completing *To the Lighthouse* which led Woolf to conceive of writing the book that would become *The Waves*. In 1926 she analyzed her "glooms" and speculated that "in part they are the result of getting away by oneself, & have a psychological interest which the usual state of working & enjoying lacks." Her "plunge into deep waters," though "a little alarming," was "full of interest." This state has "an edge to it which I feel of great importance": "One goes down into the well & nothing protects one from the assault of truth. Down there I can't write or read; I exist however. I am. Then I ask myself what I am? & get a closer though less flattering answer than I should on the surface" (*Diary* 3:112). Woolf feels called upon to write an "eyeless" book, a book beyond the domination of the subjective gaze. She wants to articulate an experience that defies classical representation and the everyday economies of pleasure and pain. She wants to trace the edge of being—that moment of "uncertainty and ambiguity" in which the subject answers the call of its own difference from itself, its own alterity. This is the call of the moth whose wings shadow reality and articulate the *jouissance* of being.

The present discussion could be described as an attempt to clarify Woolf's use of the adjective of possession, "own," both in the quoted statement about the style of *The Waves* and in her feminist classic, *A Room of One's Own*. I will try to show that when Woolf says "my own style" the possessive must be qualified by a writing practice or rhetorical strategy that divides the subject of such possession from itself and marks it with alterity in its constitution as a socially symbolic position. This alterity receives more emphatic articulation in the phrase "a room of one's own," where possession is situated in the indefinite pronoun "one." The suggestion is that by coming into her own, or finding her own style and space, Woolf does not arrive at the place of self-identity, her true being or essence both as a person and as a woman. On the contrary, she comes to herself in the place of the Other, the place of the indefinite social identity. The effect is not simply to defer difference by insisting on its difference from itself, but to reverse it, annul it, in an act of symbolic exchange. Such an act does not put an end to difference as the incommensurable or irreducible in social processes but rather annuls value and resists the absorption of differences into social hierarchies that distribute value through the mediation of a system or code. In *The Waves*, Virginia Woolf tries to privilege not the symbolic order as the Law of Culture, or the system of social values, but the Other, with a capital O.

She reverses the Law of Culture in order to disrupt the production of value.

For this context, I need to point out that in privileging the Other, Woolf privileges the unpresentable, what Lyotard has called the postmodern in the modern, or "that which, in the modern, puts forward the unpresentable in presentation itself" (*The Postmodern Condition* 81). Strictly speaking, she could not know that she was privileging the Other for the obvious reason that Lacan had not yet introduced this term, with the specific value he gives it, into the critical vocabulary of her time. She also could not know it for the subtle reason that the effects of the Other are unconscious (in Lacan's phrasing, the unconscious is the discourse of the Other). As I noted earlier, the term "unconscious" does not refer to the presence or absence of consciousness but to an effect of language that is not grounded in the logic of meaning. Woolf could possibly have intended the "unconscious" effect of her work, but *she could not have known it objectively*. Her work destroys the separation between subject and object and thus refuses the Western concept of knowledge founded on the principle of reason. In doing so, it transmits to its readers precisely what psychoanalysis transmits to those who follow its teachings: "It is called—a style" (Lacan, *Ecrits* 458). Those passages in her works which resonate with Lacanian theory suggest a compatibility of styles that does as much to clarify contemporary psychoanalysis as to clarify Woolf's fiction. In *Ulysses*, I have argued elsewhere, Joycean repression is a form of representation (see *Paperspace*). Woolf attempts to represent the Other through a repression of the symbolic order with its patriarchal code. She fails, of course. The symbolic cannot be repressed, because such a repression would be the end of repression and perhaps the beginning of schizophrenia. This is so because, as Judith Butler stresses, "the repression of the feminine does not require that the agency of repression and the object of repression be ontologically distinct. Indeed, repression may be understood to produce the object that it comes to deny" (93). To repress repression would be to eliminate the very object one wanted to liberate in the first place—in this case, the material or linguistic ground of subjectivity. All that would remain would be a subjectless or schizophrenic relation to the symbolic. Woolf's work is never schizophrenic (not even in the way that Joyce's is). On the contrary, I want to argue that in failing to repress the symbolic, Woolf reverses it and miraculously succeeds in presenting the unpresentable.

In the introduction to her influential work *Sexual/Textual Politics*, Toril Moi criticizes some feminists, most notably Elaine Showalter, for evading the political effects of Virginia Woolf's writing. She suggests that by not "locating the politics of Woolf's writing *precisely in her textual practice*," these critics project an essentialist view of writing onto her work without paying attention to its deconstructive reversals (16). They also bypass her challenge to the humanist concept of identity, especially as it applies to sexual difference. Moi aligns Woolf's textual practice with Julia Kristeva's critical theory, which she reads as a refusal of biologism and essentialism. Like Kristeva, Woolf articulates a third feminist position beyond liberal and radical feminisms, "one that has deconstructed the opposition between masculinity and femininity" (Moi 12). Finally, in advocating an antihumanist approach to Woolf, Moi identifies Perry Meisel's book *The Absent Father*, as the "only study of Woolf to have integrated some of the theoretical advances of post-structuralist thought" (17). She praises Meisel for having grasped the "radically deconstructed character" of Woolf's writing and quotes with approval his remark: "With 'difference' the reigning principle in Woolf as well as Pater, there can be no natural or inherent characteristics of any kind, even between the sexes, because all character, all language, even the language of sexuality, emerges by means of a difference from itself" (234). Although Moi's reassessment of Woolf's relation to feminism seems to me on the whole timely, I find her concluding reference to Meisel curious for several reasons. First, it ignores the context in which Meisel makes his remark: he is criticizing Woolf for not seeing the real implications of her theory of difference, for not seeing that the only difference between the sexes is difference itself (in some originary sense). Second, it fails to demarcate the patriarchal ideology that underlies Meisel's reading of Woolf and the theory of influence he espouses. By pondering this problem for a moment, I think we can begin to elaborate on Woolf's theory of difference and the critical role alterity plays within it.

In *The Absent Father*, Meisel examines the influence of Walter Pater on Virginia Woolf. In opposition to what he calls the "current political trend in Woolf scholarship" (i.e. feminism), Meisel argues for the theory of influence as "a more purely literary equation." This equation, both literary and historical, is really a paternal metaphor, which frames Woolf's text by curtailing any effects it may produce outside the boundaries of literature as an institution. Influence in this equation articulates authority as the paternal stamp. As Meisel describes it, "the exemplary pressure of Pater's precedent . . . leads Woolf to attempt to expunge his authority despite, and because of, its lawgiving powers, and it is on the questions of authors, authority, and influence itself that we shall find the real lines of battle to be drawn between them" (xv). Meisel reserves his strongest criticism of Woolf for the conclusion of his book—a brief discussion of *Three Guineas*. There, the purpose behind the paternal metaphor, with its pattern of influence and denial, is suggested. On the page immediately preceding the passage cited by Moi, Meisel asks this question of Woolf's text: "Where, then, is the difference between men and women that Woolf insists upon?" The answer lies in what Meisel calls "Woolf's strongest, in fact her only authentic, liberationist assertion in all of *Three Guineas*" (233). Leaving aside the question of Meisel's authority for knowing what is authentic liberation for women, we have to consider Woolf's words in their context. She suggests that, even if she is willing to contribute her symbolic guinea to the antifascist cause espoused by men, she is still hesitant about joining their "society," a word she leaves somewhat ambivalent. Then she questions herself: "What reason or what emotion can make us hesitate to become members of a society whose aims we approve, to whose funds we have contributed? It may be neither reason nor emotion, but something more profound and fundamental than either. It may be difference. Different we are, as facts have proved, both in sex and in education" (*Three Guineas* 103).

Meisel's response to this statement would be curious if it were not symptomatic of his response to *Three Guineas* as a whole. Woolf's arguments about the differences between men and women, he stresses, show only that there are no differences. If Woolf condemns the male propensity for making war, she recommends that women use their disinterested influence as a weapon. If she criticizes capitalism, she also insists that women gain and use their share of the wealth. According to Meisel, her rhetoric gives her away every time. For example, when Victorian men insist that a "lady" should not degrade herself by earning money, Woolf responds bluntly, "the lady must be killed" (*Three Guineas* 133). Meisel sums it up: "In her very zeal to do away with struggle, competition, war, and fascism, Woolf covertly deploys their very methods" (231). The argument is disingenuous. Woolf's antipatriarchal rhetoric, though it may employ figures drawn from the culture it opposes, does not simply repeat that culture. It appropriates the rhetoric of patriarchy and turns it to radically different ends. As I suggested earlier, Meisel insists that the difference between men and women for Woolf is difference itself: "Even the cultural 'difference' between men and women in terms of 'education' is, of course, itself the product of the more originary difference between men and women as such" (233). The word "originary" is interjected into Woolf's argument by Meisel. Nowhere in *Three Guineas* does Woolf talk about difference, even sexual difference, in these essentialist terms—though she does imply that difference, arbitrary as it is, is not such a bad thing. There is sophistry in Meisel's equation of Woolf's rhetorical violence with the physical violence of war; and even if we concede the influence of Pater on Woolf, we need not accept the paternal metaphor that erases the incommensurable difference Woolf insists upon with some originary difference-in-identity that subsumes it. Walter Pater is not the *pater*; and his presence in absence cannot account for all the effects of Woolf's text.

Meisel's literary equation tries to control the ambivalence of Woolf's writing by submitting it to the authority of a great tradition. It is ironic that in order to do so he employs the language and rhetoric of contemporary theory, particularly the concepts of Jacques Lacan and Jacques Derrida, without ever explicitly referring to these thinkers. Even Harold Bloom, whose theories of the anxiety of influence obviously support Meisel's reading of Woolf, is mentioned only twice, for insignificant reasons. Yet, this is a book that starts from a thesis about "Woolf's manifest silence on the subject of Pater": "Such repression and the reasons for the anxiety that both causes and accompanies it may be unraveled by a psychoanalysis not so much of Woolf herself as of the texts, including the biographical ones, by which we know her" (xiii). How does Meisel's manifest silence about *his* fathers relate to Woolf's manifest silence? To answer this question would be to repeat Meisel's strategy, to construct yet another paternal metaphor. As Daniel Mark Fogel observes (in a book that, if it subordinates Woolf and Joyce to the authority of Henry James, nevertheless remains self-conscious about the risk of constructing this sort of critical fiction), "all of these metaphors [of influence] may be powerful aids to thinking about influence relations, but they also have serious limitations, particularly if they are held as anything more than figurative and provisional. Insofar as they become embedded in consciousness, they can indeed victimize people, wrongly persuading us, for instance, that originality and authority are male prerogatives" (166). Institutionally, as the work of Meisel, Fogel, Sandra Gilbert and Susan Gubar, and Bloom himself should remind us, these metaphors have a compelling force; for they are applied not only to individual authors but to historical periods and movements. Freud is the father of psychoanalysis; Joyce or Pound or Eliot the father of modernism. Yet, to argue that psychoanalysis was fathered, even by its founder, contradicts its fundamental discovery that unconscious structures play a determining role in the symbolic life of individuals and civilizations. It is curious that no one ever thinks of calling Woolf the mother of modernism, though she suggested in *A Room of One's Own* that "poetry ought to have a mother as well as a father" (107). Joyce called paternity a legal fiction; but such a fiction is not without its historical determinations. There are also historical determinations for what could be called Woolf's maternal metaphor.

One such determination has to do with Woolf's relation to the university. First, by way of contrast, let me briefly consider the same relation in the work of James Joyce. I have discussed in another place the way Joyce's late texts resist the ideological foundation of the university on the principle of reason (see "Joyce's Pedagogy"). Such resistance, however, cannot take the form of opposition as long as it depends on the structure it questions, as long as it assumes that the reason of the university is one. As Derrida observes, "Nobody has ever founded a university *against* reason. So we may reasonably suppose that the University's reason for being has always been reason itself, and some essential connection of reason to being" ("The Principle of Reason" 7). In truth, the resistance to reason and its university is already inscribed within the principle of reason as its negative ontology: reason in and of itself has no reason. Joyce's challenge, his disclosure of the abyss underlying the principle of reason, therefore, actually lends to the university an ideological support, which is not simply the product of historical accident or inadvertence. Joyce was shaped not only by the English language, Irish nationality, and the Catholic church but by the university; and these institutional forces must constitute determinate limits within the overdetermination of his symptom. This is not to say that Joyce had a better education than, for example, Virginia Woolf. Joyce privileges the university (just as he privileges the patriarchal culture it reproduces) by writing for it and anticipating the institutional effect of his work. To some extent, this anticipation involves subversion, a desire to force down the throat of the university something it cannot swallow. But at the same time, the Joycean resistance allows the university to reassert itself and to demonstrate its legitimacy by monumentalizing his text, even in the name of its unreadability or indeterminacy. Today we can say of the discourses and theories that have come to surround the name Joyce what Derrida has said of such discourses as Marxism and psychoanalysis in the contemporary university:

> It is not a matter simply of questions that one *formulates* while submitting oneself . . . to the principle of reason, but also of preparing oneself thereby to transform the modes of writing, approaches to pedagogy, the procedures of academic exchange, the relation to languages, to other

disciplines, to the institution in general, to its inside and its outside. Those who venture forth along this path, it seems to me, need not set themselves up in opposition to the principle of reason, nor need they give way to "irrationalism." They may continue to assume *within* the university, along with its memory and tradition, the imperative of professional rigor and competence. ("The Principle of Reason" 17)

Like Marxism and psychoanalysis, Joyce's text has sometimes been the occasion, particularly in theoretical discussions, of reformulating institutional practices; and he continues to win the respect of the university for the "rigor and competence" his works demand from the class of professional readers. Nevertheless, some critics and scholars have begun to think beyond Joyce as an institutional signifier, even to think Joyce beyond Joyce. The work of such critics as Jane Marcus, Shari Benstock, and recently, Sandra Gilbert and Susan Gubar challenges our tendency to think of modernism as a single event or movement or writer or sex. In the face of literary history dominated by patriarchal figures (the Joycean revolution or the Pound era), feminist critics have employed a different strategy, writing as Virginia Woolf said women write: "For we think back through our mothers if we are women" (*A Room of One's Own* 79).

In positing this maternal metaphor for the process of "writing as women write," Woolf demonstrates a relation to the university as an ideological apparatus substantially different from that of Joyce or Derrida. It is not that Woolf opposes the university with some irrational force it cannot master or challenges its claims to "rigor and competence." Rather, Woolf, as someone who has been denied access to the university, simply does not have the same use for it Joyce would have. It goes without saying that the difference I am suggesting here is not insurmountable. Joyce, after all, got no nearer to Oxbridge than Woolf. But Joyce, from his corner of the British Empire, was able to stake his claim to the whole—not just to the university but to the institutional authority it reproduces. Similarly, it could be argued that Woolf's position cannot be situated completely *outside* the university any more than it can be isolated from the determinations of Western male-centered culture; but that argument need not deter us from the recognition that Woolf's historical experience of that culture and the institutions of its reproduction is marked by a difference. That difference is determined as much by sex as it is by education. Woolf reminds us that, though we may and should continue to meet the challenge of social transformation from *inside* the institution, there is a historical (and not a metaphysical) *outside*. The university neither monopolizes the principle of reason nor can claim its reason as the only foundation for thought broadly defined. For though the university founded on reason has always tried to master and delimit human thought through its powers of legitimation, it has also produced for every age in which it has existed an/other thought, a thought beyond authority, legitimacy, convention. Such a thought is Woolf's notion of "writing as women write." With this thought, Woolf anticipates the current interest in *écriture féminine*, though she never essentializes women's writing: she historicizes it. It should be possible to use Woolf, to read her and think back through her text to what no paternal signifier of modernism can assimilate. The end will not simply frame Woolf as the other of modernism but rather show modernism and its university as the other in her eye, a vision haunting the institution and subverting its authority with the thought it cannot think. In effect, Woolf forces those of us who write within the university to think and recognize the historical *outside*, the tradition and memory of what has been excluded from its foundation.

Before *The Waves*, Woolf wrote one of her most influential books, *A Room of One's Own*. Jane Marcus discusses this work as one of "Woolf's strategies for subverting patriarchal language," and certainly it can be taken as a challenge to the Western university (45). It was not the first text, however, in which Woolf eyed the university from the outside. As Jane Marcus points out, the short sketch, "A Woman's College from Outside" (probably written in 1920 and published in 1926), anticipates *A Room of One's Own* and *Three Guineas* by positioning Woolf in a marginal relation to institutional education. Marcus comments that "here the chip on her shoulder at never having had a formal education ('From the *Outside*') weighs down Woolf's shoulder and sprains her writing arm" (156). Woolf fails "to share narration with her subject and her audience" (159), fails to produce the triological structure Marcus finds in *A Room of One's Own* (a point to which I will return). Marcus's judgment of this sketch is probably undeniable, but I want to pursue the peculiarity of Woolf's gaze in this short work.

The first sentence of the sketch presents the image of the "featherywhite moon" illuminating the dark; then in the second, the wind of Cambridge courts, going "neither to Tartary nor to Arabia," lapses "dreamily in the midst of grey-blue clouds over the roofs of Newnham." The wind seems emblematic of human desire, which, though one might think it fully in the hands of the masculine ruling class in Cambridge, wanders not toward the goals of male fantasy (Tartary and Arabia) but instead accumulates like rain over the woman's college, Newnham. In the third sentence, Woolf returns her focus to the moon through the use of the pronoun "she": "There, in the garden, if she needed space to wander, she might find it among the trees; and as none but women's faces could meet her face, she might unveil it blank, featureless, and gaze into rooms where at that hour, blank, featureless, eyelids white over eyes, ringless hands extended upon sheets, slept innumerable women." This "she" possesses just enough ambivalence to conflate the initial image of the moon as an object shedding light with the eye of the author looking into this woman's world from the outside. It genders the moon's gaze and delivers the author's eye over to radical alterity, neither outside nor inside but elsewhere, different. She (the moon's/Woolf's gaze) moves freely, unveiling her being as "blank" and "featureless," while projecting onto Newnham her desire for a utopian, feminine space, the object of a blank, featureless subject, that is, a subject beyond conventions, systems of value, and the imposed order of patriarchal culture. This image lasts only a moment before the author's gaze fixes itself on the figure of Angela standing before the mirror in her room: "The whole of her was perfectly delineated—perhaps the soul. For the glass held up an untrembling image—white and gold, red slippers, pale hair with blue stones in it, and never a ripple or shadow to break the smooth kiss of Angela and her reflection in the glass, as if she were glad to be Angela" ("A Woman's College" 139). Angela (the angel in the house?) resembles Jinny in *The Waves*, who also discovers her imago in the mirror, the fantasy of wholeness and self-identity. The author's gaze, on the other hand, belongs more to Rhoda, who looks over Jinny's shoulder at the mirror and thinks, "I have no face. Other people have faces" (*The Waves* 43). Woolf marks her own faceless alterity with the simple comment that Angela gazes at and symbolically kisses the image in the mirror "as if she were glad to be Angela." With these words, the narrator withdraws her gaze, allowing the utopian vision to dissolve before the signifiers of patriarchal law: "Only Angela Williams was at Newnham for the purpose of earning her living, and could not forget even in moments of impassioned adoration the cheques of her father at Swansea; her mother washing in the scullery: pink frocks to dry on the line; tokens that even the lily no longer floats flawless upon the pool, but has a name on a card like another" ("A Woman's College" 139). The name on Angela's door reads A. Williams, a reminder that the name of the father can insinuate its authority even into this college where every woman has a room of her own. Resistance is still possible, however, and takes the form of laughter—the laughter of young women "pouring forth into the garden" like mist or vapor, "this bubbling

laughter, this irresponsible laughter: this laughter of mind and body floating away rules, hours, discipline: immensely fertilising, yet formless,
chaotic, trailing and straying and tufting the rose-bushes with shreds of
vapour" ("A Woman's College 141). The vapors of feminine laughter fuse
with the moonlight of Woolf's alterity, subverting any radical opposition
between inside and outside, since the one materializes the desire of the
other. Laughter becomes the signifier of opposition in Woolf's eye, the
subject standing apart, at a distance, shrouded in text.

Still, "A Woman's College" lacks critical density because it merely
transforms, through repression, the desire for a university education into
the dream of a feminine universe. In *A Room of One's Own*, by contrast,
Woolf deconstructs that desire, in offering a materialist analysis of wom-
en's relation to art, culture, and education. She enters the university and
assumes the position of lecturer without surrendering for a moment her
status as an outsider. Indeed, she embodies in herself the patriarchal
relation of the woman's college to the man's university; for, as she later
remarks to the male addressee in *Three Guineas*, "At Cambridge, in the
year 1937 [or nine years after Woolf gave the lectures from *A Room of
One's Own*], the women's colleges . . . are not allowed to be members of
the university" (30). The women's colleges are locked out of the university, just as Woolf is locked out of the Oxbridge library. But in *A Room of
One's Own*, where she employs fiction to dramatize the historical facts,
Woolf has a second thought: "I thought how unpleasant it is to be locked
out; and I thought how it is worse perhaps to be locked in" (24). Woolf
has no illusion that the university she seeks is the same one kept under
lock and key by the patriarchs of Oxbridge; for the historical education of
women has produced the desire for something different: "It would be a
thousand pities if women wrote like men, or lived like men, or looked like
men, for if two sexes are quite inadequate, considering the vastness and
variety of the world, how should we manage with one only? Ought not
education to bring out and fortify the differences rather than the sim-
ilarities?" (92). Woolf rejects the university of the same, that is, the one
sex, and insists on the necessity of difference, including a sexual difference
that cannot be mastered by binary logic. Later, in *Three Guineas*, she
gives this difference a political meaning by arguing for the failure of
traditional male education to inculcate the values of pacifism that would
be able to resist the seductions of fascist ideology: "Need we collect more
facts from history and biography to prove our statement that all attempt
to influence the young against war through the education they receive at

the universities must be abandoned? For do they not prove that education . . . does not teach people to hate force, but to use it?" (29). Woolf
finally differs from Derrida in claiming that even the relation to memory
and tradition are not the same for those who are *inside* and those who are
outside. To the patriarch of *Three Guineas*, she says,

> Your class has been educated at public schools and universities for five
> or six hundred years, ours for sixty. . . . Your class possesses in its own
> right and not through marriage practically all the capital, all the land,
> all the valuables, and all the patronage in England. Our class possesses
> in its own right and not through marriage practically none of the capi-
> tal, none of the land, none of the valuables, and none of the patronage
> in England. That such differences make for very considerable differ-
> ences in mind and body, no psychologist or biologist would deny. It
> would seem to follow then as an indisputable fact that "we"—meaning
> by "we" a whole made up of body, brain and spirit, influenced by
> memory and tradition—must still differ in some essential respects from
> "you," whose body, brain and spirit have been so differently trained
> and are so differently influenced by memory and tradition. Though we
> see the same world, we see it through different eyes. (17–18)

Woolf does not posit, as Meisel has suggested, some originary difference but rather claims that history makes the difference, even the supposedly "essential" differences of mind and body. The feminine collective
"we" is the effect of historical determination. Woolf theorizes an education founded on radically different principles from that of the traditional
university. Since the idea of the university has always been elaborated
within the principle of reason, however, and since Woolf will not accept
an irrationalist position, she cannot directly say what such an education
would be, except by pointing toward the effects of what it has already
been in the lives of women. She must try to discover the effects of an
education outside the university on those who have not been included
within. This attempt must finally involve an analysis of the human mind
that explores the drama of sexual difference in complex historical terms. I
quote from *A Room of One's Own*:

> Why do I feel that there are severances and oppositions in the mind, as
> there are strains from obvious causes on the body? What does one
> mean by "the unity of the mind," . . . for clearly the mind has so great
> a power of concentrating at any point at any moment that it seems to

have no single state of being. It can separate itself from the people in the street, for example, and think of itself as apart from them, at an upper window looking down on them. Or it can think with other people spontaneously, as, for instance, in a crowd waiting to hear some piece of news read out. It can think back through its fathers or through its mothers, as I have said that a woman writing thinks back through her mothers. Again if one is a woman one is often surprised by a sudden splitting off of consciousness, say in walking down Whitehall, when from being the natural inheritor of that civilisation, she becomes, on the contrary, outside of it, alien and critical. Clearly the mind is always altering its focus, and bringing the world into different perspectives. But some of these states of mind seem, even if adopted spontaneously, to be less comfortable than others. In order to keep oneself continuing in them one is unconsciously holding something back, and gradually the repression becomes an effort. But there may be some state of mind in which one could continue without effort because nothing is required to be held back. (101)

Over ten years before she began to read Freud (that is, if we care to believe her late autobiographical essay, "A Sketch of the Past"), Woolf produces her own analysis of the mind's relation to unconscious processes (*Moments of Being* 108). There is no unity of the mind, she says, because the mind has the principle of alterity inscribed within it. The mind's divisions, those "severances and oppositions," are directly correlated with repression; its power of concentration disables it from equality of concentration, knowledge is bound to ignorance. The mind can connect itself or detach itself from others—either through symbolic identification or through alienation, the perception of self as other (with a small *o*). Alienation or identification is determined by how one relates to the symbolic, by whether one is thinking back through one's mothers or through one's fathers, indeed by the historical relation to sexual difference. If one is a woman, one is surprised by the splitting off of consciousness, by one's separation from the symbolic, not only in the sense that one is excluded, pushed outside of it into the position of alien, but in the sense that one becomes critical of it, recognizing its alterity. Some states of mind are more comfortable than others. If the thinking subject is constituted from within the symbolic order, and if the symbolic is dominated by the constraints of patriarchal ideology, then thinking through one's fathers requires less repression than thinking through one's mothers. If a woman experiences the symbolic as other, then she represses her own identity as a speaking subject (in the patriarchal frame of reference) in order to think through her mothers, through their historical difference. The greatest risk of such thinking is that it may succeed, that one may repress the symbolic, repress repression, or, to use Lacan's technical term, foreclose the name-of-the-father, and lose the sense of being a subject altogether. The safeguard against such a loss is the difficulty of imagining a state of mind in which "nothing is required to be held back."

The words I have quoted and explicated immediately precede, within the same paragraph, Woolf's controversial theory of androgyny. The sight of two people, a man and a woman, getting into the same taxi makes Woolf ask "whether there are two sexes in the mind corresponding to the two sexes in the body" (102). In the man's brain, she says, the male predominates over the female; and in the woman's brain, the female predominates over the male. Still, the larger context I have described suggests that these sexes in the brain do not signify an essential identity. The woman in the brain is the relation to the symbolic as other, a relation both critical and alienating; the man in the brain is the relation to the symbolic as identity, law, and power. This sexuality of symbolic relations, as *A Room of One's Own* makes perfectly clear, is historical; it is the psychic effect of patriarchal culture and civilization. This is not to say that, were patriarchy somehow overthrown, the mind would cease to be divided, sexual difference would cease to function as a signifier of symbolic relations. It means simply that these would not be the relations of patriarchy as we know them.

Sexual difference in the brain, it follows, is a social text. In patriarchy, identification with the symbolic as One signifies the masculine; alienation from the symbolic as the big Other signifies the feminine. The normal state of affairs in patriarchal culture would be the repression of the second position by the first: the assumption of unified identity in language and culture, the production of a sex which sees itself as One, represses the big Other, that relation to language and culture through nonidentity or alterity. The historical correlative of this repression is the domination of one sex by another, through the insistence that there is only one sex which is not One. In the everyday use of language, these relations support the normative structure of communication which, according to Roman Jakobson, can be divided into six elements: addresser, addressee, message, code, contact, and context. This structure, despite its apparent complexity, articulates a binary relation between self and other which mirrors the sexual relations defined by patriarchal ideology. The big Other overthrows this binary economy through an infraction that Lacan would call the insistence of the signifier and Woolf calls, in her late autobiographical writings, the "third voice":

I fumble with some vague idea about a third voice; I speak to Leonard; Leonard speaks to me; we both hear a third voice. Instead of labouring all the morning to analyse what I mean, to discover whether I mean anything real, whether I make up or tell the truth when I see myself taking the breath of these voices in my sails and tacking this way and that through daily life as I yield to them, I note only the existence of this influence; suspect it to be of great importance; cannot find how to check its power on other people. (*Moments of Being* 133)

The third voice would appear to be that dimension of language that resists meaning and signification, that exceeds the intention of the addresser and escapes the decoding of the addressee. No code can master its message. The third voice would be the voice of language as language, its material dimension, which comes into play, for example, in the act of translation. Walter Benjamin writes, "In all language and linguistic creations there remains in addition to what can be conveyed something that cannot be communicated; depending on the context in which it appears, it is something that symbolizes or something symbolized. It is the former only in the finite products of language, the latter in the evolving of the languages themselves" (*Illuminations* 79). Applying Benjamin to Woolf—hearing the third voice means hearing something that symbolizes without signifying, or rather, hearing beyond signification the symbolized toward which every language as language, as that which symbolizes, moves. The third voice is the whole that is not equal to the sum of its parts. As such, it articulates language as interminable process.

It seems to me that Woolf's university, or what she chose to call in *Three Guineas* the Society of Outsiders, is founded on this relation to language as the Other. Jane Marcus's work suggests that *A Room of One's Own* exemplifies this relation through the complex rhetoric of its triological structure. Here Woolf "deconstructs the lecture as a form" and "invents human intercourse on a model of female discourse, as a conversation among equals" (145–46). Woolf saw in the traditional lecture what Mikhail Bakhtin would call monological discourse—a discourse of the master, of patriarchal authority and value. She challenges it, initially, by refusing to speak with authority, with the pretence of the one who is supposed to know, for example, in the first sentence of *A Room of One's Own*: "But, you may say, we asked you to speak about women and fiction—what has that to do with a room of one's own?" (3). As Marcus points out, this sentence is the continuation of an interrupted conversation in which [Woolf] is only an equal partner. . . . The reader is included in the "you," so the text becomes a three-sided conversation between the woman writer, the women students in the audience, and the woman reader. . . . Our role as readers is to collaborate in this conversation, to conspire with the woman writer and the women students to overthrow the formal rigidity of the lecture as an "educational device." It is not a monologue. It is not even a mock Platonic dialogue, but a *trio-logue.* (148–49)

There is also a fourth position, that of the male reader, who must change himself by identifying with the position of the female reader in order to enter the triological structure of the text. Woolf does not intend to speak as one subject to another subject or even to a group or class of subjects who would be the receivers of her message. On the contrary, she subordinates the content of her message to its social production: "One can only show how one came to hold whatever opinion one does hold. One can only give one's audience the chance of drawing their own conclusions as they observe the limitations, the prejudices, the idiosyncrasies of the speaker." This speaker should not be construed as a unitary subject in full possession of the meaning it wants to convey. As she goes on to say, the "I" or subject of her discourse "is only a convenient term for somebody who has no real being" (*A Room* 4). This feminine subject is a fiction; and the story "she" will tell is a fiction, though it may lead or point to the truth. For the truth of this "I"—"call me Mary Beton, Mary Seton, Mary Carmichael or by any name you please" (5)—lies in the Other, the collective, the anonymous. By showing how she came to the position she holds, Woolf gives ground to the discourse of the Other, to all those forces that determine her speech, to Influence writ large, not as the influence of this or that literary father or mother but as the complex overdeterminations of history itself. This "I" of the Other has usually been the historical marker of the woman writer, the one who signed herself "Anonymous." But it is the Other in the "I," that is, an alienated relation to the symbolic order with its patriarchal law, that defines the sexuality of this position. The "I" of the Other resembles the eye of the narrator/moon in "A Woman's College from Outside"; it possesses the alterity, the materiality, of the third voice. Either through the utopian fantasy of the sketch or through the critical analysis of *A Room of One's Own*, the gaze of Woolf's eye/I represents the possibility of going beyond the patriarchy and *its* principle of reason, of seizing the material language on which it is founded and transforming it.

Returning to *The Waves*, I would contend that from the very beginning, in her earliest conception of that work, Woolf wanted to articulate
something like the third voice or the Other. For example, there is the well-
known diary entry for September 30, 1926. Here, in the midst of her
depression after completing *To the Lighthouse*, the impulse behind *The
Waves* appears as she ponders "how it is not oneself but something in the
universe that one's left with. It is this that is frightening & exciting
in the midst of my profound gloom, depression, boredom, whatever it is:
One sees a fin passing far out. What image can I reach to convey what I
mean? Really there is none I think." A few lines later she comments, "By
writing I dont reach anything"; and then she concludes, "I want to watch
& see how the idea at first occurs. I want to trace my own process"
(*Diary* 3:113). In other words, *The Waves* begins with the sense that
writing fails to reach anything, least of all the expression of that "something in the universe that one's left with." Nevertheless, Woolf refuses to
accept a sense of linguistic futility as the last word. She will trace *or write*
her own process. Accepting the impossibility of writing as absolute fulfillment, she will write the impossible as impossible, in the moment of its not
reaching what no image can convey: a fin passing far out. As we know
from her diary entry for February 7, 1931, after completing *The Waves*,
Woolf believed that she had achieved what she wanted: "I have netted
that fin in the waste of waters" (*Diary* 4:10).

The fin carries us directly into the text of *The Waves*, where Bernard
writes the phrase in his notebook: "Fin in a waste of waters" (189). Here I
simply want to read the word "fin" in the context of the last chapter, the
final soliloquy (Deborah Wilson gives a more detailed consideration of
the fin in Woolf's work in an unpublished essay, "The Fin and the Fish").
Bernard's discourse is the fin of *The Waves*. To exploit the bilingual pun in
fin, it is *le fin*—the end, the aim, the conclusion, of this book of "dramatic soliloquies" (*Diary* 3:312). Woolf called them soliloquies, but one
misses the novel's texture if one employs that word in its conventional
sense. These soliloquies are addressed not to the self but to the other, to a
"you," if only implied. They are more like Browning's typical dramatic
monologues, although this description misses something too. For these
monologues occupy a space between self and other, "I" and "you";
though they express the "I" and address the "you," they exceed these
positions and the context that informs them. The lives of the six characters—Bernard, Neville, Louis, Susan, Jinny, and Rhoda—make up the
content of these monologues; but that content is abstracted or emptied
out as the characters become types or positions in an indeterminate dis-

course. "I" and "you" and the syntax framing them become empty forms. As Makiko Minow-Pinkney points out, "though Woolf does not dislocate syntax . . . she goes a long way towards *emptying* syntax of its function of articulation across the novel as a whole" (172). The effect is to foreground the materiality or *jouissance* of language, that which symbolizes something beyond meaning—in Lacanian terms, *the discourse of the Other*. Woolf sets out to capture this process—the fin or end of her work.

Bernard is the fin of *The Waves*; like Molly Bloom in Joyce's *Ulysses*, he gets the last word. Yet, these characters are not symmetrical: Molly is not to Joyce as Bernard is to Woolf. If we hear the third voice in Molly's soliloquy, we hear it through Joyce's representation of the feminine, through the mask of Molly's abjection, which produces its own real-effect. Joyce may hide behind the mask, but the sexual identity of the mask is foregrounded. Molly represents Joyce the subject (that is, Joyce's conception of a female or Joyce as a female) for another signifier, namely, patriarchal culture. Bernard does not represent Woolf; and the peculiar style of *The Waves* subverts any real-effect. Bernard is the end at which Woolf aims, not in speaking for Woolf or in her speaking through him, but in articulating the third voice, the voice of the human collective. Bernard becomes this voice, formally, only at the novel's conclusion; he becomes the end that in retrospect was there from the beginning, even in the poetic interludes. At the same time, Bernard's sexuality becomes undecidable; for as a character he is emptied out, like the fin emerging from the waste of waters. One day, as he leans over a gate "looking down over fields," the self refuses to answer his call. "Nothing came," he says, "nothing. I cried then with a sudden conviction of complete desertion, Now there is nothing. No fin breaks the waste of this immeasurable sea. Life has destroyed me. No echo comes when I speak, no varied words. This is more truly death than the death of friends, than the death of youth" (*The Waves* 284).

The fin is not the full signifier or the signifier of power. For in articulating the fin as the signifier of the Other, Woolf cadaverizes it, reduces it to the shell of meaning. Before she began work on *The Waves*, she wrote that she meant "to eliminate all waste, deadness, superfluity: to give the moment whole; whatever it includes. . . . Waste, deadness, come from the inclusion of things that dont belong to the moment; this appalling narrative business of the realist: getting on from lunch to dinner: it is false, unreal, merely conventional" (*Diary* 3:209). Woolf sets out to eliminate convention, or patriarchal law, and thus to repress the symbolic order that constrains her writing process. Within the fiction, she has to kill Percival (in Bernard's words, "He is conventional; he is a hero" [*The Waves* 123]), for he allegorically embodies the ideology of British imperialism (one empire for one race and sex), that Holy Grail which unites him with Kurtz from Conrad's *Heart of Darkness*. What Woolf calls the "moment whole" turns out to include the other hole—the one Lacan calls "the locus of the signifier." When she opens her net, Woolf discovers not the fin but the big Other, which cannot be represented. Ironically, as the privileged signifier of the Other, the fin attempts to repress the symbolic order from which it emerges. It is, if you will, the antiphallus. But this repression necessarily fails because the signifier of the Other cannot support the Law and constitute itself as One. As Lacan remarked, "there is no Other of the Other," there is no metalanguage transcending the arbitrary law of the father (*"Ecrits": A Selection* 310–11). The fin eliminates in order to articulate the waste. The fin surfaces only to submerge itself in the third voice; and the third voice, as Bernard makes clear at another point in his monologue, is the voice of silence, which is "now and again broken by a few words, as if a fin rose in the wastes of silence; and then the fin, the thought, sinks back into the depths spreading round it a little ripple of satisfaction, content" (*The Waves* 273). The fin is a thought not constrained by the principle of reason—a word that must be uttered only to articulate the silence of the Other, the letter as litter. Elsewhere Bernard speaks of the need for "a little language such as lovers use, words of one syllable such as children speak." That is, he needs as little language as possible, "a howl, a cry," but no "false phrases." He says, "I have done with phrases" (*The Waves* 295). Just a little language, enough to rise and fall and make a ripple of satisfaction—a wave. This little language is not the phallus, for the phallus produces pleasure only through repression. This little language is the discourse of the Other, the waves.

That discourse, it should be said, has been there all along, on the margins of the text. Woolf's university, the school of the Other, always occupies a space close to, sometimes inside sometimes outside, the official institution. As a child, Bernard shows Elvedon to Susan, where they see the lady writing between two windows and the gardeners sweeping the lawn. The real significance of this scene emerges only in Bernard's final monologue:

> On the outskirts of every agony sits some observant fellow who points; who whispers as he whispered to me that summer morning in the house where the corn comes up to the window, "The willow grows on the turf by the river. The gardeners sweep with great brooms and the lady sits

writing." Thus he directed me to that which is beyond and outside our own predicament; to that which is symbolic, and thus perhaps permanent, if there is any permanence in our sleeping, eating, breathing, so animal, so spiritual and tumultuous lives. (*The Waves* 248–49)

Beyond the symbolic order nurtured and reproduced by the offical university, beyond the laws of patriarchy with their claim to permanence and universality, lies the real permanence of the symbolic Other. This is the symbolic not as it has been inscribed with meanings by a given culture but as the material trace, the historical condition of the possibility of meaning. The woman writing embodies the relation to the symbolic as radically other, material, subject to historical reshaping; and she writes where the gardeners, that is, the subaltern classes, sweep up the remains of patriarchal culture (like the housekeeper Mrs. Moffat, of whom Bernard says, "Oh, Mrs. Moffat, Mrs. Moffat, I say, come and sweep it all up" [*The Waves* 186]). Nothing is wasted on the woman writer because she transforms the waste into utopia, Elvedon, a protest against not only patriarchal power but any power that presents itself as the form of totality. The woman writing occupies the border of the symbolic, the place of its alterity—the place of Rhoda's resistance when she balks the rules, the theorems, the social positions thrust upon her by institutional order: "How you chained me to one spot, one hour, one chair, and sat yourselves down opposite! How you snatched from me the white spaces that lie between hour and hour and rolled them into dirty pellets and tossed them into the wastepaper basket with your greasy paws. Yet those were my life" (*The Waves* 204). Rhoda's suicide may represent the risk of any woman writer (or any writer thinking back through one's mothers) who discovers within the university of the fathers, perhaps buried in the archives, the university of the Other. Historically, as Woolf dramatically shows in *A Room of One's Own*, women have had little choice: only one university was accepting them. But now that the doors have been jarred open, women have entered the archives to unfold those white spaces, those paper pellets, and read the truth that no university has been willing to speak.

The end of *The Waves*, its fin, is not this sex which is One or which is not One. It is this sex which is not. I mean by that: this sex which has not been *thought* because it cannot be *thought* within the confines of Western reason. Luce Irigaray remarks, "Woman's desire would not be expected to speak the same language as man's; woman's desire has doubtless been submerged by the logic that has dominated the West since the time of the

Greeks" (25). There has always been a world beyond the West, however, and, Woolf's writing suggests, beyond the Greeks—a world of more than one sex, more than two sexes—a world in which the differentiation of irreducible desire becomes radically possible. Irigaray knows as much when she suggests, along with Woolf I believe, that the sexuality of a woman is *plural* (28). Furthermore, to give Irigaray's analysis of feminine sexuality a figurative reading, this idea of plural sexuality should be seen as a challenge to the dichotomy masculine/feminine on which patriarchal representations of sexuality hinge. As I suggested before, Irigaray is re-structuring the rhetoric of patriarchy in order to think of a sexuality beyond the phallus, that is, beyond the drive toward metaphysical unity and Oneness animating Western civilization. The same can be said of Woolf. By thinking through her mothers, she reaches toward the unpre-sentable in language, the locus of the signifier before it is captured by the symbolic rule of patriarchy. She reaches toward the possibility of change, its material ground, beyond the laws of binary thinking. Bernard suggests such a place when he imagines himself persuading Rhoda to go on living: "In persuading her I was also persuading my own soul. For this is not one life; nor do I always know if I am man or woman, Bernard or Neville, Louis, Susan, Jinny or Rhoda—so strange is the contact of one with another" (*The Waves* 281). Jane Marcus suggests that "the male reader is forced to deny the superiority of his gender if he is to read *A Room of One's Own* sympathetically" (159). Perhaps a text like *The Waves*, if it is read sympathetically or at least critically, can become the occasion for challenging the university on the superiority of its knowledge and expos-ing the determinations of that knowledge by gender and class. Such a text is not a cultural revolution in and of itself, but it does make a wave.

In her writing, Woolf traces her own process as the discourse of the Other. She writes her *jouissance* beyond the economies of pleasure and pain. This discourse is not the signifier of modernism within the institu-tional context of the university. Instead, it signifies something beyond, something elsewhere, something at which all languages aim. Woolf's language aims at what I call the university of the Other, the university in her eye—that is, an education founded not on the principle of reason but on difference and process (which need not exclude reason). Woolf, writing from the *outside* to those of us *inside*, describes her alterity, her differ-ence, as the true gift of the Society of Outsiders: "Any help we can give you must be different from that you can give yourself, and perhaps the value of that help may lie in the fact of that difference. Therefore before we agree to sign your manifesto or join your society, it might be well to discover where the difference lies, because then we may discover where the help lies also" (*Three Guineas* 18). In Meisel's or Fogel's reading, Woolf's difference hides a secret identity. But the identity was never a secret. It is the language we all speak and which speaks through us beyond our intentions, beyond our message. Woolf does not try to expunge the influence of Pater or James or any other father; she situates those influences as determinate moments in a historical process. It is the history that must be elaborated before it can be overcome and give ground to the future of difference.

5

. . . and the Other Modernism: From Conrad to Rushdie

"I see India," said Bernard. "I see the low, long shore; I see the tortuous lanes of stamped mud that lead in and out among ramshackle pagodas; I see the gilt and crenellated buildings which have an air of fragility and decay as if they were temporarily run up buildings in some Oriental exhibition. I see a pair of bullocks who drag a low cart along the sun-baked road. The cart sways incompetently from side to side. Now one wheel sticks in the rut, and at once innumerable natives in loin-cloths swarm round it, chattering excitedly. But they do nothing. Time seems endless, ambition vain. Over all broods a sense of the uselessness of human exertion. There are strange sour smells. An old man in a ditch continues to chew betel and to contemplate his navel. But now, behold, Percival advances; Percival rides a flea-bitten mare, and wears a sun-helmet. By applying the standards of the West, by using the violent language that is natural to him, the bullock-cart is righted in less than five minutes. The Oriental problem is solved. He rides on; the multitude cluster round him, regarding him as if he were—what indeed he is—a God."

—Virginia Woolf, *The Waves*

This passage from *The Waves* articulates as well as any passage in modern British literature what Edward Said has called latent Orientalism, "an almost unconscious (and certainly an untouchable) positivity," which results from "the distillation of essential ideas about the Orient—its sensuality, its tendency to despotism, its aberrant mentality, its habits of inaccuracy, its backwardness—into a separate and unchallenged coherence" (*Orientalism* 205–6). The underlying assumptions of Said's groundbreaking research are that not only fields of learning but works of individual artists "are constrained and acted upon by society, by cultural traditions, by worldly circumstance, and by stabilizing influences like schools, libraries, and governments; moreover, that both learned and imaginative writing are never free, but are limited in their imagery, assumptions, and intentions" (*Orientalism* 201–2). *The Waves*, despite its critique of the Western patriarchal subject, is no exception to the rule. The novel is virtually riddled with references to Orientalism or to its Africanist counterpart. Even in the framing imagery of the poetic interludes, the ideology of imperialism asserts itself through the figure of a British sun that rises and sets over the waves. At the end of the third interlude, the waves drumming on the shore are likened to "turbaned warriors . . . turbaned men with poisoned assegais who, whirling their arms on high, advance upon the feeding flocks, the white sheep" (*The Waves* 75). In the fifth interlude, the sun "risen to its full height" gives

> to everything its exact measure of colour; to the sandhills their innumerable glitter, to the wild grasses their glancing green; or it fell upon the arid waste of the desert, here wind-scourged into furrows, here swept into desolate cairns, here sprinkled with stunted dark-green jungle-trees. It lit up the smooth gilt mosque, the frail pink-and-white card houses of the southern village, and the long-breasted, white-haired women who knelt in the river bed beating wrinkled cloths upon stones. (*The Waves* 148)

The sun disseminates civilization or those "standards of the West" that are able to determine the "exact measure of colour," or of human geographies, across the globe. The force of the sun, like the language of imperialism, is violent; but that violence would seem to be natural and necessary if the world is to be reduced to a unified perception, a coherent whole. Civilization, like the masculine sex, must be One, that is, must be Western; and everything that is not Western must not be One, that is, not a civilization, or, at best, must be an imperfect image or reflection of the true civilization.

If this reading of Woolf's imagery seems too arbitrary, one does not have to go far in the text to find verification in the voices of the characters. As Jinny enjoys the metropolitan spectacle of London, she thinks, "This is the triumphant procession; this is the army of victory with banners and brass eagles and heads crowned with laurel-leaves won in battle. They are better than savages in loin-cloths, and women whose hair is dank, whose long breasts sag, with children tugging at their long breasts. These broad thoroughfares . . . are sanded paths of victory driven through the jungle" (*The Waves* 194). Or near the end of the novel, contemplating the "unborn selves" of his inner being, Bernard says, "There is the old brute, too, the savage, the hairy man who dabbles his fingers in ropes of entrails; and gobbles and belches; whose speech is guttural, visceral—well, he is here. He squats in me" (*The Waves* 289). As I will show later, these passages resonate with the words of Marlow in Conrad's *Heart of Darkness*. They not only identify Africa and India as the savage *other* of the West but associate them with the prehistory of civilization and the unconscious of the European subject. In *The Waves*, this subject finds its most complete manifestation in Percival. Bernard, Neville, Louis, Susan, Jinny, and Rhoda all identify with this figure of the imperialist as with the form of their own subjectivity, and they interminably mourn his death. Bernard, in particular, idealizes Percival as the instrument of Western justice, the Holy Grail that he should have borne to the rest of the unilluminated world:

> He was thrown, riding in a race, and when I came along Shaftesbury Avenue tonight, those insignificant and scarcely formulated faces that bubble up out of the doors of the Tube, and many obscure Indians, and people dying of famine and disease, and women who have been cheated, and whipped dogs and crying children—all these seemed to me bereft. He would have done justice. He would have protected. About the age of forty he would have shocked the authorities. No lullaby has ever occurred to me capable of singing him to rest. (*The Waves* 243)

In effect, the world without Percival is without a stable center of social value. He alone commands the natural authority that could shed some light on the subjectless being of those hungry and diseased Indians, women, children, and dogs, who without him have no voice to appeal to justice and to protect them from ruthless and illegitimate authorities. In Bernard's discourse, Percival emerges as a figure reminiscent of T. E. Lawrence, who in his writings came to identify the Arab Revolt with his own personal experience of it. As Said states it, "Lawrence equates himself fully with the struggle of the new Asia to be born"; and in narrating the failure of the revolt, he "*becomes* both the mourning continent and a subjective consciousness expressing an almost cosmic disenchantment." To the reader he presents "an unmediated expert power—the power to be, for a brief time, the Orient" (243). Bernard's narrative transforms Percival into the subjective consciousness of the colonial world, and his death merely monumentalizes the authority that his life would have actualized. By identifying with Percival, the other characters authorize themselves and their own voices; they assume Percival's knowledge of the world beyond Europe as a transparency rooted in their autonomous subjectivity.

None of the characters in *The Waves* ever develops a critical consciousness of the imperialism that Percival embodies. Nevertheless, Woolf marginalizes this character and the authority he stands for in several ways that point toward an implicit if not fully developed critique of imperialism. Percival has no voice. Although he symbolizes the authority that empowers the speech of the other characters, he is denied any word of his own. If the reader hears him nevertheless, it is as the voice of social convention and political power in the discourses of the six characters. I do not mean that we can trace the imperialist ideology of these characters back to Percival as their origin, only that the name Percival signifies in their discourses a system of unquestioned truths and values, a form of cultural hegemony, that we can identify with imperialist ideology. Percival signifies the Orientalism that Said describes as "a system of truths, truths in Nietzsche's sense of the word"—that is, in Nietzsche's own words, "illusions about which one has forgotten that this is what they are" ("On Truth and Lie" 47). According to Said, such a system is so compelling for any European of the nineteenth century that it is possible to say that "every European, in what he could say about the Orient, was consequently a racist, an imperialist, and almost totally ethnocentric" (Said, *Orientalism* 203–4). If Woolf could not entirely evade this hegemonic predisposition in her own work, she could at least frame it in such a way as both to make visible and to destabilize its authority. She exposes the discourse of hegemony to its own radical alterity. The sovereign European subject speaks from the dead as the discourse of the Other in the voices of the others, that is, the social collective. I don't mean to say that Woolf self-consciously saw through this problem. Rather, she points toward the limits of her own social representation by marking in Percival the blank space that lies beyond the transparency of an ideology. Percival (like his medieval precursor) may be the sun-god at the center of a novel framed by the symbolic rising and setting of the sun over a world dominated by

Western power. Nevertheless, he is also presented as a social fiction not reducible to any transparent reality, just as the poetic interludes that frame the book dramatize the figurative power of language when it mediates between human subjects and the "real."

The contradictions that emerge from reading such a modernist text anticipate some of the issues raised by Pierre Bourdieu and Gayatri Spivak from radically different perspectives. Both address the problem of counterhegemonic discourse, that is, a speech act that challenges and somehow tries to escape the determinations of *dominant* language and culture. Bourdieu argues bluntly for a radical discontinuity between "ethos and logos, practical mastery and verbal mastery." To him, "if the members of the dominated classes frequently produce a discourse that is in contradiction with itself, with the meaning of their practice and with their objective condition, this is because they have to talk politics without possessing the instruments of production of their discourse, without having control over their 'political tongue'" (461). Though it may seem farfetched to think of Virginia Woolf as a member of a dominated class, as a woman she is marked by social exclusions and hegemonic articulations; and as a writer she may have to resort to language and discursive formations that directly or indirectly contradict her own attempt to disclose and subvert hegemonic representations of sexual difference. For example, while she analyzes the ideology of sexual difference within the European framework, she may leave unquestioned or transparent the inscription of colonized men and women by imperialist or Orientalist discourse. This problem assumes historical significance when we consider that Woolf has become a symbolic spokesperson for women precisely through her double canonization as a feminist writer and an English novelist. Bourdieu suggests that the experience of the dominated is intercepted, before it can reach verbal expression, by the "professional producers of discourse," a group that includes those shaped and supported by the literary institution:

> The dominated, whose interests are bound up with the raising of consciousness, i.e., with language, are at the mercy of the discourses that are presented to them. . . . The dominant language discredits and destroys the spontaneous political discourse of the dominated. It leaves them only silence or a borrowed language. . . . It forces recourse to spokesmen, who are themselves condemned to use the dominant language." (461–62)

Bourdieu's hyperdeterminism probably should be criticized—but not before cultural critics carefully consider the strongest and most negative reading of their own institutional emplacement, particularly if they want to locate the positive and socially transforming dimensions of intellectual work. From the perspective I have tried to sketch, hegemonic culture can be said to operate in the imaginary register. It is not that such culture merely represents the interests of a ruling class but that it postulates a system of meanings and social values that become the ground for communication throughout the whole of society and across the classes. It has only secondarily the effect of legitimating class society with all its attendant hierarchies according to gender, race, sexual orientation, and the general panoply of social distinctions. Any time a subject speaks in such a way as to be understood *immediately*, through the production of a transparent signifier, he or she runs the risk of endorsing, legitimating, and reinforcing the very structure of symbolic value that must be overthrown if the "raising of consciousness"—or the construction of counterhegemonic political consciousness—is to take place. To some extent, of course, this risk has to be taken; otherwise, criticism would only lend itself to mystification, creating the illusion that intellectual work is beyond the reach of those who have not been properly initiated into the institutional order. It would support the illusion that those *empowered* to know *really do know* and those who cannot understand have been legitimately excluded from understanding. It would reinstitute the hierarchy between legitimate and illegitimate knowledge. Still, a pedagogical effect that would challenge this hierarchy cannot emerge without the risk of confusion and misunderstanding because the spokespersons of the oppressed have the ethical imperative to call into question their own authority to speak for others. The pedagogical effect questions the political autonomy of the speaking subject which makes the position of the spokesperson possible in the first place.

Spivak makes a related point when she analyzes the radical criticism of Michel Foucault and Gilles Deleuze. These writers try to sound a revolutionary note by insisting that "the oppressed can know and speak for themselves." This claim, however, "reintroduces the constitutive subject on at least two levels: the Subject of desire [in Deleuze's work] and power [in Foucault's] as an irreducible methodological presupposition; and the self-proximate, if not self-identical, subject of the oppressed." But in this framework the intellectual's own position is left unquestioned or transparent, "for they merely report on the nonrepresented subject and analyze (without analyzing) the workings of (the unnamed Subject irreducibly presupposed by) power and desire" ("Can the Subaltern Speak?"

279). Spivak suggests, it seems to me, that the subject of the oppressed, when it is constructed by Western intellectuals as an autonomous force capable of self-determination in some global political context, can be only a projection by identification with the Western imperialist "Subject" harbored by the terms "power" and "desire." To the extent that Western intellectuals leave unquestioned the ground of their claim to know the "subject of the oppressed" as the site of a determinate will, they align themselves with imperialist knowledge: "The produced 'transparency' [of the unnamed subject of power and desire] marks the place of 'interest'; it is maintained by vehement denegation: 'Now this role of referee, judge, and universal witness is one which I *absolutely refuse* to adopt'" ("Can the Subaltern Speak?" 279–80). In refusing to speak for the other subject, they assume that the other can speak for itself in such a way as to be understood by the Western subject. They take for granted their own power to hear the other as another subject. Spivak exposes the transparency of these assumptions by rearticulating the question from another perspective:

> According to Foucault and Deleuze (in the First World, under the standardization and regimentation of socialized capital, though they do not seem to recognize this) the oppressed, if given the chance (the problem of representation cannot be bypassed here), and on the way to solidarity through alliance politics (a Marxist thematic is at work here) *can speak and know their conditions*. We must now confront the following question: On the other side of the international division of labor from socialized capital, inside *and* outside the circuit of the epistemic violence of imperialist law and education supplementing an earlier economic text, *can the subaltern speak?* ("Can the Subaltern Speak?" 283)

I cannot begin to do justice to the complexities of this question in the context of Spivak's groundbreaking essay. To say that she answers it negatively (she concludes, "The subaltern cannot speak" [308]) does not demonstrate the effect of the unexpected that characterizes this writing. That the subaltern cannot speak does not mean that the being behind the name "subaltern" has no voice. It means that the subaltern *as subaltern*—the subject of the oppressed constructed through the mirror of production—cannot really be thought outside the economy of the ethnocentric European subject. This latter is an imaginary construction like the ego (*moi*) which appropriates the other *as a whole self or identity* through its own reflection or image. Even to pose the question of autonomous subaltern speech recasts the third-world subject in the image of the

European subject. It does not construct a social tie, nor does it aim at or reach the true Others.

Over the superficially liberationist rhetoric of Deleuze and Foucault, Spivak chooses the more constrained "writing" of Jacques Derrida because its "Nietzschean, philosophical, and psychoanalytic, rather than specifically political, choices" at least suggest "a critique of European ethnocentrism in the constitution of the Other." The object of Derrida's philosophical critique is not "a general problem, but a *European* problem." Rather than extend the imperialism of the European subject by constructing the third-world subject in its image, Derrida wants "to demote the Subject of thinking or knowledge as to say that *'thought is . . . the blank part of the text'*; that which is thought is, if blank, still *in the text* and must be consigned to the Other of history" ("Can the Subaltern Speak?" 293–94). Furthermore, the passage Spivak quotes and comments upon says emphatically, "*In a certain sense, 'thought' means nothing. . . .* This thought has no weight. It is, in the play of the system, the very thing which never has weight. Thinking is what we already know we have not yet begun" (Derrida, *Of Grammatology* 93). Thought in this context has the function of utopia: it is nowhere. It is the pedagogical effect of language, which displaces the structure of meaning and value by bringing human subjects up against the alterity of a "*text-inscribed blankness.*" Through this relation to language as the Other, the Other within us, the real possibility of a social tie or symbolic exchange between the European and the postcolonial critic emerges. This exchange is consigned to the Other of history not as a negation of history but as the recognition that history is a situated discourse. Symbolic exchange ruptures that discourse as value and opens it to radical transformation, to the possibility of a rewriting and redefinition of the historical in terms of immediate conflicts and struggles. As Spivak stresses,

> That inaccessible blankness circumscribed by an interpretable text is what a postcolonial critic of imperialism would like to see developed within the European enclosure as *the* place of the production of theory. The postcolonial critics and intellectuals can attempt to displace their own production only by presupposing that *text-inscribed* blankness. To render thought or the thinking subject transparent or invisible seems, by contrast, to hide the relentless recognition of the Other by assimilation. It is in the interest of such cautions that Derrida does not invoke "letting the other(s) speak for himself" but rather invokes an "appeal" to or "call" to the "quite other" (*tout-autre* as opposed to a self-consolidating other), of "rendering delirious that interior voice that is the voice of the other in us." ("Can the Subaltern Speak?" 294)

The "*text-inscribed* blankness" that Spivak describes could be said to rupture the order of communication. It also ruptures the hierarchy between the hegemonic subject and the subject of the oppressed by breaking the mirror through which they are produced as functions of each other. By calling attention to the international division of labor (which, I would emphasize, cuts across the so-called first and third worlds), Spivak reminds us that the voice of theory—whether we have in mind the first-world theorist of the third world or the spokesperson of the dominated in either world—must depend for its production on socialized capital derived, ultimately, from the expropriated labor of the oppressed. Furthermore, postcolonial intellectuals like Spivak (and she points this out herself) do not escape this necessary condition for the production of legitimate speech under the dispensation of multinational capitalism. The radical intellectual who would be heard as a counterhegemonic voice within the frame of a global hegemonic culture must necessarily enter into a state of contradiction. By speaking for the others or insisting that the others speak for themselves, intellectuals take for granted and leave unquestioned the autonomy of the speaking subject. This figure is a cultural force identifying each individual as a unity reducible to a particular value within the system of social differences. If intellectuals fail to take into account the contradiction in their position, they lend authority to the mirror of production that gives ground to every hegemonic speech act. The "essential indeterminacy of the relationship between experience and expression" which Bourdieu recognizes also makes possible another kind of discursive effect, however (461). The spokespersons or hegemonic subjects can use speech to deconstruct the autonomy of their own positions. They can direct speech away from its communicative functions toward that "*text-inscribed* blankness." This redirection may involve nothing more than allowing the material dimension of language to emerge so as to reveal the emplacement of the speaking subject within a social process that inevitably fractures the unity of the ego (*moi*), that point of structural identity. I do not mean that radical intellectuals should stop trying to communicate or articulate the unequal and exploitative relations between the two sides of the international division of labor. But I do mean that they must be willing to scrutinize and question their own construction of models of social and cultural differences. As Spivak writes in a recent essay,

The operation of value makes every commitment negotiable, however urgent it might seem to be. For the *long* haul emancipatory social intervention is not *primarily* a question of redressing victimage by the assertion of (class- or gender- or ethno-cultural) identity. It is a question of developing a vigilance for systematic appropriations of the social capacity to produce a *differential* that is one basis of exchange into the networks of cultural or class- or gender-identity.

In other words, the struggle for liberation (even the concept of "liberation") cannot be justified solely through appeals to history or political philosophy. "You take positions in terms not of the discovery of historical or philosophical grounds, but in terms of reversing, displacing, and seizing the apparatus of value-coding" ("Poststructuralism, Marginality, Postcoloniality, and Value" 228). It is not enough to communicate the truth to/of the other; one must call to the "quite-other" (Lacan's big Other) within us—must find in the symbolic, viewed from the side of the Other, the intersubjective ground that ties subject to subject through the wall of language.

This call to radical alterity has left its trace in the history of the English novel, by which I mean the history of novels written in English. Such a distinction reminds us that the language of colonization has always been subject to strategies of appropriation, reversal, and displacement by colonized subjects. Hegemony is never a one-way street; and even from within the ethnocentric enclosure of European culture, there are ways in which a writing practice can resist its own "colonizing" effect. For it is important to remember that in the historical process of articulating a global hegemony the languages of imperialist powers not only colonize the immediate victims of European conquest and domination but also those *hegemonized* subjects that are constructed as European. As direct domination eventually gives place to cultural hegemony, particularly in the postcolonial or neocolonial era, those intellectuals who legitimately speak as third-world subjects in the languages of the colonizers must come to terms with the hegemonizing effect of their own discourses and subject positions. As I have stressed about *The Waves*, modernism, even at that point where it can be said to expose its alterity in challenging traditional representations of social identity and sexual difference, also encounters the limit of that challenge in the unthought transparency of its representations of Asia and Africa. Nevertheless, this "unthought" representation can become the trace of "real" or utopian thought—"what we already know we have not yet begun," as Derrida says—insofar as it is presented as the edge that limits the political play of the text. It becomes a "*text-inscribed* blankness." This merely says that Woolf's work, like

Woolf the subject, is constituted in contradiction. The same can be said about other modernist texts (including *Absalom, Absalom!*, *Ulysses*, and *Finnegans Wake*) as well as about postmodern and postcolonial responses to the modernist project. In this context, I want to consider two modernist attempts to represent the "experience" of imperialism and two postcolonial responses to that representation, which struggle to reverse the hegemonic effect of the language in which they are written—English. This analysis should reveal not only the ethnocentrism of modernism but the text-inscribed blankness in modernist and postmodernist works that point toward the Other modernism within modernism. This Other modernism may include the postmodern within the modern and after the modern; but it also links the postmodern and its retrospective reading of the modern to the postcolonial experience as the historical ground of its emergence. The first place to look for this radical alterity within modernism may be in the heart of Joseph Conrad's *Heart of Darkness*.

In *The Political Unconscious*, Fredric Jameson makes a case for "reading Conrad not as an early modernist, but rather an anticipation of that later and quite different thing we have come to call variously textuality, *écriture*, post-modernism, or schizophrenic writing" (219). Although Jameson is thinking primarily of *Lord Jim*, Patrick Brantlinger claims that the same reading strategy could be applied to *Heart of Darkness*. He speculates that Jameson would see in both works "a symptomatic split between a modernist will-to-style, leading to an elaborate but essentially hollow impressionism, and the reified, mass-culture tendencies of romance conventions." Jameson might suggest a reading of *Heart of Darkness* that tries to reconcile traditional Western academic views of it as a critique of imperialism with its condemnation as a racist text by the Nigerian writer Chinua Achebe. Brantlinger spells out the chief difficulty he has with Jameson's argument:

> The will-to-style in Conrad's text is also a will to appropriate and remake Gothic romance conventions into high art. On some level the impressionism of Conrad's novels and their romance features are identical—Conrad constructs a sophisticated version of the imperialist romance—and in any case both threaten to submerge or "derealize" the critique of empire within their own more strictly aesthetic project. As part of the project, providing much of the substance of impressionism, the romance conventions that Conrad reshapes carry with them the polarizations of racist thought. (265)

I don't altogether disagree with the substance of this analysis, although it seems to me that Brantlinger has missed the point of Jameson's use of a term like "postmodernism." Making Jameson stand in for contemporary literary theory in general, Brantlinger insists that for the latter "words themselves have almost ceased to have external referents." The will-to-style is not only applicable to Conrad; it "devours literary critics, too, leaving structuralists and deconstructionists, Althusserians and Foucauldians." While Brantlinger supplies the historical context of Conrad's novella with skill and sophistication, he misses the historicity of the text in itself when he rejects its "schizophrenic writing" as one more vagary of contemporary theory.

Jameson, if I am reading him correctly, suggests something subtler than Brantlinger is willing to admit—something that has a bearing on how we read *Heart of Darkness*. If Conrad is able to "overleap the now classical Jamesian moment and become post-modernist," he does it not by exploding the referent through some sort of autonomous linguistic free play; rather, he bypasses or dissolves the ideology underlying the Jamesian "point of view." While James remains "theoretically locked into nonsymbolic, essentially 'expressive' categories," which make point of view "a psychological matter, a matter of consciousness," Conrad discovers the symbolic: "If the multiple narrative shifts in Conrad are to be seen as textbook exercises in point of view, then we must add something which changes everything: they are point of view conceived as being inseparable from speech, from the materiality of language" (Jameson, *Political Unconscious* 224). For Brantlinger, Conrad's style is an act of evasion that reflects "the patterns of reification underlying both commodity fetishism and literary modernism—the deliberate ambiguity and refusal of moral and political judgment at the heart of an impressionism and a will-to-style that seem to be ends in themselves" (264). Against this sort of Lukácsian judgment, Jameson argues that Conrad's impressionism "projects a unique sensorium of its own" which provides a wall of resistance to the capitalist process of reification. Yet, the "ultimate ambiguity [of this style] lies in its attempt to stand beyond history." Brantlinger would agree that there is, as Jameson puts it, "a reflexivity, a self-consciousness" about symbolic processes in Conrad (*Political Unconscious* 237); but the end result too closely resembles the imperialist rhetoric of Kurtz's pamphlet for the International Society for the Suppression of Savage Customs, which, although Marlow describes it as "a moving appeal to every altruistic sentiment," ends with the scribbled sentence: "Exterminate all the brutes!" (Conrad, *Heart of Darkness* 51). Like the pamphlet, the novel finally "cancels out its own best intentions" (Brantlinger 272).

It seems to me that the historicity of *Heart of Darkness* (to which both Jameson and Brantlinger point) lies in the way it dramatizes its own resistance to historical emplacement. Rather than focus on Kurtz—who, like Percival in *The Waves*, actually has no voice in this novel since whatever we know or hear of him is mediated by Marlow's narration—I would rather look at Marlow and, in particular, at that moment in the story when his monologue seems to confront its own discursive authority. "We penetrated deeper and deeper into the heart of darkness," he says, and imagines himself "on a prehistoric earth." The dances and other social forms of the native community appear to him as "a black and incomprehensible frenzy." He and his business associates are "cut off from the comprehension of our surroundings" because they cannot remember this "night of first ages, of those ages that are gone, leaving hardly a sign—and no memories" (*Heart of Darkness* 37). The past leaves no sign and has no voice, ironically giving Marlow unlimited powers of speech:

> The earth seemed unearthly. We are accustomed to look upon the shackled form of a conquered monster, but there—there you could look at a thing monstrous and free. It was unearthly and the men were. . . . No they were not inhuman. Well, you know that was the worst of it— the suspicion of their not being inhuman. It would come slowly to one. They howled and leaped and spun and made horrid faces, but what thrilled you was just the thought of their humanity—like yours—the thought of your remote kinship with this wild and passionate uproar. Ugly. Yes, it was ugly enough, but if you were man enough you would admit to yourself that there was in you just the faintest trace of a response to the terrible frankness of that noise, a dim suspicion of there being a meaning in it which you—you so remote from the night of first ages—could comprehend. And why not? *The mind of man is capable of anything—because everything is in it, all the past as well as all the future.* What was there after all? Joy, fear, sorrow, devotion, valour, rage—who can tell?—but truth—*truth stripped of its cloak of time.* Let the fool gape and shudder—the man knows and can look on without a wink. But he must at least be as much of a man as these on the shore. He must meet that truth with his own true stuff—with his own inborn strength. Principles? Principles won't do. Acquisitions, clothes, pretty rags—rags that would fly off at the first good shake. No. You want a deliberate belief. An appeal to me in this fiendish row—is there? Very well. I hear, I admit, but I have a voice too, and for good or evil *mine is the speech that cannot be silenced.* (*Heart of Darkness* 37–38, my emphasis)

This speech betrays Marlow's refusal to situate his experience in any actual historical context. The ideology of European imperialism is seemingly reduced to a purely natural and inevitable perception. The earth is not the earth when it is allowed to run free in all of its monstrosity—that is, when it has not been remade in the image of Europe. By representing the relation between Europe and the Congo as that between a "conquered monster" and a "thing monstrous and free," Marlow simply erases the historical developments that gave birth to what Brantlinger calls "the myth of the Dark Continent." This myth "was shaped by political and economic pressures, and also by a psychology of blaming the victim through which Europeans projected onto Africans their own darkest impulses." After the abolition of the British slave trade in 1833, which had its own economic motives, "the myth of the Dark Continent defined slavery as the offspring of tribal savagery and portrayed white explorers and missionaries as the leaders of a Christian crusade that would vanguish the forces of darkness" (Brantlinger 195; all Brantlinger's chapter 6 [173–97] is relevant to this discussion). Once blame for the slave trade had been shifted from Europeans to Africans, abolitionist rhetoric was easily modified to serve the interests of the imperialist scramble at the end of the century. Marlow's "suspicion of their not being inhuman" reverses the function of the abolitionist argument for the slave's humanity. It enables him to justify the domination of his own gaze over that of the native "other" because this other is only a dimension—a prehistoric trace—of the European subject. Marlow, in penetrating the heart of darkness, is able to see through the "uproar" and the "noise" of native culture to its real meaning. Without comprehending the languages or social forms of this culture, he intuitively grasps its significance as the unconscious "other" of his own culture, which is, of course, civilizaton itself. Though he has no memory or direct knowledge of this prehistoric "night of first ages," he can immediately grasp its essence.

The first sentence I have emphasized in the quotation economically expresses the core of Eurocentric ideology. Whose mind is capable of everything? Surely not that of the native who does not know his or her own destiny. Marlow may not comprehend the concrete material culture of the native "others," but he knows what their future will be insofar as the European mind is the goal of all "human" history and therefore contains "all the past as well as all the future" as the immanent principle of its own becoming. The European mind is capable of anything and contains everything because it is One, the only One; and whatever approaches it becomes a part of it. Marlow is a hesitant Hegelian in that, while suspecting the other's humanity, he is also deeply shocked and appalled by the inhumanity of what he cannot comprehend. And why should he comprehend the particular when the truth transcends "the cloak of time," those geographical boundaries or historical contexts? What cannot be comprehended in native culture is inessential to those fundamental human emotions that transcend the European culture that foregrounds them. Everywhere Marlow looks he sees the same, the One culture and mind of which he, like Kurtz, is the ambassador. He meets the One truth with the same, "his own true stuff."

It goes without saying, perhaps, that this imperialist discourse is couched in phallocentric language. Darkness and penetration are not only governing metaphors in the literary sense; they are metaphors used to govern, that is, to create a discursive field making it possible to construct the colonial subject and then govern it. Therefore, it is possible to speak of an imperialism of the metaphor rooted in a patriarchal language that conflates racial difference with sexual difference in the field of Western representations. Marlow identifies his manhood with the manhood of those he sees on the shore. But it would be a mistake to see this as a gesture toward equality in difference. It is the erasure of difference through the assimilation of the native "other" to the paradigm of the European subject. The manhood like the "humanity" of the native only foregrounds his inhumanity and inevitable subordination to Western standards. As Marlow suggests, in order that the European male should be able to face the heart of darkness with its combined force of feminine seduction and inhuman corruption, he must have something beyond mere principles and symbols of the West: he must have a conscious belief in the universal "truth" of Western standards and values. He must see the native as a prehistoric image of himself. It is no accident that at the juncture in his discourse when he seems to recognize the other as another version of himself, Marlow suddenly stops to explain to his audience of European men the appeal to him in this "fiendish row" of native culture. In effect, he reaffirms his alignment with these men as the collective social ground of his own discourse, of his power to represent the other through assimilation to Western ideology. The word "fiendish" subordinates native culture to the standards of the West through the implementation of what Abdul JanMohamed calls the "manichean allegory": "a field of diverse yet interchangeable oppositions between white and black, good and evil, superiority and inferiority, rationality and sensuality, self and Other, subject and object" ("Economy of Manichean Allegory" 82). Finally, Marlow reemphasizes the autonomy of his own word. He not only has a voice too; there is really no other voice in this text. For his is "the speech that cannot be silenced"—that is, an imperialist discourse that governs every position within the field of hegemonic discursivity.

When I say that Marlow's is the only voice in Conrad's text, I don't mean that he is the only narrator, since obviously there are at least two other levels of narration: that of the frame narrator who describes the scene of storytelling on the deck of the *Nellie* and, ultimately, that of Conrad himself, whose own narrative, or biography, is a framing context for the novel as a whole. Nevertheless, Marlow's voice as contained by the frame narrator as contained by Conrad is a unified expression of Eurocentrism, and there is nothing in the text that seriously challenges its representational authority. For this reason, Edward Said identifies *Heart of Darkness* as the paradigm of Eurocentric discourse, noticing "how totalizing it is, how all-enveloping its attitudes and gestures, how much it shuts out even as it includes, compresses, and asserts a great deal." It leaves out "the traces . . . that comprised the immensely detailed and violent history of colonial intervention . . . in the lives of individuals and collectivities, on both sides of the colonial divide" ("Intellectuals in the Post-colonial World" 48). Of course, it could be argued that these traces survive to some extent in the human heads on the fence surrounding Kurtz's compound and in the dying laborers, judged by the Company to be criminals, whom Marlow encounters at the Outer Station. The latter, in my opinion, actually do point toward the real relations of power underlying the colonial experience; and it is probably no accident that Marlow sees them after finding a discarded boiler and an overturned "railway truck" (*Heart of Darkness* 19), which could be read as symbols of the Industrial Revolution that gave new impetus to the colonial ambitions of the West. But the human heads do not so much represent the violent treatment of the native peoples in the Congo Free State by the emissaries of King Leopold II of Belgium, as they manifest the white man's paranoid fear of "going native," of allowing the savagery of the Dark Continent to contaminate the humanity of the imperialist. Conrad's representation of the West is ambivalent, but he consistently associates colonialism with a hypocritical death drive. The Company's offices are in a European city that makes Marlow think of a "whited sepulchre" (*Heart of Darkness* 13); and traveling down the African coast, he contemplates "the merry dance of death and trade" (*Heart of Darkness* 17). As Said insists, however, Marlow's narrative "leaves us with a quite accurate sense that there is no way out of the sovereign historical force of imperialism, and that it has the power of a system representing everything within its dominion." Nevertheless, Conrad is "different from all the other colonial writers." He "is self-conscious about setting and situating the narrative in a narrative moment, thus allowing us to realize after all that far from swallowing up its own history, imperialism has in fact been placed and located by history, one that lies outside the tightly inclusive ring on the deck of the yawl *Nelly* [*sic*]" ("Intellectuals in the Post-colonial World" 48–49). In this sense, Conrad's text inscribes a crucial blankness that is the sign of its own historical contingency. Christopher Miller observes that "Africa" is never named as the referent of this text (*Blank Darkness* 172–75). Perhaps more important, the Congo River is never named, nor are we given any specific knowledge of or names for the peoples who live on its shores. Everything particular is drowned out by the metaphor "heart of darkness." Kurtz himself is not so much a character as an extension of this figure of speech. His words are "the pulsating stream of light or the deceitful flow from the heart of an impenetrable darkness" (*Heart of Darkness* 48). It is because nothing escapes the imperialism of this metaphor that we can see the discursive system within which it operates.

It would seem that things are very different in a novel like *A Passage to India* where early on the Englishman is confronted with his own will to power. When Mrs. Moore suggests to her son that he talks of India as if he were a god, he snidely remarks, "India likes Gods." She responds, "And Englishmen like posing as Gods" (*Passage to India* 50). E. M. Forster may go a long way toward exploding the myth of Percival, to coin a phrase; but it is an ironic commentary on Mrs. Moore's criticism of her son that she is the one who is eventually transformed into Esmiss Esmoor, a new goddess for Indian myth, during the trial of Dr. Aziz. Forster, says Abdul JanMohammed, attempts to find a syncretic solution to the "manichean opposition of the colonizer and the colonized" ("Economy of Manichean Allegory" 85). According to JanMohamed, this use of syncretism in Forster's text distinguishes its "symbolic" approach from an "imaginary" or blatantly imperialist approach to colonial contradictions: "The 'symbolic' text's openness toward the Other is based on a greater awareness of *potential* identity and a heightened sense of the *concrete* socio-political cultural differences between self and Other" ("Economy of Manichean Allegory" 92–93). As JanMohamed also stresses, however, the limit of Forster's novel may lie in the fact that his "depiction of racial and cultural difference is ultimately based on a rational, intellectual concern" (96). This observation identifies *A Passage to India* as a specific type of "symbolic" fiction, one which "overlaps . . . with the 'imaginary' text" in such a way that "those portions of the novel organized at the emotive level are structured by 'imaginary' identification, while those controlled by cognitive intentionality are structured by the rules of the 'symbolic' order" ("Economy of Manichean Allegory" 85).

To some extent, the ambiguity of the Marabar Caves reproduces the same manichean economy as Conrad's imperialist metaphors in *Heart of Darkness*. The caves have the same destructive effect on the European subject as Conrad's jungle has on Kurtz. Adela Quested nearly destroys Dr. Aziz when she encounters her own repressed sexuality in the mirror of this Indian heart of darkness. Mrs. Moore resembles Marlow in her recoil from the experience of the caves, whose echo threatens "to undermine her hold on life": "Coming at a moment when she chanced to be fatigued, it had managed to murmur, 'Pathos, piety, courage—they exist, but are identical, and so is filth. Everything exists, nothing has value'" (*Passage to India* 149). Fielding shows little interest in the caves before the crisis, and afterward he "experienced nothing" while gazing at them: "It was as if someone had told him there was such a moment, and he was obliged to believe" (*Passage to India* 191). Forster explains the threat posed to Western value systems by the culture of the colonized through an appeal to the metaphysical difference that the caves seem to manifest. This has the effect of naturalizing social differences and occluding the real violence of cultural hegemony, which may far exceed the overt racism of colonial officials. Fielding epitomizes Forster's rationality and tolerance and, therefore, comes the closest to establishing a relationship of equality with the Indian community. Nevertheless, he eventually recoils from Indian "chaos" and on his return to Europe rediscovers his cultural identity: "The Mediterranean is the human norm. When men leave that exquisite lake, whether through the Bosphorus or the Pillars of Hercules, they approach the monstrous and the extraordinary; and the southern exit leads to the strangest experience of all" (*Passage to India* 282). The final scenes between Fielding and Dr. Aziz insinuate that cultural differences are an insurmountable barrier. The newfound Indian nationalism of Assiz and Fielding's reaffirmed identification with the British Empire are presented not as conscious political choices but as inevitable cultural facts. They want to be friends, but Indian culture rises up to say, "'No, not yet,' and the sky said, 'No, not there'" (*Passage to India* 322).

Edward Said interprets the conclusion of *A Passage to India* as one more example of the "crisis of modernism," which responds to "alterity and difference" in the form of "women, natives, and sexual eccentrics" with "paralyzed gestures of aestheticized powerlessness, for example, the ending of *A Passage to India* in which Forster notes, and confirms the history behind, a political conflict between Dr. Aziz and Fielding— Britain's subjugation of India—and yet can neither recommend decolonization, nor continued colonization" ("Representing the Colonized" 222–23). Nevertheless, in comparison with Conrad's, Forster's text is less dominated by the modernist will-to-style, and ironically this may be one of the weaknesses of its representation of imperialism. JanMohamed classifies *Heart of Darkness* as a second type of "symbolic" fiction, one that "realizes that syncretism is impossible within the power relations of colonial society." This fiction frees itself from the manichean allegory by "confining itself to a rigorous examination of the 'imaginary' mechanism of colonialist mentality" ("Economy of Manichean Allegory" 85). Stated simply, Conrad's language never forgets itself or allows us to forget its scene of production vis-à-vis Marlow's storytelling in a circle of "white" European men. The figure "heart of darkness" is always a figure that hollows out a gap between its own rhetorical force and the referent it is meant to define. I do not mean that Chinua Achebe mistakenly identifies Conrad as a "thoroughgoing racist." As he suggests, the racism of Conrad's rhetoric has been "glossed over in criticisms of his work" because "white racism against Africa is such a normal way of thinking that its manifestations go completely unremarked" (*Hopes and Impediments* 8). Hegemony is nothing other than this normal way of thinking. Still, to the extent that Conrad articulates his "racism" as a rhetoric and not as a transparent expression, he makes visible the blankness that rhetoric inscribes. Forster, by contrast, employs a greater charge of realism by situating the Indian heart of darkness in the actual Marabar Caves without situating the voice of the narrator. As the characters approach the caves, the narrator says, "A new quality occurred, a spiritual silence which invaded more senses than the ear. . . . Everything seemed cut off at its root, and therefore infected with illusion" (*Passage to India* 140). It is possible to see beyond this illusion, as Homi K. Bhabha does, to the threatening nonsense of the colonial signifier that momentarily disrupts the hegemonic gaze: "Cultural difference, as Adela Quested experienced it, in the nonsense of the Marabar caves, is not the acquisition or accumulation of additional cultural knowledge; it is the momentous, if momentary, extinction of the object of culture in the disturbed artifice of its signification, at the edge of experience" ("Articulating the Archaic" 206). In other words, the Marabar Caves disrupt the manichean allegory as a structure of value by articulating an irreducible difference that defies represention within any specific economy. Bhabha points to the caves as the place where the novel's system of representations breaks down, but the narrator of the novel hardly shares this insight when he suggests that the irreality of Indian culture is the effect not of rhetoric but of the "real" itself. For this reason, while Forster may not be the "thoroughgoing racist" Conrad is, his writing remains almost completely blind to its own hegemonic functions. The blankness his text inscribes is not open to revision or rewriting, because it claims to occupy an "actual" place in "neutral" historical time.

The rhetoric of representation takes on a very different value when we shift to the postcolonial context. Chinua Achebe's *Things Fall Apart*, published a year after the independence of Ghana and two years before Nigerian independence in 1960, also employs a style of realism—but for very different ends. JanMohamed, in his *Manichean Aesthetics*, has already discussed the *negative* influence of English literature on the African writer who rejects "the colonial depiction of Africa" (153). Achebe insists on the duty of the African writer to restore the dignity of the African past that was nearly destroyed by colonialism. This becomes a sociological imperative that demands not only recovery of the past but realistic representation of it. The writer is a social being whose work is necessarily determined by his or her relation to others. "The tool that we use," says Achebe "the basic tool which is language, is made by society and therefore you cannot really arrive at whatever it is you are looking for by gazing inwards" (quoted from a personal interview by JanMohamed, *Manichean Aesthetics* 155). At the same time, Achebe is perfectly aware that the question of community can be very complex for the African writer in the "wide-open, multicultural and highly volatile condition known as modern Nigeria." For example, he directed these questions at his own political and historical situation in 1984: "If I write novels in a country in which most citizens are illiterate, who then is my community? If I write in English in a country in which English may still be called a foreign language, or in any case is spoken only by a minority, what use is my writing?" ("The Writer and His Community," *Hopes and Impediments* 40). In 1964, however, Achebe had already decided that "for me there is no other choice. I have been given this language and I intend to use it." English, he felt then, "will be able to carry the weight of my African experience," but "it will have to be a new English, still in full communion with its ancestral home but altered to suit new African surroundings" (*Morning Yet on Creation Day* 62). All these statements appear years after the composition of *Things Fall Apart* but support the assumptions already implicit in that work.

Achebe's realism is self-conscious and intertextual. JanMohamed compares Achebe's situation to that in which "the French realists found themselves when their hopes in the future of the revolution were dashed by the enthronement of the bourgeoisie." But before "the promise of [Nigerian] independence . . . turned out to be hollow" like that of the

French Revolution, Achebe was already engaged in a struggle with the imperialist rhetoric of such writers as Joseph Conrad (JanMohamed, *Manichean Aesthetics* 155–56). This struggle does not necessarily take the form of a system of allusions to Conrad; rather, it displaces the rhetoric of imperialism that so thoroughly informs Conrad's text. This is the goal of Achebe's realism: to undo the imperialism of the metaphor and to articulate the concrete particularity of African life that imperialist discourse occludes. To some extent, this goal means rewriting Conrad's "controlling" figures in ways that resituate them in an African context they no longer mystify but describe:

> The night was very quiet. It was always quiet except on moonlight nights. Darkness held a vague terror for these people, even the bravest among them. Children were warned not to whistle at night for fear of evil spirits. Dangerous animals became even more sinister and uncanny in the dark. A snake was never called by its name at night, because it would hear. It was called a string. And so on this particular night as the crier's voice was gradually swallowed up in the distance, silence returned to the world, a vibrant silence made more intense by the universal trill of a million million forest insects. (*Things Fall Apart* 7)

The directness of this description may belie its rhetorical self-consciousness. Not only does it rewrite Conrad's central metaphor as a metonymy that no longer reduces the totality of African experience to a univocal representation, but it challenges the moral tone of Conrad's style. Compare it to Marlow's description of the silence of the Congo: "An empty stream, a great silence, an impenetrable forest. . . . And this stillness of life did not in the least resemble a peace. It was the stillness of an implacable force brooding over an inscrutable intention. It looked at you with a vengeful aspect" (*Heart of Darkness* 36). For Marlow, Africa is always "other," which makes it demonic in relation to Western values. Because the Western mind is "capable of anything" and the measure of everything, whatever it cannot measure or comprehend must be morally evil, that is, "implacable" and "inscrutable." Achebe's style is radically different. He describes the point of view of "these people" without judging it. The terror of darkness is not questioned or interpreted, only mentioned. The "fear of evil spirits" is not presented as the response to some "implacable force" but as a concrete experience of everyday life. The dangerous animals and the darkness are problems that can be managed through very specific social and linguistic strategies, such as calling a snake a string. The narrator's point of view is not coincident with that of the people he describes, for they would not be able to speak the language he uses to tell their story. But his position does not transcend their experience either. There is, if you will, an effort of translation, a fitting of the English language to subject positions that are completely "foreign" to the Eurocentric discourse of Conrad. This translation requires making that language foreign to itself, making it participate in the "foreignness of languages" that Benjamin describes and that, according to Homi Bhabha, makes it possible "to inscribe the specific locality of cultural systems— their incommensurable differences—and through that apprehension of difference, to perform the act of cultural translation" ("DissemiNation" 315). The words "dark" and "darkness" are repeated throughout the novel in multiple contexts that self-consciously destroy the associations Conrad's style invested in them. One chapter begins with the sentence, "The night was impenetrably dark" (*Things Fall Apart* 67); and although this episode explores the fear of forces beyond individual human control, the overall effect is not to enhance fear but to dissipate it. While Ekwefi awaits the return of her daughter from the priestess who has taken her away for the night, she is joined by her husband Okonkwo. Together they wait out the night, while Ekwefi recalls her first sexual encounter with Okonkwo, which gave a different meaning to the word "darkness": "He just carried her into his bed and in the darkness began to feel around her waist for the loose end of her cloth" (*Things Fall Apart* 76). Darkness is no longer a ruling metaphor but an incommensurable particular.

These effects may seem minute and almost irrelevant, but they are crucial to the African writer of novels in English who feels the effect of Conrad's language as an impediment to the construction of an African experience that does not simply mirror the European subject. Because Achebe concedes that Conrad "is undoubtedly one of the great stylists of modern fiction and a good storyteller into the bargain," he cannot ignore the effectiveness of his work in reducing Africa to the evil twin of Europe: "Africa is to Europe as the picture is to Dorian Gray—a carrier onto whom the master unloads his physical and moral deformities so that he may go forward, erect and immaculate." The lesson of Kurtz is transparent: "Keep away from Africa, or else!" ("An Image of Africa," *Hopes and Impediments* 2, 12). Achebe destroys this transparency by stealing darkness away from Conrad's abstractions and giving it back to the concrete world. He sweeps away the Eurocentric view of African culture as "a black and incomprehensible frenzy" by carefully delineating its social forms without subsuming them under European models. He even situates his own storytelling within an African framework that refuses to replicate the Eurocentric claim to universal truth. After hearing about the massacre of the people of Abame by "white men," Obierika says, "We have heard stories about white men who made the powerful guns and the strong drinks and took slaves away across the seas, but no one thought the stories were true." Uchendu responds, "There is no story that is not true. . . . The world has no end, and what is good among one people is an abomination with others" (*Things Fall Apart* 99). *Things Fall Apart* does not aim at producing a universal value, not even a universal representation of Africa—except insofar as it translates one incommensurable African perspective into a language that can be exchanged through the circuits of multicultural social ties. It does, however, try to suggest ways of displacing or resituating Conrad's text-inscribed blankness. The name "Africa" does not appear until the last paragraph of the novel, which could be read as a return to the Eurocentric perspective of *Heart of Darkness*. The commissioner, who has "toiled to bring civilization to different parts of Africa," contemplates his own version of Okonkwo's story, that is, of the novel Achebe has written, to be included in his work, *The Pacification of the Primitive Tribes of the Lower Niger*. This title, of course, recalls Kurtz's pamphlet for the International Society for the Suppression of Savage Customs. According to Achebe's commissioner, "The story of this man who had killed a messenger and hanged himself would make interesting reading. One could almost write a whole chapter on him. Perhaps not a whole chapter but a reasonable paragraph, at any rate. There was so much else to include, and one must be firm in cutting out details" (*Things Fall Apart* 147–48). The European tendency to subordinate every reality to the discourse of "One" civilization necessarily requires the erasure or "cutting out" of details, and it is these details that Achebe tries to restore. He does not idealize the African. As JanMohamed summarizes, "Okonkwo is an inflexible monomaniac who destroys himself through his compulsive preoccupation with martial values" (*Manichean Aesthetics* 179). Achebe does not shy away from the patriarchal structure of African communalism, though he insists that Okonkwo's tragedy should not be governed by the generalizing authority of the European gaze. According to Achebe, "in the course of the last four hundred years . . . the white man has been talking and talking and never listening because he imagines that he has been talking to a dumb beast" ("Impediments to Dialogue between North and South," *Hopes and Impediments* 15). Marlow's insistence on the legitimacy of his monologue, "the speech that cannot be silenced," implies that dialogue between Europe and Africa is impossible; and it is the ground of this impossibility that Achebe rejects by taking such a strong stand on the racism of Conrad's text. *Things Fall Apart* finally has its own text-inscribed blankness—the history of colonialism (including its neocolonial forms) and, beyond it, the hope of a future we have not yet begun to think.

By way of concluding this chapter, I want to consider briefly a "postmodern" response to modernist contradictions. Even to label Salman Rushdie's *Midnight's Children* a postmodern work should draw attention to the historical unthinkability of "postmodernism" outside the nexus of events that we call postcolonialism, though, as Said stresses, "the break between the colonial and the post-colonial period is [not] that great" ("Intellectuals in the Post-colonial World" 69). What has emerged from the explosion of postcolonial fiction, along with the expansion of feminist, African-American, and other "minority" writing in America and Europe, is the increasing awareness of modernism's political limitations, particularly its ethnocentrism. As Rushdie formulates it, in the present world-historical context, "we see that it can be as false to create a politics-free fictional universe as to create one in which nobody needs to work or eat or hate or sleep" ("Outside the Whale" 137). Modernism can be said to aim at such a "politics-free" universe not by totally excluding political issues from its representations but by attempting to transcend them at the level of style and form. Conrad's will-to-style enables him to react aesthetically to the politics of imperialist discourse that his work so carefully records. Forster, on the other hand, realistically depicts the racism behind British rule in India but then tries to root this political conflict in a cultural mysticism that enables him to evade taking a position. In other words, his representation aims at universality through a construction of human nature that transcends political debate. Other writers—for example, Joyce and the later Woolf—anticipate the postcolonial writer precisely to the extent that they themselves, *as subjects*, have been colonized by hegemonic discourses to which they offer specific forms of linguistic resistance. Nevertheless, as I have suggested already, these representations are inconsistent and contradictory. Even Achebe, who tries to reverse the negative effects of colonialist representations in English, cannot fully resolve the contradictions that arise from what he comes to see as "the fatalistic logic of the unassailable position of English in our literature" (*Morning Yet on Creation Day* xiv). Rushdie, as the "postmodern" and "postcolonial" writer in English, confronts the same problem with yet another stylistic strategy.

Midnight's Children undertakes the impossible task of representing the whole of Indian history in the twentieth century. At the same time, it rewrites the European novel from Cervantes to Günther Grass, not so much with allusions as with structural echoes of *Tom Jones, Tristram Shandy, Wuthering Heights, Heart of Darkness, Kim, A Portrait of the Artist as a Young Man, In Search of Lost Time, A Passage to India,* and *The Tin Drum.* But of course the master text behind all these and the point of symbolic exchange between East and West on which Rushdie gambles is the *Arabian Nights,* to which there is a reference at the beginning of the book: "I have no hope of saving my life, nor can I count on having a thousand nights and a night. I must work fast, faster than Scheherazade, if I am to end up meaning—yes, meaning—something" (*Midnight's Children* 4). Saleem Sinai, the first-person narrator of the book, knows that ultimately his desire for meaning is insatiable, that he suffers from "an Indian disease, this urge to encapsulate the whole of reality" (*Midnight's Children* 84). In fact, he attempts to encapsulate the totality of a written culture whose hegemonic functions would seem to be realized in his own mode of self-representation. According to Richard Cronin, the disease Saleem refers to is peculiar to those "who write about India in English." Ironically, he says, "the Indian novel, the novel that tries to encapsulate the whole of Indian reality can, as yet, be written only in English" (201). This is the case not because the languages of India, including its other national language, Hindi, confer a regional identity on the Indian writer (what kind of identity does English, which is used as a primary language by less than 2 percent of the population, confer?); it relates to the cultural diversity of India that Dr. Aziz in Forster's novel insists upon in his conversation with Miss Quested: "Nothing embraces the whole of India, nothing, nothing" (*Passage to India* 145). By the end of *A Passage to India,* however, Aziz has made a political about-face: "India shall be a nation! . . . Hindu and Moslem and Sikh and all shall be one!" (322). In effect, Aziz has been converted to Indian nationalism by his confrontation with the racism of British culture. Saleem Sinai knows that the India which was born at midnight on August 15, 1947, is also a reaction to the history of colonialism. On that day, there was "a new myth to celebrate, because a nation which had never previously existed was about to win its freedom, catapulting us into a world which, although it had five thousand years of history, . . . was nevertheless quite imaginary" (*Midnight's Children* 129–30).

The imaginary India is the effect of imperialism, and the language that expresses that effect is English. But precisely because the imperialism of English is rooted in the imaginary, it is possible to turn it back against itself, to use the language of empire against its own imperialist aims (as Joyce did in *Ulysses* and *Finnegans Wake*). Rushdie suggested as much himself in 1982: "English . . . now grows from many roots; and those whom it once colonized are carving out large territories within the language for themselves" ("The Empire Writes Back"). In *Midnight's Children*, if India is imaginary, so is the child who is said to mirror it, Saleem himself. His genealogy makes his national identity a nearly insoluble puzzle. Having been switched with his psychic twin Shiva at birth, he is raised as the child of Indian Muslims, Ahmed Sinai and Amina Aziz (who eventually emigrate to Pakistan); and his grandfather bears the allusive name, Dr. Aziz. His biological father, however, is an Englishman descended from the East India Company officer who first had the dream of a British Bombay. The modern William Methwold seduces Saleem's Hindu mother, Vanita, the wife of a street singer with another allusive name, Wee Willie Winkie. Saleem's enormous nose, the seat of his telepathic powers, belongs to his English father and his grandfather Aziz and also to his mythological father, Ganesh. Though his identity is historically bound to postindependence India, it is genealogically indeterminate. He is the symbolic child of England, India, and Pakistan, of Hindu and Moslem, of imperialism and nationalism, of European and Indian literature.

Like Stephen Dedalus (who has his own symbolic fathers), Saleem tries to forge the conscience of his race. We can apply the double meaning of the word "forge" to both Joyce and Rushdie, since their use of the English language—that is, the language of their conqueror—makes their representations of "race" into a forgery. Because Saleem's complicated genealogy calls the whole notion of "race" into question, he is more self-conscious than Stephen Dedalus about the limits of his self-representations. He questions himself at one point: "Am I so far gone, in my desperate need for meaning, that I'm prepared to distort everything—to re-write the whole history of my times purely in order to place myself in a central role?" (*Midnight's Children* 198). But if Saleem occupies the central role, he also represents more than a single identity: "I have been a swallower of lives; and to know me, just the one of me, you'll have to swallow the lot as well" (4). Although he longs to be One (just as his India longs to be one nation), he knows that he is not-One, since he is falling apart even as he writes to assert his self-identity: "I ask you only to accept (as I have accepted) that I shall eventually crumble into (approximately) six hundred and thirty million particles of anonymous, and necessarily oblivious dust" (37). As the representative or spokesman of all Indians (630 million at the time of writing), Saleem must consign his own identity to oblivion, for whoever would speak for the whole must articulate an illusion in a language of illusions.

Saleem directly confronts this power of illusion when he voyages into yet another version of the heart of darkness, the impenetrable forests called the Sundarbans. After the death of nearly all his family during the 1965 Indo-Pakistani War, Saleem, who has been brained by the family spittoon, loses his memory and falls out of history. He becomes the human tracker dog for the West Pakistan army. His nickname, the buddha, means that he is old before his time while suggesting that he has experienced some form of enlightenment: "Emptied of history, the buddha learned the arts of submission, and did only what was required of him. To sum up: I became a citizen of Pakistan" (418). This appellation also aligns him with Conrad's Marlow, who is twice compared to the Buddha (*Heart of Darkness* 10, 76) and who, despite his irony, always remains a more or less obedient company man. Saleem as the buddha participates with his intelligence team in the brutal suppression of the Bangladesh independence struggle in 1971. It is in the mindless process of doing what he has been trained to do, "pursue-relentlessly-arrest-remorselessly," that the buddha and his team escape into "a mission without an end, pursuing a foe who endlessly eludes them" (428). Though only the buddha knows it, they are running away from history. Appropriately, before entering the Sundarbans, the buddha is chased by a man resembling Father Time, who soon "lies dead in a rice-paddy," killed by Saleem's comrades (429). With time virtually murdered, the team enters the jungle, which "closed behind them like a tomb" (432). Their military mission "acquires in the altered light of the Sundarbans a quality of absurd fantasy which enabled them to dismiss it once and for all" (434). Ironically, the jungle, by tormenting them with their misdeeds, leads them toward "a new adulthood" of social responsibility. The buddha is bitten by a snake, which brings back his memory: "He was reclaiming everything, all of it, all lost histories, all the myriad complex processes that go to make a man" (436–37). Moving farther into the "dense uncertainty of the jungle," hearing "the accusing, pain-filled voices of their victims," the men come finally to "a monumental Hindu temple," where they take refuge from "the endless monsoon" before the "towering statue of a black dancing goddess," Kali (438). Through a process of multicultural hybridization, this Hindu goddess of devouring destruction and creative power takes the form of four Muslim houris who appear every night and bring "the lost quartet to an incredible united peak of delight." Finally, the day comes when they looked at each other and realized they were becoming transparent, that it was possible to see through their bodies, not clearly as yet, but cloudily, like alarm they understood that this was the last and worst of the jungle's tricks, that by giving them their heart's desire it was fooling them into using up their dreams, so that as their dream life seeped out of them they became as hollow and translucent as glass. (439)

They see through Kali's illusions to the "four funeral pyres" that indicate her real design on them. In fleeing, they are swept up by a tidal wave and "borne out of the heart of the jungle of dreams" back into history (440).

This dream-jungle is the text-inscribed blankness at the heart of Rushdie's novel. Saleem enters the Sundarbans in the midst of a war that destroys his sense of reality and his belief in the power of language to articulate the "real." In describing the displacement of ten million human beings across the border of East Pakistan-Bangladesh into India, Saleem speaks of the "futility of statistics": "Comparisons do not help: 'the biggest migration in the history of the human race'—meaningless" (*Midnight's Children* 427). At the moment when history becomes unbearable and unspeakable, Saleem escapes to the place where history collapses. In this realm of illusions, he is able to recover his own personal past; but this recovery also suggests that personal history is an illusion and an escape from the self-crushing truth of "real" history. The jungle is also a metaphor for Saleem's art of storytelling and for the aesthetic and sexual pleasure, the *jouissance*, it bestows on both speaker and listener. Art becomes a way of saying the unsayable, of directly confronting death as the literal goal behind the various constructions of human desire. In the jungle of art, the historical subject becomes transparent; he finally achieves the meaning he has sought and escapes the historical absurdity he has feared. But this transparency is also the form of death—the end of the quest for meaning, the end of ambivalence. The last trick of the jungle of illusions and of art is to sweep these subjects back into the reality they fear, back into the world where nothing is transparent and where death can never be predicted, much less seen through. In the dream-jungle, Rushdie turns Conrad's will-to-style inside out. He shows that art can only lead us to the moment when we reject it even as it rejects us—that is, we reject it as the form of reality and it rejects our reality as the object of its form. In the jungle, Saleem rediscovers his own history as the discourse of the Other, and it is not insignificant that he remembers everything from the past except one detail, his own first name.

Saleem's voice cannot be silenced. And Rushdie knows that the imperialist's language cannot be silenced, though it can be subverted by the subject positions it is made to speak for: "The [English] language needs to be decolonized, to be remade in other images, if those of us who use it from positions outside Anglo-Saxon culture are to be more than artistic Uncle Toms" ("The Empire Writes Back"). To be an artistic Uncle Tom is to remain in the jungle of illusions with the hollow men, Marlow and Kurtz. Still, a postcolonial intellectual such as Rushdie cannot afford too many illusions about what it takes to step out of the jungle. If, as he has recently argued in defending *The Satanic Verses*, his determination is "to create a literary language and literary forms in which the experience of formerly-colonized, still-disadvantaged peoples might find full expression" ("A Pen against the Sword" 52), in literary practice he recognizes the extreme difficulty, if not impossibility, of this goal. Throughout *Midnight's Children*, Saleem is reading his story to his female Sancho Panza— a low-caste Indian woman who works in the chutney factory. Padma, the dung-lotus who associates writing with shitting, is the subaltern whom Saleem cannot speak for, even though she takes pity on him and proposes marriage after learning of his castration. For a moment, Saleem is "assailed by the demented notion that it might be possible, after all, that she may be capable of altering the ending of my story by the phenomenal force of her will, that cracks—and death itself—might yield to the power of her unquenchable solicitude... " Padma may point the way out of the jungle of illusions, but not for politically and sexually impotent Saleem, who knows too well that "love does not conquer all, except in the Bombay talkies" (530). Padma is the reality that Saleem has tried to seduce with his storytelling, but in the end it is this reality that destroys him. The future belongs to those who have no real voice in Saleem's history, those who are represented only by the blankness, the jungle of illusion, at the heart of his text. Uma Parameswaran sees in "Saleem the writer, with his English father, Indian mother, Mission schooling and Catholic ayah, an analogue of Indo-English writing" (40); and his fate implies the hope for something beyond this hegemonic discourse.

Rushdie implies that the truth of his Indian-English novel is not the imaginary India but the "real" that this representation rigorously misses. In other words, the only way out of the jungle of illusions may be the way in, so that the transparencies of hegemony are made to reveal the shit of writing. To say that writing is shitting suggests that there is a writing that transgresses the laws of value—even an English that disrupts its own values and decolonizes its ethnocentric traditions. This idea supports the conclusions of Timothy Brennan in his important study *Salman Rushdie and the Third World*. For Brennan, the attack on linear form in Rushdie's novel tries to resolve the "Saleem-Shiva duality," that is, the conflict between a creative and a destructive nationalism. This duality alludes to the mythological rivalry between Brahma and Shiva, who represent two aspects of the creation process: "Brahma . . . is the god who *dreams* the world. Shiva . . . is the god who allows it to exist by declining to use his immeasurable power for destroying it" (Brennan 113). In *Midnight's Children*, this duality takes shape as a violent historical contradiction between the desire for liberation and the longing for national form. If any resolution is possible, it is through the production of "a third element— Ganesh, whose style amounts to the chaotic 'sum total of everything'— an appropriate paradigm for India's national form, not simply because of India's mammoth diversity, but because all-inclusiveness finally undermines the idea of national distinctions themselves" (Brennan 117). In the novel, the grandfather Aadam Aziz, Saleem, and his son (through Shiva's biological intervention) Aadam Sinai are all identified with the elephant-headed Ganesh, who embodies good fortune and fecundity. He also symbolizes "India's *elephantiasis* of style," which, Brennan says, Rushdie wants to reproduce in his novel (116). Such a writing may figure forth the ambivalent legacy of the children of independence who had "the privilege and the curse . . . to be both masters and victims of their times" (*Midnight's Children* 552). Rushdie seems to be saying that the only resolution to the contradictions of postcolonial nationalism is the emergence of a new "postmodern" internationalism.

Postcolonial writers such as Achebe and Rushdie transform the concept of the modern by making visible the ethnocentrism and imperialism of the modernist will-to-style. Though they may implicate themselves in the cultural hegemony of modernism, they also complicate it with the inscription of its postmodern moment by introducing what Rushdie calls "new rhythms, new histories, new angles on the world" into the English language ("The Empire Writes Back"). They make it possible to read the postmodern in the modern—for example, to read the decolonizing effect of Joyce's writing or the critique of gender essentialism in Woolf's— which is rooted in a historicity that has concrete relations to the situation of the postcolonial intellectual. Modernist style is no longer transparent, no longer merely a question of form; it has to be read as a historical symptom marked by contradictions. The postmodern text starts from these assumptions and is written within the framework of a more or less conscious dialogue with the postcolonial situation. Although postcolonialism should not be construed as signifying the end of colonialism, it does identify the historical possibility of a *symbolic exchange* between the so-called first and third worlds.

6

Texts between Worlds:
African Allegories

Five days later—or exactly six weeks after the banning of
Ngaahika Ndeenda [*I Will Marry When I Want*]—I was in
cell 16 at Kamītī Maximum Security Prison as a political
detainee answering to a mere number K6,77. Cell 16 would
become for me what Virginia Woolf had called *A Room of
One's Own* and which she claimed was absolutely necessary
for a writer. Mine was provided free by the Kenya government.

—NGŪGĪ WA THIONG'O, *Decolonising the Mind*

These words of Ngūgī wa Thiong'o demonstrate the
necessary irony underlying the relation of the
postcolonial writer to European literature and literary
ideologies. The reference to Woolf is meant not to de-
legitimate her insight but to emphasize the gap in historical circumstances that gives the phrase "a room of
one's own" such a different meaning when it comes
from the pen of an African writer. Something along
these lines could also be said of Salman Rushdie who
lives under the threat of death for having written *The
Satanic Verses*. At the time of the publication of *Shame*,
Rushdie was confronted with a view of the third-world
writer that ironically contextualizes his own situation.
Here is the interviewer's question with the author's
answer:

Q: If modern literature is largely a literature of
alienated man, written by Western cosmopolites

and emigrés, do you think that with books like yours and those of Gabriel Garcia Marquez, Wole Soyinka, Chinua Achebe, V. S. Naipaul, alienation is being increasingly expressed within third-world contexts?

A: I think that's almost right. It seems to me that the idea of rootlessness has certain problems. I know it is something that explains a kind of Western intelligentsia. But I don't think that migration, the process of being uprooted, necessarily leads to rootlessness. What it can lead to is a kind of multiple rooting. (Rushdie, "Author from Three Countries" 23)

The interviewer takes it for granted that "modern literature" finds its norm in the West, even if third-world literature gradually approaches that norm by reproducing the theme of alienation. Rushdie makes a canny response by suggesting that the interviewer's position is "almost right." It is not that the term "alienation" cannot be meaningfully applied to postcolonial literature, but it must be redefined and resituated if it is to have an effect different from that of assimilating the postcolonial other to the standards of the West. The uprooting of the postcolonial intellectual from his or her native culture has resulted in a "multiple rooting" that must be distinguished from the rootlessness dramatized by Western writers like Hemingway or Fitzgerald or even Graham Greene. The alienation of the Western writer has been contained by the horizon of an ethnocentrism that sanctions Western ignorance of non-European cultures and languages. Ngũgĩ, now living in England, has had to work in a multicultural context where the decision to write in his native language results in political imprisonment and exile. Rushdie, also living in England, has become a house prisoner in his adopted country because of his fictional experiments in cultural syncretism. Achebe has tried to adapt his fund of European culture to the circumstances of Nigeria. Although the titles of his first two novels are drawn from poems by Yeats and Eliot, in his hand these phrases assume totally different significations. *Things Fall Apart* deflates Yeats's apocalyptic rhetoric in "The Second Coming" by shifting the focus from the collapse of the Christian West as a universal tragedy to the destruction of Ibo communities in West Africa by British colonialism as a regional tragedy that calls into question Yeats's universalism. *No Longer at Ease* borrows the words that Eliot uses to describe the Magi returning to their kingdoms after witnessing the birth of Christ: they are "no longer at ease here, in the old dispensation, / With an alien people clutching their gods." Obi Okonkwo, the grandson of the hero of

the first novel, is "no longer at ease" in a Nigeria where he is torn
between Ibo communalism and the new African materialism underwrit-
ten by Western capital. In postcolonial fiction, cultural elitism and spiritual alienation are not inevitable realities but the effects of social contradiction.

Recently, several scholarly discussions of postcolonial literature have
made clear the pitfalls of generalizing, even with progressive intentions,
about such diverse and culturally complex phenomena as African, Indian,
or South American fiction. For example, Fredric Jameson, in his
essay on this subject, contends that third-world novels are "necessarily . . . allegorical" and should be read as "national allegories." This
fiction, he says, lacks one historical determinant of the Western realist
and modernist novel: namely, "a radical split between the private and the
public, between the poetic and the political, between what we have come
to think of as the domain of sexuality and the unconscious and that of the
public world of classes, of the economic, and of secular political power: in
other words, Freud versus Marx." Without this split, third-world fictions
can all be reduced to the same fundamental narrative strategy. As
Jameson states it, "The story of the private individual destiny is always an
allegory of the embattled situation of the public third-world culture and
society" ("Third-World Literature" 69). Ultimately, Jameson argues that
third-world commitment to nationalist ideology is the only practical alternative to "some global American postmodernist culture" ("Third-
World Literature" 65).

In response to Jameson's argument, Aijaz Ahmad claims that such
sweeping generalization ignores the political allegory in American novels
such as Thomas Pynchon's *Gravity's Rainbow* and Ralph Ellison's *Invisible Man*, not to mention the political dimensions of personal experience
in the work of Richard Wright and other black and feminist authors (15).
But Jameson's argument actually relies on an assumption not about the
presence or absence of allegory in different areas of contemporary fiction
but about *the relation to* allegory; he argues that the allegorical structures
of first-world texts are unconscious, but "third-world national allegories
are conscious and overt: they imply a radically different and objective
relationship of politics to libidinal dynamics" ("Third-World Literature"
80). Several troubling assumptions underlie this generalization. According to Jameson, because first-world cultural texts are *unconscious* political allegories, they call for interpretive elaboration entailing "a whole
social and historical critique of our first-world situation" ("Third-World
Literature" 79). By implication, third-world texts would be transparent,

conscious expressions of political desire, requiring no social and historical critique, apart from the determination of the author's intention.
Jameson probably would not accept these assumptions as his own; but as
Ahmad suggests, they do follow from the rhetoric of otherness he uses
throughout his essay.

The slippage of Jameson's rhetoric into such a homogenized view of
the cultures that we label "third-world" points toward a problem in
articulating the social relation to language. For example, the works I
discuss in this chapter are mostly written in English, though one is in
French and another is an English translation by the author of his Gĩkũyũ
original. How does African literature in English and French relate to the
languages in which it is written and the cultures from which those languages historically derive? In trying to answer such a question, the Western critic discovers the task Jameson set for himself: that of translating the
experience of third-world literature into the critical language of the West.
Such a gesture cannot avoid recapitulating the hegemonic structure of
Western thought, though it also exposes that thought to dialogical response. In this case, Jameson's essay becomes the occasion for challenge
and one possible opening for a discourse whose ends and political effects
may exceed those of the initial position. If it is arguable that such critical
language subjects the "third world" to Western ideologies, it also forces
the radical thought of the West to open its ear to the discourse of the
"third world." The real question is whether Jameson's position is suffi-
ciently dialogical, that is, whether it calls for an opening or a closing of
discourse. I think Aijaz Ahmad's essay demonstrates that it has become
an opening in a much larger dialogue whose force is felt everywhere in
world literature today. For example, with respect to African literature in
French, Christopher Miller defines the situation of contemporary criticism in these terms: "The challenge now is to practice a kind of knowledge that, while remaining conscious of the lessons of rhetorical theory,
recognizes European theory as a *local phenomenon* and attempts dialogue with other localized systems of discourse" (*Theories of Africans* 8).
I want to agree with Miller about the need for a literary anthropology
that would offer the reader of African literature "not just ethnographic
'facts' but also access to modes of understanding that emanate from other
cultures" (*Theories of Africans* 21). But in this return to anthropology it
is essential that critics not use traditional African culture as the "final
determining instance" of the African present: they should not silence
African literature by situating its voice within a narrowly defined "nativ-
ism" of their own design. As Miller knows, anthropology has a place in

the history of ethnocentrism; and European theory remains a local phenomenon *even when it is conscious of its limits.* It would be naive to think
that it could ever simply transcend those limits, which would be to transcend its history. Rather than evade his or her position within hegemonic
culture, the Western critic should display it, expose it, question it, and put
it into relation to the "third-world" culture he or she needs to hear. This
is the first step toward unlearning the privileges of imperialist culture.
(Miller, I should note, more or less says so himself. In the way he accounts
for the limits of his work, he has been an exemplary Western critic of
African literature, though he is "Western" for all that. But I don't want to
leave the reader with the impression that the limits of his work somehow
justify the gaps in *my* knowledge and the very severe limits of this preliminary intervention in the field of African literature.)

From the perspective I have sketched, therefore, it is my intention not
to refute Jameson but to qualify and elaborate on one term of his discourse: namely, "allegory." This term could be useful in describing the
relation to language one finds in third-world and other oppositional
writing. Classically, allegory is described for Western literature as the
concrete representation of abstract ideas or values, that is, as Goethe
suggested, a method of deriving the particular from the general. With the
Romantics, however, allegory is challenged by the theory of the symbol,
which derives the general from the particular, transcendent truth from the
sensuous reality of nature. Several thinkers of the present century have
analyzed the natural referent that grounds the romantic symbol, showing
it to be an illusion whose truth is a historically determined set of meanings and values. In other words, the symbol itself signifies through a
process of *allegoresis.* Walter Benjamin, in particular, elaborated a theory
of allegory, which, according to Peter Bürger, owes something to the
experience of the avante-garde work of art in the early twentieth century
(68). Allegory, for Benjamin, reflects a cultural situation in which "any
person, any object, any relationship can mean absolutely anything
else. . . . In the field of allegorical intuition the image is a fragment, a
rune" (*German Tragic Drama* 175). Stated differently, allegory arises in a
culture for which the real world has become meaningless, devoid of intrinsic value, fragmented yet mysterious. The allegorist merely arranges
the fragments of this world, its images, in order to produce a meaning the
fragments could not produce by themselves—a meaning irreducible simply to the intention of the allegorist but reproducing his or her relation to
the given historical context. As Bürger notes, "This is posited meaning; it
does not derive from the original context of the fragments" (69). The

result is not a finished whole but a process of signification that never reaches a final closure. Allegory possesses an "obviously constructed quality" because it is rooted in temporality, in the unfinished world of everyday life (*German Tragic Drama* 179). Such writing expresses not the transcendent truth of the organic work of art but the critical relation to history of the nonorganic work; it shows history as a process of decay and ruin, the *facies hippocratica* or deathmask, "a petrified, primordial landscape" (*German Tragic Drama* 166). Allegory represents history as the concrete relation to death underlying the human situation. Though Benjamin describes this relation to history as one of melancholy, the more appropriate term is probably "alienation." But such alienation, as Marx understood, becomes the motive for social change, since it empowers the allegorist to ascribe new values and meanings to the things of his or her world: "If the object becomes allegorical under the gaze of melancholy, if melancholy causes life to flow out of it and it remains behind dead, but eternally secure, then it is exposed to the allegorist, it is unconditionally in his power. That is to say it is now quite incapable of emanating any meaning or significance of its own; such significance as it has, it acquires from the allegorist." (*German Tragic Drama* 183–84)

In its allegorical potential, language is situated in the place of the big Other. This Lacanian term, it is worth noting, has cropped up in recent criticism of African literature, particularly in the work of Christopher Miller and Abdul R. JanMohamed. But these writers, like Jameson, give the term a strictly binary interpretation that goes against the grain of Lacan's insistence that "there is no Other of the Other" (*"Ecrits": A Selection* 311), no metalanguage, no master narrative, that governs it. In his theory of allegory, Benjamin describes the process by which language is emptied out of "natural" meaning, abstracted from its ideological framework, and reduced to radical alterity: the substance of history as the support of any conceivable, socially determined meaning. As Bürger stresses, Benjamin's allegory "represents history as decline" (69); but this is not a Spenglerian notion but a recognition of meaning's historicity. The signifier, in ceasing to be natural, becomes the field of historical intervention, the place from which radical meaning-effects can emerge in opposition to the hegemonic authority of some master-slave dialectic. Unlike the Hegelian other, which is only a detour from the subject, the big Other is radical, irreducible alterity, underpinning every position insofar as it is historical. Such alterity dissolves even the distinction between first and third worlds, or rather reduces that difference to the historical dimensions that enable us to project the possibility of transformation. It articulates the unity in difference that Indian philosophy would seem to privilege, and it is no accident that Lacan's Rome discourse concludes with references to the *Upanishads* (*"Ecrits": A Selection* 106–7). In relating to language as the Other, third-world writers enter into the "dialogic relation" with hegemonic discourse which JanMohamed specifies in the following terms: "The Third World's literary dialogue with Western cultures is marked by two broad characteristics: its attempt to negate the prior European negation of colonized cultures and its adoption and creative modification of Western languages and artistic forms in conjunction with indigenous languages and forms" ("Economy of Manichean Allegory" 103–4).

Benjamin's theory, therefore, should not be a formula for the reductive generalization of all third-world writing. But it can be juxtaposed to the efforts of some third-world authors to confront and break through the wall of Western ideology with which colonialism has surrounded their specific cultures. For example, Wole Soyinka, resisting the sublimation of African into European culture, comments that his book *Myth, Literature, and the African World* "is engaged in what should be the simultaneous act of eliciting from history, mythology and literature, for the benefit of both genuine aliens and alienated Africans, a continuing process of self-apprehension whose temporary dislocation appears to have persuaded many of its non-existence or its irrelevance . . . in contemporary world reality" (xi). Ironically, these words anticipate the controversy that has recently surrounded Soyinka's work, the attack on his "mythocentric/traditionalist" position by an overly dogmatic left-wing criticism both from Africa and Europe (see Gugelberger). The object of this criticism has been Soyinka's reinterpretation of the Yoruba gods, particularly Ogun, the creator god of the hunt, fire, iron, and war. In an interview at Louisiana State University, Soyinka remarked, "I use the Yoruba gods as creative metaphors. Sometimes as metaphors for my own existence. One in particular called Ogun" ("Seminar on *Aké*" 512). The question as to whether Soyinka "believes" in African gods (in the Western sense of that word) hardly seems relevant to the larger context of his project—certainly no more relevant than the issue of Joyce's belief or disbelief in Catholicism to an understanding of his work. Ogun as creative metaphor functions within a particular matrix of thought, or symbolization, which derives not so much from some universal mind of Africa as from the symbolic material of Yoruba ritual, a fragment abstracted from a seemingly natural order and reinformed by personal and social desire. Ogun signifies not only African consciousness but the symbolic relation of Africans to the great historical shifts of the postcolonial era. In the context of Yoruba tragic drama, the past and the future are contained in the present, and tragic terror arises from the experience of severance or division within the temporal continuum. Ogun is the god who must create a bridge across the abyss that opens up in time: "The weightiest burden of severance is that of each from self, not godhead from mankind, and the most perilous aspect of the god's journey is that in which the deity must truly undergo the experience of transition" (*Myth, Literature, and the African World* 153). This nontranscendent god is the first actor in the battle against social dissolution; and "Yoruba tragic drama is the re-enactment of the cosmic conflict" (*Myth, Literature, and the African World* 149–50). One can recognize the relative material autonomy of Soyinka's rethinking of Yoruba mythology, and yet at the same time hear in it dialogical resonances with Benjamin's theoretical description of German tragic drama: "Allegory established itself most permanently where transitoriness and eternity confronted each other most closely" (*German Tragic Drama* 224). In his fiction, Soyinka transforms the Ogun figure, alienated by cultural imperialism, into the warrior against Western hegemony; such a figure, crossing the abyss of historical transition, is the main character of *Season of Anomy*, Ofeyi, who employs the remnants of African communal culture to undermine and wage war against the neocolonial Corporation. Ofeyi cannot separate personal desire from collective action, as he searches for the kidnapped woman Iriyise (who perhaps symbolizes the social regeneration of Africa?) in the midst of class war: "I'm sure every man feels the need to seize for himself the enormity of what is happening, of the time in which it is happening. Perhaps deep down I realise that the search would immerse me in the meaning of the event, lead me to a new understanding of history" (218).

Benjamin's concept of allegory, in other words, can be useful as an instrument for analyzing the allegorical tendency of third-world literature—one tendency among others. It enables us to hear resonances that, otherwise, we might not be open to. Since my concern here is with African writing, I want to set aside the term "third world," while recognizing that even the term "African" lacks univocal meaning with reference to the fiction under consideration. Even texts by Yambo Ouologuem from Mali, Ayi Kwei Armah from Ghana, Ngũgĩ wa Thiong'o from Kenya, Wole Soyinka from Nigeria, and Bessie Head from South Africa have been described by Ngũgĩ not as "African" but as "Afro-European" because they are written in the languages of the colonizers. They are part of "an Afro-European literary tradition which is likely to last for as long as Africa is under this rule of European capital in a neo-colonial set-up" (*Decolonising the Mind* 27). In this statement, Ngũgĩ demonstrates the allegorical gesture that enables him to reappropriate the term "African" from a hegemonic literary tradition and language and inform it with new value and meaning. Behind such an act lies the historical alienation of the postindependence, neocolonial intellectual who has undergone the transformation that Frantz Fanon described in *The Wretched of the Earth*. After having been shaped by colonial education, which implants in his brain "a vigilant sentinel ready to defend the Greco-Latin pedestal," he has entered into the struggle for liberation which turns "this artificial sentinel . . . into dust." In Fanon's words, "All the Meditteranean values,—the triumph of the human individual, of clarity and of beauty— become lifeless, colourless knick-knacks. All those speeches seem like collections of dead words; those values which seemed to uplift the soul are revealed as worthless, simply because they have nothing to do with the concrete conflict in which the people is engaged" (46–47). These words articulate the historical alienation that Benjamin calls melancholy—a term having nothing to do with simple sadness or depression but with the perception of historical transience and destruction. In the case of the colonial or neocolonial subject, it has to do with the perception of the historicity of those eternal truths and, most particularly, of those eternal values (including those called aesthetic), which mask the domination of Western culture. It challenges the principle of canon ("the Greco-Latin pedestal") as reflective of a natural aesthetic order outside the realm of politics and desire.

The brief readings and more extended discussion of Ngũgĩ that follow are not intended to provide an overview of African fiction or to do justice to the literary complexities of individual novels. I merely want to isolate a few moments in African literature which demonstrate the challenge of such writing to the hegemonic order of value in the West even as it uses that order as its own negative "literary" starting point. I want to give some space to the cultural differences that emerge in these texts, without reducing these differences to a constituted or assimilated "other" of Europe. Homi Bhabha, calling for an "interdisciplinarity of cultural texts," has warned against contextualizing "the emergent cultural form by explaining it in terms of some pre-given discursive causality or origin." Rather, he says, "We must always keep open a supplementary space for the articulation of cultural knowledges that are adjacent and adjunct but not necessarily accumulative, teleological, or dialectical. The 'difference' of cultural knowledge that 'adds to' but does not 'add up' is the enemy of the *implicit* generalization of knowledge or the implicit homogenization of experience" (313). To me, this statement suggests that the differences of postcolonial fictions are not strictly inside or outside the closure of hegemonic culture; they "supplement" that culture in a way that calls into question the priority of the West and the exclusivity of its master narratives. They destabilize the difference between the inside and the outside of culture, that is to say, the principle of the cultural norm in itself. This destabilization should not blind us, however, to the overt political purpose of these writings or their insistence on the necessity of opposition or critique. Part of the challenge of recent African fiction is that it refuses to allow either the "normative" subject of imperialism or the "marginalized" subject of the colonized any aesthetic safe harbor from the violence of history in this era of late capitalism. There is even, in some instances, a conscious refusal of ambivalence when it pertains to the representation of the social and political relations that exist in the contemporary neocolony. This ambivalence nevertheless resurges in the disclosure of such literature as "writing," as something obviously constructed, rather than as a transparent representation. The tendency toward allegorization qualifies the transparencies of political engagement without abstracting the literary work from the space of its political responsibility. In other words, it is the allegorical effect of these writings that enables them to add something to the fund of cultural knowledge without its adding up to the totality of some universal "human" culture.

At the end of Armah's novel, *The Beautyful Ones Are Not Yet Born*, the central character, who is called simply *the man*, gazes upon an advertisement painted on the back of a bus. Forming an oval shape are these words: "The Beautiful Ones / Are Not Yet Born." Within the oval is "a single flower, solitary, unexplainable, and very beautiful" (*The Beautyful Ones* 183). This advertising slogan with its image is the signature of neocolonial power in Armah's home state of Ghana. After independence (1957), this power was supported by the bourgeois nationalists of the United Gold Coast Convention despite the socialist aspirations of Kwame Nkrumah and the Convention People's party. Armah's novel paints a bitterly disenchanted portrait of the corrupting influence of that power on Ghana, where human "goodness" and autonomy, epitomized by *the man*, suffer from the overdeterminations of historical violence. Under pressure from family and colleagues, *the man* suffers throughout the novel, both physically and mentally, for his resistance to "the gleam" of commodity culture. In a final ironic gesture, he aids a corrupt official of the Nkrumah government to escape during the coup; in effect the victim is compelled by his own concept of humanity to save the victimizer. Nevertheless, another hope emerges out of the ashes of disenchantment. The advertising slogan has become meaningless as a signifier of the social and economic order that produced it in the language of colonial power (with the "y" in "beautyful" to signify the difference between the colonizer and the colonized); but in the gaze of *the man* it is transformed into the double-edged instrument of social criticism and desire. The words and the emblematic flower are subjected to a reinvestment of value and meaning. Earlier in the novel, after learning of the coup, *the man* thinks: "Someday in the long future a new life would maybe flower in the country, but when it came, it would not choose as its instruments the same people who had made a habit of killing new flowers. The future goodness may come eventually, but before then where were the things in the present which would prepare the way for it?" (*The Beautyful Ones* 159–60). Although *the man* discovers few if any signs of "future goodness" outside himself, he does project his "inward" sense of beauty and ethical value into the dead and reified language of the advertisement, transforming the symbols of neocolonial domination into the emblems of future social movements for African liberation. As Neil Lazarus remarks,

> *The Beautyful Ones* is transparently a moral work. . . . This sense of moral earnestness ought not, however, to be interpreted as idealistic, for it stems not from any abstract consideration as to how the 'good' or the 'just' life might be led, but rather from an appraisal of what was actually possible in Ghana after decolonization—of what seemed, indeed, to be prefigured in the style of the decolonizing movement itself. (55)

Stated differently, *the man's* utopian desire, though buried inside him, derives from social determinations that could bring about a transformation of the collective will and a reorganization of the "historical bloc" (to use Antonio Gramsci's term) that determines it. *The man* shows that the conditions that prepare the way for liberation in the future exist *now*— that is, exist in the brain of the neocolonial subject who can transform the dead letters of hegemonic culture into the instruments of social revolution.

Revolutionary hope through pessimistic social vision also takes shape in the rewriting of African history. Two novels of considerable importance in this area are Ouologuem's *Bound to Violence* (*Le devoir de violence* in French) and Armah's *Two Thousand Seasons*. Both novels project a vision of African history from the period of the Arab domination of northern Africa in the thirteenth century to the postcolonial era. Ironically, Ouologuem, whose novel received the Prix Renaudot in 1968, was later accused of plagiarism for his so-called borrowings from André Schwartz-Bart, Graham Greene, and Guy de Maupassant; but Christopher Miller has usefully argued that the book is really "an assault on European assumptions about writing and originality" (*Blank Darkness* 219). To my mind, Ouologuem engages in a compelling act of postmodern pastiche which attacks the authority of the Western master narrative by mirroring its violence and demystifying its claim to universal truth. As James Olney stresses, Ouologuem not only inverts and displaces Western representations: "This stylistic pastiche, which combines elements from the historical traditions of family and village, from *griot* 'archives,' and from Arab chronicles, is matched . . . by a geographical and cultural pastiche, the elements of which Ouologuem draws from all over Africa; here again he freely mixes the real with the imaginary and the historic with the mythic to produce a new historic amalgam with a new interpretation." The result is the "symbolic autobiography of a continent" (241–42). In this autobiography, Ouologuem not only does not condemn violence; he expresses the "duty of violence" as offering the only possibility of a solution to the social contradictions of African history; or as Miller suggests, he "posits destructive violence and theft as origin itself" (*Blank Darkness* 219) not only of history but of any historical representation. In the end, his book is a ruse in a complicated game, like the game of chess between the black king Saif and the white bishop Henry in the last chapter, "Dawn." To Saif's remark, "You play the game. But you don't let yourself be made game of," Henry responds,

> But keep your eye on the other man's play. . . . You must learn to know it and to know yourself in it. Say to yourself, . . . *I want to play as if they did not see me playing*, entering into my game without ostentation, appearing to be in accord with myself and with them, making use of their guile without ever seeming to face it head on or trying to divert it, exposing the intricate trap, but with caution, never touching anything until I have fathomed its hidden mechanism. Without such caution, my friend, can you hope to kill your adversary... in a game? (176–77)

Surprisingly, Ouologuem puts these words into the mouth of a white Christian. For his work seems to imply that only through a sort of literary ventriloquism can the neocolonial subject subvert the voice of European culture, which has foreclosed African voices from symbolization. Such a reappropriation attempts to reverse the pattern of historical relations between Africa and the West. No doubt, Ouologuem's incorporation of fragments from Greene and Maupassant, as well as his satirical portrayal of Western scholars such as Frobenius (who appears in the book as Shrobenius), follows the same pattern of reversal and reappropriation—a strategy indicating both the strength and the limitations of his achievement. As Lyotard implies in *The Postmodern Condition*, the master narrative of Western culture, including its colonialist and neocolonialist chapters, can be viewed, in its symbolic dimension, as a game—indeed, a language game—that can be deconstructed by reducing it to the status of one language game among others. Ouologuem's "duty of violence" proposes the duty of African literature to strip all master narratives of their global authority by exposing them as allegories of power. But it remains silent as to the possibility of actually overthrowing cultural hegemony through the construction of a "new" African voice or a nonhegemonized subjectivity.

In *Two Thousand Seasons*, through the style of "mythical realism," Armah tries to articulate that voice and the historical conditions of its coming-to-be. Although the book has been described as the fictional equivalent of Walter Rodney's *How Europe Underdeveloped Africa* (Ngara 55), Armah concerns himself less with producing the unwritten history of a continent than with carving out a vision of the African past that creates the possibility of a future for the whole of Africa. In doing so, he fuses the personal voice of his social alienation with the more traditional voices of Africa, which Robert Fraser describes as "a class of griots, poet-historians whose vision of their role has far more in common with that of the Yoruba Ijala singer or Ewe lyricist than with the self-conscious *angst* of many a Western artist" (69). While consciously inverting the manichean structure of colonial ideology—so that "whiteness" comes to signify the death-inflicting bestiality of colonialism and "blackness" the redemptive truth of African history—he also subverts in advance any naïve relation to the past as pure origin:

> How the very first of us lived, of that ultimate origin we have had unnumbered thoughts and more mere fables passed down to us from those gone before, but of none of this has any of us been told it was sure knowledge. We have not found that lying trick to our taste, the trick of making up sure knowledge of things possible to think of, things possible to wonder about but impossible to know in any such ultimate way. (*Two Thousand Seasons* 4)

So much for Hegel's absolute knowledge. For Armah, knowledge of the past is necessarily allegorical; that is to say, it comes to us in fragments that must be arranged and for which a meaning must be posited through human agency. The past is not, as in the most common version of Christianity, the divine revelation of a lost wholeness or unity of being. Rather, "Of what is revealed, all is in fragments. Much of it was completely lost in that ashen time when loneliness, bringer of madness, nearly snapped the line of rememberers" (13). Revelation is a fragment; and out of these fragments Armah the allegorist constructs "the way" not simply as a return but, in its "closer meaning," as "destruction's destruction" and "the search for paths to that necessary beginning" (233). The destruction of destruction requires not only revolution and the "duty of violence" but also revising the master-slave dialectic at the center of Western historiography by constructing a collective subject of African history that depends not on the recognition of the master but on the rearticulation of the present in constellation with a distinctly African past. Like Benjamin's historical materialist, Armah "recognizes the sign of a Messianic cessation of happening, or, put differently, a revolutionary chance in the fight for the oppressed past. He takes cognizance of it in order to blast a specific era out of the homogeneous course of history" (*Illuminations* 263). The book has been criticized for its racialism and negative depiction of Arabs and white Europeans, and there is no question that Armah sees his book as a weapon and an antidote against the cultural domination of Africa both before and after the colonial era (for the best discussion of these problems, see Lazarus 222–24). In relation to such hegemonic culture, the book implicitly argues that Africa cannot sublimate or be sublimated; on the contrary, the destroyers must be destroyed (or, at least, as Spivak has frequently insisted, they must unlearn their privileges) before the roots of relative cultural autonomy can flower. Armah's "duty of violence," consequently, does not limit itself to the symbolic (as Ouologuem's appears to do) but calls for armed struggle and insurrection.

Soyinka's *Season of Anomy*, Ngũgĩ's *Petals of Blood*, and Bessie Head's *Question of Power*—these novels employ an allegorical realism that projects African history onto the plane of contemporary postcolonial experience. The communalism of the African past is pitted against the violence of multinational capitalism in Ngũgĩ's and Soyinka's work, while for Bessie Head the season of anomy stages itself in the mind of a South African woman struggling for a new communal life against the pull of history's nightmare, a scene of masculinist power and racist violence. The characters in these novels all find themselves "enmeshed in a surreal world," to cite the words of Munira in Ngũgĩ's *Petals of Blood* (100); and the reader encounters another mode of surreality in the postmodern narrative techniques that disrupt his or her position as knowing subject. Soyinka leaves out critical information that would tend to rationalize the brutal violence he depicts; Ngũgĩ employs multiple narrative techniques, combining detective fiction with historical epic, to challenge any linear view of social progress; Bessie Head refuses to make any strict divisions in narrating the contents of everyday reality and the unconscious. Perhaps Head best exemplifies the relation of these fictions to the cultural phantasmagoria of Western and Eastern gods and myths erected over African culture. In *A Question of Power*, the central character contemplates her own mental division as the result of colonialist ideology:

> So harsh was the present face-to-face view of evil that in a subconscious way Elizabeth found her mind turning with relief to African realism: a woman was simply a woman with legs; a man simply a man with legs, and if good and noble they earned a certain courteous respect, just as Christianity and God were courteous formalities people had learned to enjoy with mental and emotional detachment—the real battlefront was living people, their personalities, their treatment of each other. (66)

Elizabeth struggles against the manichean allegory implanted in her mind by colonial and patriarchal culture—an allegory that must be overthrown before she can reenter and help to create an African community for the future. As JanMohamed stresses, such an allegory reduces the African subject as "native" to his or her exchange value in the colonialist symbolic: they are "fed into the manichean allegory, which functions as the currency, the medium of exchange, for the entire colonialist discursive system" ("Manichean Allegory" 83). Of course, the manichean allegory tries to hide its true character by denying its "constructed quality" and insisting that its "posited meaning" is universal and natural. African fiction, therefore, has to expose this "allegory" and open the symbolic field to ideological struggle. It must challenge the system of exchange values and overthrow the process of human commodification by redefining social ties, even those "courteous formalities" and languages taken over from the West, as incommensurable—that is, "African realism" over against the Western canon. What counts is the symbolic tie between people and not their worth on a scale manufactured in Europe and America. But the "evil" still remains, and the overthrow of its invisible system of values has to be repeated continually as a part of everyday life in the neocolony.

One of the most significant experiments in political allegory to have appeared in postcolonial African fiction is Ngũgĩ's *Devil on the Cross*. This novel represents a genuine break in the development of Ngũgĩ's work and responds directly to the concrete historical situation of postindependence Kenya. But before I proceed any further I should make clear that in discussing this work, particularly in the context of "Afro-European" fiction, I am aiming at an understanding not of the original but of the translation, though a translation with a special claim to signatory status when we read below Ngũgĩ's name on the title page of the Heinemann edition: "Translated from the Gĩkũyũ by the author." As Ngũgĩ has written, his decision to write his novel in the Gĩkũyũ language was a political one that arose out of both regional (Kenyan) and more general (African) historical conditions. Originally, it was Ngũgĩ's work in a village cultural center that led him to write literature in his native tongue for the first time. After fifty peasants and factory workers in the Kamĩrĩĩthũ literacy program had learned how to read and write in Gĩkũyũ, "it was time . . . to enter the second phase of our program—that is, cultural development with theatre at the center." Ngũgĩ and his associate, having been asked to write a play, felt compelled to ask: "In what language were we going to write?" The answer was self-evident ("one writes in the language that the people use"), but that the question had even to be posed drove home to Ngũgĩ "how far gone we were." The play was written and performed; it became immediately popular with peasants and workers; and the "political result of this popularity was that the Kenyan regime reacted and after nine performances the play was stopped. I myself was put into political detention for a year in 1978." Realizing that the "whole point of a neo-colonial regime putting a writer into prison is really to keep him out of touch with the people," Ngũgĩ took the offensive and wrote *Caitaani Mũtharabainĩ* (*Devil on the Cross*) ("Tension" 5–6).

Elsewhere, Ngũgĩ has emphasized the importance of his decision to write Gĩkũyũ literature in the context of African culture as a whole. Those who questioned his decision forced him to the conclusion that

in choosing to write in Gĩkũyũ, I was doing something abnormal. But Gĩkũyũ is my mother tongue! The very fact that what common sense dictates in the literary practice of other cultures is being questioned in an African writer is a measure of how far imperialism has distorted the view of African realities. It has turned reality upside down: the abnor-

mal is viewed as normal and the normal is viewed as abnormal. Africa
actually enriches Europe: but Africa is made to believe that it needs
Europe to rescue it from poverty. Africa's natural and human resources
continue to develop Europe and America: but Africa is made to feel
grateful for aid from the same quarters that still sit on the back of the
continent. Africa even produces intellectuals who now rationalise this
upside-down way of looking at Africa. (*Decolonising the Mind* 27–28)

Ngũgĩ understands the act of writing Gĩkũyũ literature as part of the
antiimperialist struggle; and of course this struggle informs the content of
his work, as it either directly or indirectly informs the work of all the
writers I have discussed in this chapter. But by writing in his native
tongue, Ngũgĩ positions himself in relation to a particular audience or
what American critics would call an "interpretive community." He positions himself in relation to their world, their history, and their language.
He need not produce a static image of that community; nor is he bound
to reproduce any but a dynamic view of the African past or present.
Writing in Gĩkũyũ, Ngũgĩ no longer translates Kenyan experience into a
colonial tongue or oral narrative into purely written idioms. At the same
time, he has no reason to fear writing or to fear contamination by those
components or fragments of Western and world culture that have become
a part of the African experience in the colonial and postcolonial eras.
Everything is grist for the mill of the postcolonial allegorist, and Ngũgĩ
accepts even the influence of Conrad, apparent in all his novels, because
"the story-within-a-story was part and parcel of the conversational norms
of the peasantry. The linear/biographical unfolding of a story was more
removed from actual social practice than the narrative of Conrad and
Lamming." Knowing what would be familiar to ordinary Kenyans impels
him to borrow "heavily from forms of oral narrative, particularly the
conversational tone, the fable, proverbs, songs and the whole tradition of
poetic self-praise or praise of others. I also incorporated a biblical
element—the parable—because many literates would have read the
bible" (*Decolonising the Mind* 76–78). Finally, having long been in-
trigued by the Faust theme in literature and suspecting that "the story of
the good man who surrenders his soul to evil for immediate earthly gains
of wealth, intellect and power was universal and was rooted in the lores of
the peasantry," Ngũgĩ is able to fuse the Christian embodiment of evil,
the Devil, with more traditional figures of evil from Gĩkũyũ orature, such
as the man-eating ogre: "Marimũ[s] were supposed to possess two
mouths, one in front and the other at the back. The one at the back was

covered with long hair. They were cruel, very greedy, and they lived on the labour of humans. What about the latter day Marimūs? Would the Marimū characters provide me with the image I sought?" (*Decolonising the Mind* 80–81).

This work of fusion and reconstruction results in a novel of allegorical realism that both identifies and analyzes the neocolonial setup while it displaces traditional African values toward a future beyond the present stage of imperialism. *Devil on the Cross* differs from Ngũgĩ's other novels in that its central character is a woman who must struggle against both the patriarchal structures native to Africa and neocolonial exploitation. Through flashbacks and stories within the story, we first learn Jacinta Waríinga's history as the victim of wealthy men of the *comprador* class and then see her transformed by fantastic events into a *relatively* autonomous figure (she becomes a mechanic and a student engineer) and finally into a revolutionary. The plot of the novel, however, focuses on the events taking place over a period of roughly twenty-four hours and then briefly discloses their aftermath two years later. Waríinga loses her job in Nairobi when she refuses to become Boss Kĩhara's mistress, a repetition of her adolescent experience with a Rich Old Man. Her lover doesn't believe that she has been innocent in this relationship and leaves her. She decides to go home to Ilmorog, but on the way to the *matatū* stop she momentarily despairs and nearly steps in front of a city bus, another repetition from her past. She is stopped by a voice and then a young student appears who gives her an invitation to attend the Devil's Feast in Ilmorog where there will be a competition to choose seven experts in theft and robbery. She travels to Ilmorog on a *matatū* in which she meets a professor of music at the university, a worker, an unemployed woman, and a businessman. The driver of the *matatū* turns out to be a thug who will sell his treachery to the Devil for any price. In Ilmorog, they discover that the Devil is really the capitalist class of Kenya and the international financiers who bankroll them and scoop off most of the profits from African labor. Each member of the competition elaborates new and utterly fantastic techniques for expropriating the wealth produced by working people. Finally, these people rise up and try to throw the neocolonial devils out; but almost immediately the ringleaders, who turn out to be the working man and the unemployed woman from the *matatū*, are arrested and the status quo is reconfirmed. Two years later Waríinga has decided to marry the music professor. When she meets his father, however, she recognizes the Rich Old Man who originally victimized her and almost drove her to suicide. After he threatens to do the same again, she shoots him with the gun handed to her for safekeeping by the revolutionary worker. This time Wariinga chooses revolution instead of suicide, and the future promises "the hardest struggles of her life's journey" (*Devil on the Cross* 254).

This plot summary, unfortunately, cannot do justice to the stylistic force of this novel, which is constructed on the tension between the tragic shape of Wariinga's history and the satirical thrust of Ngũgĩ's depiction of the agents, both native and international, of neocolonialism. Wariinga achieves some autonomy in the closing scenes, but the novel offers no illusion as to what the final price of her freedom may be. The history of postcolonial Kenya has become a nightmare; and Ngũgĩ depicts it as such, aiming in this book less at producing the effect of reality than at capturing the surreality of everyday life in a neocolony. Such a reality, "stranger than fiction," is "what confronts a novelist in a neo-colony vis-à-vis the audience most adversely affected by that reality" (*Decolonising the Mind* 78). In the case of Wariinga, Ngũgĩ creates a character whose revolutionary impulses reveal themselves unconsciously long before they are consciously recognized by her. Throughout her life she has had a recurrent nightmare related to her early experience of the Catholic church. As a girl, when she looked at the pictures on the walls and windows of the church, she saw that the "Virgin Mary, Jesus and God's angels were white, like Europeans, but the Devil and his angels were black." In her dreams, Wariinga reverses this Western symbolism:

> Instead of Jesus on the Cross, she would see the Devil, with skin as white as that of a very fat European she once saw near the *Rift Valley Sports Club*, being crucified by people in tattered clothes—like the ones she used to see in Bondeni—and after three days, when he was in the throes of death, he would be taken down from the Cross by black people in suits and ties, and, thus restored to life, he would mock Wariinga. (*Devil on the Cross* 139)

This Devil on the cross eventually speaks to Wariinga in a waking dream and teaches her something that experience will confirm later. In addition to the two worlds she has witnessed, the worlds of "the oppressor and the oppressed, of those who eat what has been produced by others and the producers themselves," there is a third world of "the revolutionary overthrow of the system of eating and being eaten" (186–88). Wariinga enters this world at the novel's end when she takes up for herself the "duty of violence." Like Soyinka's Ogun, she must progress through the abyss of transition, or history, to struggle against the agencies of both economic and cultural hegemony.

Obviously, *Devil on the Cross*, in spite of its popularity in Kenya (where it was absorbed through public readings in families as well as on buses, taxis, and in bars [*Decolonising the Mind* 83]), is not a work that can expect a popular reception in the West or even with those Africans sympathetic to Western culture and education. The work is polemical and committed and challenges Western aesthetic theory and its canon from every angle. So the question arises as to why Ngũgĩ bothered to translate it himself—that is, why does he give the translation signatory status for the Eurocentric reader? Since I began this essay with Benjamin's theory of allegory, it may be useful at this point to consider his theory of translation. For Benjamin understood that a translation possesses a different mode of intentionality from an original. It does not reproduce the meaning of the original and, thereby, its social and historical context. The reader of Ngũgĩ's text in English cannot claim to grasp the full implications, the concrete value of the Gĩkũyũ original, cannot claim to have entered the space of African literature, which remains irreducible and, to some extent, indecipherable to the purely Western viewpoint and methodology. But a translation can produce another effect that may have its own political significance, the effect of literalness that avoids "the desire to retain meaning" in any absolute sense. Benjamin describes this effect with an analogy:

> Fragments of a vessel which are to be glued together must match one another in the smallest details, although they need not be like one another. In the same way a translation, instead of resembling the meaning of the original, must lovingly and in detail incorporate the original's mode of signification, thus making both the original and the translation recognizable as fragments of a greater language, just as fragments are part of a vessel. (*Illuminations* 78)

The greater language in which Gĩkũyũ and English are implicated—the whole of language, which is not equal to the sum of its parts, that is, languages—could be called the Other, the material signifier or the mode of signification that remains beyond meaning. Stated differently, Ngũgĩ's translation of his work does not give his English-speaking reader the meaning of the original but rather shows the place of the original. The translation signifies the difference constituting what is incommensurable in the African experience, what cannot be translated into any other tongue and is irreducible to any other system of values. At the same time, the translation subverts the binary *other* within which a naïvely Western view wishes to locate and contain African history and culture. In effect, the English and the Gĩkũyũ versions are dialogically related to each other, in communication with each other, and contaminated by each other. But there is no question which language has the upper hand. It is the Gĩkũyũ text that governs the English text and which now impacts on the history of the English language. Ngũgĩ's translation is not reverse domination but a subtle displacement of the authority of English. It situates the original not as the transparent referent but as, after Spivak and Derrida, the *blank part of the text*.

By writing in Gĩkũyũ and translating into English, Ngũgĩ discloses and exploits his own contradiction as a postcolonial intellectual writing texts between worlds. He reveals the duality of his voice as both native Kenyan and Afro-European. In Gĩkũyũ, he does not speak *for* African subjects *to* a European or Afro-European audience. He does not *represent* Africa as the Other for the subject of hegemonic culture. Rather, he speaks to Africans from the position of contradiction he occupies as a teacher and a writer: he represents them only in speaking as one of them but not for all of them. He engages in a symbolic exchange with the community whose language he shares. In English, on the other hand, his text inscribes the Other of history as that which cannot be represented except as Spivak's "*text-inscribed* blankness." He presents the English-speaking world not with an Africa to be assimilated to its ethnocentric concepts of humanity, human nature, and universal human psychology but rather with "*the* place of the production of theory" (Spivak, "Can the Subaltern Speak?" 294). Theory in this context means a performative articulation of what Lyotard calls the *differend*, "the unstable state and instant of language wherein something which must be able to be put into phrases cannot yet be. This state includes silence, which is a negative phrase, but it also calls upon phrases which are in principle possible" (*The Differend* 13). Although the *differend* cannot be assimilated or made transparent in the context of hegemonic culture, it can induce Western and African intellectuals to question the transparency of their own positions as speaking subjects and to recognize the complicity of their theories with ideological processes. Ngũgĩ's translation *as text* articulates this differend or *space between* ideological and cultural differences. As such, it epitomizes without prescribing the politically self-conscious relation of African writing to the hegemonic culture of Europe.

An unidentified reader of an early verson of this chapter pointed out that I "fall into the trap of assuming that writing in English means writing to an English/American audience, ignoring or not realizing the enormous role English plays as a means of communication in countries like Kenya and across Africa." I did not think I had made that assumption, but this is an important issue to keep in mind. Ngũgĩ argues simply that when he writes in English he writes in a language "which is understood by a very tiny minority in each of the [African] nationalities." In Gĩkũyũ, on the other hand, he reaches "at least some peasants and workers" ("Interview" 163–64). Ngũgĩ suggests elsewhere that by writing in English, African intellectuals contribute to "the development of what could be called an Afro-Saxon literature" ("On Writing" 151). He is suggesting, I believe, that Afro-Saxon literature may inadvertently support and legitimate the authority of hegemonic Eurocentric culture. He also insists that it is possible to reach more Africans by writing in native African languages. Ngũgĩ's convictions are born out by the commercial success of his first Gĩkũyũ novel and play: "So in less than a year—from April to December of 1980—they [Heinemann] had to print about fifteen thousand copies of each of these works, which for them was a record in the sale of any novel or play—be it in English or any other language—for the same period of time" ("On Writing" 154).

It should be noted that Ngũgĩ has not personally translated his second Gĩkũyũ novel, *Matigari*, into English. That he has not does not necessarily contradict my argument about the political effect of the translation of his first Gĩkũyũ novel. Such an effect, however, is not the only one possible, nor should the English translation be privileged in any way over the original or any other translation. To my knowledge Ngũgĩ has never underestimated the importance of translation, though he has political reasons for wanting to dethrone English from the position of mediator beween different African languages. As he comments, "You can write, let's say, in the Gĩkũyũ language, or in Igbo language or in Luo. You can then have the work translated into other languages and for the first time, you will have the different languages of our different nationalities communicating within themselves instead of always having a foreign language to mediate between them" ("Interview" 164). This perspective pushes the political significance of translation further so that it becomes a process of symbolic exchange without any privileged linguistic audience. This significance is reinforced by the content of *Matigari*, which, rather than reproduce contemporary Kenyan experience in the realist mode, aims at a level of allegorical abstraction that lends itself to translation into other languages and cultures without, however, succumbing to the European tendency toward abstract universalization. The author makes the function of *Matigari* clear in the prologue: "The story is imaginary. / The actions are imaginary. / The characters are imaginary. / The country is imaginary - it has no name even. / Reader/listener, may the story take place in the country of your choice" (ix). The reader is asked to situate the story in his or her own social-historical context, to make it serve her or his own political needs. Nevertheless, the book is never ambiguous in its critique of multinational capitalism, its agents, and the *comprador* classes that support it in third-world countries. The book explodes with the "impassioned sarcasm" that Gramsci identified as the "appropriate stylistic element for historical political action" (quoted by Brennan 49). The central figure, Matigari ma Njirũũngi (which means "the patriots who survived the bullets," that is, the liberation war), is endowed with ambivalence not to signify the mystique of personality but to translate the desires of a broadly conceived human collective into an emblem of hope: "They all shared the same hope: that a miracle should take place. But at the same time all wondered: who really *was* Matigari ma Njirũũngi? A patriot? Angel Gabriel? Jesus Christ? Was he a human being or a spirit? Was Matigari a man or was he a woman? A child or an adult? Or was he only an idea, an image, in people's minds? *Who Was He?*" (*Matigari* 158).

Ngũgĩ's use of translation suggests that cultural and linguistic hegemony is never total, that it has the principle of reversibility inscribed within it. Translation foregrounds, to quote Derrida's reading of Benjamin, "the being-language of the language, tongue or language *as such*, that unity without any self-identity" ("Des tours de Babel" 201). Such a view defines language in its radical alterity, which enables the writer to take a critical relation to it and thus transform it. Through the pulverization of language informed by ideology, through its cadaverization as fragment, pastiche, myth, or allegory—the writer is able to seize language as the discourse of the Other, of collective human desire, which she or he reshapes and virtually translates. Thus, the writer transforms the substance of history, its raw signifiers, into the language of revolutionary hope and seeks the truth at which all languages aim beyond their immediate signification. He or she also pronounces the necessity of struggle; for culture can never be reshaped as long as the organs of social reproduction are monopolized by a dominant class.

So, having quoted English translations of three different languages (Ngũgĩ's Gĩkũyũ, Benjamin's German, and Derrida's French), my writing can do no more than suggest a relation to African fiction as world literature which future scholarship will either make concrete or reject. As I have already suggested, crucial to this historical elaboration will be the recognition that what Western thinkers have termed the "postmodern condition" must be grounded in the "postcolonial condition" (a term I borrow from Prabhakara Jha) not only of the third world but of those pockets of opposition within European and American culture. For postcolonial African literature shares some common symbolic ground with postmodern oppositional writing in Europe and America. Whether the novels I have discussed are realistic or surrealistic, they are postmodern in their self-conscious understanding of the political functions of language and literature. To quote Lyotard, narrative "determines in a single stroke what one must say in order to be heard, what one must listen to in order to speak, and what role one must play (on the scene of diegetic reality) to be the object of a narrative" (*The Postmodern Condition* 21). Such a view challenges the ideologies of modernism, just as third-world literature as a whole exposes the Eurocentrism at the heart of modernist internationalism. It also challenges the aesthetic imperialism at the core of Western education. As Ngũgĩ points out, "In literature there have been two opposing aesthetics: the aesthetic of oppression and exploitation and of acquiescence with imperialism; and that of human struggle for total liberation" (*Writers in Politics* 38). Barbara Harlow argues that this distinction has important implications for literary criticism in the West. It "contests the ascendancy of sets of analytic categories and formal conventions, whether generic, such as novel, sonnet, tragedy, etc.; national-linguistic as in French, German, or English literature; literary-historical; or even so simple a distinction as that which is still conventionally maintained between fiction and non-fiction." To these formal or analytic categories, Ngũgĩ opposes a different organization of criticism—one that is "'participatory' in the historical processes of hegemony and resistance to domination" (Harlow 9).

In this redefinition of the political responsibility of the critic, another ground for dialogue between postmodern and postcolonial cultures opens up. Fredric Jameson's call for "a pedagogical political culture which seeks to endow the individual subject with some new heightened sense of its place in the global system" offers a prescription, no doubt utopian under the present organization of Western education, for the critical practice of radical teachers in America and Europe ("Postmodernism" 92). Although such a radical pedagogy will involve the teaching and disseminating of third-world texts, it also involves redefining the institution of criticism with its implicit assumptions about the nature and purpose of literature itself. It requires a challenge to the aesthetic hierarchies and systems of value that have been predominant in the West, particularly since Kant. As Gayatri Spivak stresses in *The Postcolonial Critic*, it is not simply a question of refusing to speak for the other: "What we are asking for is that hegemonic discourses, the holders of hegemonic discourse should de-hegemonize their position and themselves learn how to occupy the subject position of the other rather than simply say, 'O.K., sorry, we are just very good white people, therefore we do not speak for blacks'" (121). In dehegemonizing their subject positions, Western critics obviously have something to learn from postcolonial critics such as Spivak or Ngũgĩ who have had to struggle against their own subject positions in order to speak through the historical contradictions that constrain their discourses. Without this kind of radical self-critique, teaching third-world texts becomes only another mode of assimilating the Other.

In summary, Jameson is not wrong to see an allegorical tendency in the postcolonial literature of Africa, but I think he makes a mistake in positing this as the condition of African or third-world otherness. The Afro-European writers I have discussed could and should be read in a dialogical relation to other writers, whether from the first or the third world, who address and struggle against cultural hegemony—writers as different as Ishmael Reed, Kathy Acker, Monique Wittig, Salman Rushdie, or Gabriel Garcia Marquez. None of these writers is free from contradiction, but their works at least try to articulate the text-inscribed blankness (what global capitalist culture mystifies as its own self-reflection) by weaving a texture of relations, or forms of symbolic exchange, between irreducibly different worlds. Their works could be thought of as the *discourses of the Other*, though in using the term "Other" with a capital O I refer not to the imaginary alterity of binary logic but to the dialogical force of contemporary world literature, which calls into question such global distinctions as the three worlds theory. As Lacan suggested, the big Other has no Other. On the contrary, it underpins every discourse as the place (without place) of the signifier before it enters into the symbolic realm of signification. The Other is the ground of all translation and the place (without place) from which the language of allegory emerges.

7

Apocalypse and Sexual Difference: Monique Wittig in the Poststructuralist Context

Try to say "come"—it can be said in every tone, every tonality. And you will see, you will hear, the other will first
hear—perhaps or not. It is a gesture in the word [*parole*],
that gesture which does not let itself be recovered [*reprendre*]
by the analysis—whether linguistic, semantic, or rhetorical—of a word.
—JACQUES DERRIDA, "Of an Apocalyptic Tone"

In this last chapter, I want to examine an act of literary
resistance *within* the closure of European culture—the
voice of a postmodern feminist writing that challenges
even as it speaks to the context of poststructuralist
theory. The word "come," as I understand it, is what
such writing tries to say against the constraint of ideology. According to Louis Althusser, "Ideology 'acts' or
'functions' in such a way that it 'recruits' subjects
among the individuals (it recruits them all), or 'transforms' the individuals into subjects (it transforms them
all) by that very precise operation which I have called
interpellation or hailing, and which can be imagined
along the lines of the most commonplace everyday po-
lice (or other) hailing: 'Hey, you there!'" (162–63).
Ideology determines the production of each subject as
an identity that bears the imprint of its social origins—

male or female, black or white, rich or poor, and so forth. Every mark of identity is a mark of value. Still, there is a beyond of value that can be solicited by a use of language, a use of the symbol, which causes to appear as "writing" everything that value represses. This act or gesture has no formula and is not reducible to a pure style. In the postcolonial context, it can take the shape of Achebe's realism, Rushdie's surrealism, or Ngũgĩ's allegory. For example, insofar as Conrad's modernist impressionism hails Africa and Africans as *the other of Europe*, Achebe's realism intertextually subverts that call by diverting English away from its imperialist rhetoric toward the constitution of an African referent. It is not that he simply effaces a Conradian style in order to produce a transparent discourse but that he actively constructs a new referent for English—for the language of the colonizer—which strictly speaking did not exist in that context before. He transforms Conrad's interpellation of Africa as the "heart of darkness" into the call to "come," to open language and discourse up to its own potentiality for referential play and translation. In itself, this gesture is ambivalent. On the one hand, it could be said to expand the territory of the cultural empire of English. On the other, it destroys the unity of that empire and, as the example of Ngũgĩ demonstrates, diverts it away from univocal representations toward an interminable translatability based on symbolic exchanges between different languages and cultures. Such an opening calls into question any essentialist or reductive concept of racial, class, or national identity. It also presupposes the necessarily political ground of any ontological difference, including sexual difference itself.

To say "come"—a writing that says "come"—offers itself as a gesture, not a communication. It does not speak directly to you or me, and it cannot speak for us. It is not, precisely, an invitation to speak. It is a disruption, a break in the communication circuit, an overturning of the subject-object, sender-receiver dyad. This gesture in itself has no meaning (though it can take shape within a discourse that means something); rather, as Derrida suggests, it has a tone. It has that tonal effect which Nietzsche recognized as fundamental to language: "All degrees of pleasure and displeasure—expressions of *one* primal cause unfathomable to us—symbolise themselves in *the tone of the speaker*. . . . In so far as that primal cause is the same in all men, the *tonal subsoil* is also the common one, comprehensible beyond the difference of language." Nietzsche saw in the union of music and lyric an effect that capitalized on *"the duality in the essence of language"* ("On Music and Words" 30–32). The word "come" as a call or appeal exploits this duality of language—the radical alterity underlying every speech-act as a social practice. Derrida further remarks:

> "Come" cannot come from a voice or at least not from a tone signifying "I" or "self," a so-and-so (male or female) in my "determination." "Come" does not address itself, does not appeal, to an identity determinable in advance. It is a drift [*une dérive*] underivable from the identity of a determination. "Come" is *only* derivable, absolutely derivable, but only from the other, from nothing that may be an origin or a verifiable, decidable, presentable, appropriable identity, from nothing that may not already be derivable and arrivable [*arrivable*] without "rive" [without the source, spring, *rivus*]. ("Apocalyptic Tone" 94)

This "come"—through its radical derivation from the Other—reverses the identity of its origin. The Other neither *is* an origin nor *has* an origin. Therefore, the "come" is derivable only from that which cannot "be" or "have" an origin, that which is only derivable. Thus, it reverses or deconstructs the act of interpellation by destroying the economy within which it operates: "*Come* does not exchange anything, it does not communicate, it does not say anything, show, describe, define, declare anything, at the moment when it is pronounced, nothing which would be something or someone, object or subject" (Derrida, "Pas" 26). "Come" does not exchange anything through an economy of equivalences because it precedes the very possibility of exchange as value; it gestures toward the "thought" (in the strictly Derridean sense, that which has not yet begun—the threshold) of the exchange beyond value, or *symbolic exchange*. It cannot be derived from the order of language because it precedes that order as the signifying potential that is the "unconscious" and the precondition of every linguistic system. "Come" speaks to no object from no subject. It precedes the mark of sexual difference or *re-marks* a sexual difference that precedes the institution of the dyad man-woman. If we continue to speak of a subject, it must be one written under erasure—"Being" or "God."

"Come" enables us to articulate, or translate into discourse, what Derrida has called the apocalyptic tone, which can be related back to Nietzsche's "tonal subsoil" as a precondition of all discourse, as long as we understand "precondition" or Nietzsche's "primal cause" as figures for the thought of a radical alterity irreducible to any actual origin or predetermination. If "apocalypse" means "unveiling" or "revelation"— if it points toward some disclosure of repressed or hidden truth—then the apocalyptic tone is the "revelator of some unveiling in process." It does not so much tell the truth as invite the truth to come or invite someone (you? us?) to come to the truth. "The apocalyptic tone naturally wants to attract, to get to come or arrive at itself, to seduce in order to lead to itself, or to the place where the first vibration of the tone is heard, which is called, as will be one's want, subject, person, sex, desire (I think rather of a pure differential vibration, without support, unbearable)" (Derrida, "Apocalyptic Tone" 84). Truth, subject, person, male, female, desire—each in itself and in the other comes, is coming, culminates in the "coming" that is *jouissance*, neither subject nor object, irreducible, unsayable—"a pure differential vibration." The pleasure and displeasure that Nietzsche associates with the tone of language is the truth that "come" calls or appeals to—beyond the ontological difference. The truth in this context is not objective or verifiable. It is the pleasure/displeasure of the call to alterity.

Apocalyptic writing uncovers what Philippe Lacoue-Labarthe calls the typography of the subject of Western discourse. This word is meant to deconstruct the philosophical transparency of such originary terms as "ontology," "onto-theology," "onto-psychology," and "onto-typology," with the notion of a subject that is written or "typed," that is stamped or marked from the outside—constituted by material discourse. The subject neither precedes the language it learns from the m/other nor proceeds deterministically from the Law of Culture. In a reading of Lacoue-Labarthe's use of the French verb *désister* and the noun *désistement*, Derrida has proposed the term *désistance* for the typography of the subject, a "(de)constitution rather than a destitution. . . . It puts off (from itself) any constitution and any essence" (Introduction to Lacoue-Labarthe, *Typography* 2). This subject is constituted without essence—therefore, without formal constitution. In the Althusserian sense, something in the subject remains unhailed and irreducible to the marks of social identity—sex, race, class, nationality, and so forth. This something is nothing in itself in that it cannot even know itself as the mirror reflection of the other. It cannot imitate self-consciously. On the contrary, "mimesis is the effect of the *typo-graphy*," which makes possible the thought of a subject whose engenderment is implicitly bracketed as "being necessarily of the order of the figure and of the fictive in general":

An entire Western *discourse* on the subject—a discourse that after all could well be Western discourse itself—right away seems to find its limit here . . . in *the necessary reversibility of the motifs of engender-*

ment and of the figure, of conception, and of the plastic, or, if you will, in this kind of reciprocal and insurmountable metaphorical (figural) exchange between the concepts of *origin* and *fiction.* (Lacoue-Labarthe, *Typography* 127–28)

The engenderment of the subject, its formation or *Bildung*, cannot be thought outside the space of a rhetoric, a figurative language, that makes this thought both possible and impossible. It is not simply that subjectivity is rooted in fictionality as opposed to truth. Deconstruction gives play to a process of symbolic exchange that bridges the gap between truth as origin and truth as fiction. The transcendental or apocalyptic structure of language is fictive not in the sense that it negates or covers the truth; rather, the truth of the origin can be approached only through the rhetorical dimension of language, which then constitutes its own ground through the engendering of the speaking subject as figure or fiction. Rodolphe Gasché identifies this ground as the space of a general metaphoricity that results from "a destruction of metaphor, and *eo ipso* of the proper and the literal" (295). Lacoue-Labarthe puts it in the form of a question: "How would it be possible for the figure of engenderment to have not always figured the engenderment of the figure?" The mimetic function of the subject—its representation as self-presentation in language—must be rethought from this question:

> There is, as Lacan would say, a "preinscription of the subject" in the structure or order of the signifier that marks the symbolic order's first domination of the subject. But the "subject," traversed from the very beginning by a multiple and anonymous discourse (by the discourses of the others and not necessarily that of *an* Other), is not so much (de)constituted in a cleavage or a simple *Spaltung*—that is, in a *Spaltung* articulated simply in terms of the opposition between the negative and presence (between absence and position, or even between death and identity)—as it is splintered or dispersed according to the disquieting instability of the improper. (*Typography* 128)

An apocalyptic discourse discloses the construction of the subject through this uncontrollable because ungrounded "mimetism" or typography. It displays the impropriety of the subject, the undecidability of its position, and the threat of a mimesis that has haunted Western philosophy from Plato to the present:

An effect of discourses, the "self"-styled "subject" always threatens to "consist" of nothing more than a series of heterogeneous and dissociated roles, and to fraction itself endlessly in this multiple borrowing. Thus, the mimetic life is made up of *scenes from the life of one who is suited for nothing*—or of a Jack-of-all-trades. Let us say that the "subject" *de-sists* in this, and doubly so when it is a question of the man (of the male), since there the roles, which are themselves fictive, are moreover passively recorded, received from the mouths of women. In short, what is threatening in mimesis is feminization, instability—*hysteria.*   (*Typography* 129)

The threat of mimesis, the threat of the feminine, the threat of the rhetorical and the fictional—these are all symptoms of a repression that the apocalyptic tone promises to unveil even as it veils, even as it hides behind the fiction of the subject. It is not women in themselves who threaten (that is, threaten the patriarchal order that interpellates the masculine subject as the One sex, the absolute sex) but the possibility that sexual difference is not given by a law of originary Being. Women threaten insofar as their lips articulate (and, in a different sense, are articulated by) the apocalyptic tone. As a work such as Conrad's *Heart of Darkness* suggests, the voice of the racial other presents the same sort of threat. Marlow tries to build a wall of language against the dissolution of sexual and racial difference; but in the process, he resorts to an apocalyptic style that discloses the fictionality of the Western (male) subject as a function of that which it must exclude from its narrative in order to ground its own authority. Conrad's modernist will-to-style—in its refusal of the radical alterity that threatens it from both the outside and the inside—can be linked to the history of onto-typology (the metaphysics of the subject) and the rejection of mimesis that determines it. Marlow repeats the Platonic *double bind* when he says, "The mind of man is capable of anything—because everything is in it, all the past as well as all the future" (Conrad 38). Everything to be known is already in it, already imprinted on it; and yet it is completely original and autonomous in the production of its knowledge and its truth. Just as Plato had to banish the poets in order to write his own myth, Marlow has to banish the voices of the others (Africans and women) in order to speak for them, in order to figure them metaphorically. Marlow's identity as a member of the exclusively male society of the *Nellie* must root itself in the construction of a fiction, not only the lie he tells at the end of his story but the story itself.

The other (sex, race, etc.) becomes a reflection of the fiction of the self, the true imperialism of the metaphor. Virginia Woolf was not wrong to see a connection between Western patriarchy and fascism. As Lacoue-Labarthe suggests, "An entire tradition (the one that culminates in Nazism) will have thought that the political is the sphere of the *fictioning* [i.e., fashioning, modeling, constructing] of beings and communities" (*Heidegger* 82).

Against the voice of masculine and imperialist authority, Gayatri Spivak cites Derrida's "'appeal' or 'call' to the 'quite-other' (*tout-autre* as opposed to a self-consolidating other)" ("Can the Subaltern Speak?" 294). For Kant, as Derrida reads him, such an appeal induces in the speaking subject a state of confusion that perverts

> the voice of reason, by mixing the two voices of the other in us, the voice of reason and the voice of the oracle [i.e., the apocalyptic tone]. . . . The overlordly tone [of this appeal] dominates and is dominated by the oracular voice that covers over the voice of reason, rather parasitizes it, causes it to derail or become delirious. To raise or set the tone higher, in this case, is to make it jump, make the inner voice delirious, the inner voice that is the voice of the other in us. ("Apocalyptic Tone" 71)

It might be possible to say this another way. The voice of reason always presents itself as the voice of truth, an unequivocal expression of the self-adequacy of the principle of reason. Everything has its reason; and reason's own reason is reason itself, which is given by the nature of things, by Being or God. Reason can be called into question only when its tone is unveiled as "a pure differential vibration, without support, unbearable" ("Apocalyptic Tone" 84). This unveiling occurs when the voice of reason is parasitized by its other so that it is no longer possible to draw a strict line between reason and the irrational or the oracular. The voice of reason becomes delirious or even hysterical. The apocalyptic tone then gives rise to a discourse that calls reason's monological rule into question. This tone in Western philosophy—if it is still possible to speak of philosophy once the principle of reason has been dethroned or decentered— challenges the classical divisions, concepts, and categories of rational thought without constituting an irrational other, since the other we speak of here haunts the interior of rational discourse itself. It untunes the system and thus unveils or discloses the conventionality of thought that refuses to analyze its own implication in what remains *unthought*.

One signifier for what has not been thought is "sexual difference." Both Derrida and Lyotard have taken up this signifier, in different and untranslatable forms, in the context of thinking the relation between politics and philosophy, the necessity of which has arisen from the so-called *affaire* Heidegger (see Kronick, "Dr. Heidegger's Experiment," for an illuminating overview of the complex debate about the philosophical implications of Heidegger's Nazism). For Lyotard, the term "sexual difference" names something forgotten—"this scene that has not taken place, that has not had a stage, that has not even *been*, but which *is*." It refers not to an anatomical difference but to "an excess," "the name of a furor, of pleasure and pain mixed, . . . the name of that which dispossesses the [psychic] apparatus, excises and surpasses it, which deprives it of speech" (*Heidegger and "the jews"* 19–20). Lyotard uses the silence of sexual difference, its unnamability, to describe the concept of originary repression, which he believes has historical implications. In originary repression and in the representations of sexual difference, something is forgotten because it was never "experienced," because it exceeds representation as the ground of experience. The historical implications of this Forgotten emerge in the consideration of an unsayable event such as the Shoah: "Obviously, a 'politics' of extermination exceeds politics. It is not negotiated on a scene. This obstinacy to exterminate to the very end, because it cannot be understood politically, already indicates that we are dealing with something else, with the Other" (Lyotard, *Heidegger and "the Jews"* 25). Derrida explores this Other in the concept of *Dasein*, which, in Heidegger's text, remains neutral with respect to sexuality. This neutrality as a form of repression, however, succeeds only in radicalizing the concept of sexual difference by enabling Derrida to pose this question: "What would a 'sexual' discourse or a discourse 'on-sexuality' be without evoking farness [*éloignement*], an inside and an outside, dispersion and proximity, a here and a there, birth and death, a between-birth-and-death, a being-with and discourse?" It turns out that the thought of sexual difference requires the general structure of *Dasein* (being-there, being-with, the between-birth-and-death) even if that structure tries to neutralize "less sexuality itself than the 'generic' mark of sexual difference, belonging to one of *two* sexes" (Derrida, "*Geschlecht*" 82–83). Derrida dramatizes the irreduciblity of sexual difference by insisting on the inscription of the untranslatable, the German word *Geschlecht*: "No word, no word for word will suffice to translate this word that gathers in its idiomatic value stock, race, family, species, genus/gender, generation, sex" ("*Geschlecht* II" 183). *Geschlecht* seems to gather into itself the difference of difference, the genus of difference, the condition of the ontological difference, that is, the condition of its own condition. Such an untranslatable word (perhaps it can be called, after Gasché, a *"quasitranscendental"* [295]) introduces a discord into conventional thinking which has implications for more than philosophy.

For Monique Wittig, ontology is politics. In the field of feminist theory, she works to undermine the conventional signs of sexual difference in her analysis of what she calls the "straight mind." This term refers to those "philosophical and political categories of the discourses of the social sciences" which "function like primitive concepts in a conglomerate of all kinds of disciplines, theories, and current ideas. . . . They concern 'woman,' 'man,' 'sex,' 'difference,' and all of the series of concepts which bear this mark, including such concepts as 'history,' 'culture,' and the 'real.'" These concepts of science and theory "act materially and actually upon our bodies and our minds." As a discourse they constitute "one of the forms of domination, its very expression, as Marx said. I would say, rather, one of its exercises" ("The Straight Mind" 106–7). As Wittig's general reception indicates (and as I suggested earlier), the apocalyptic tone becomes particularly threatening to the hegemony of Western reason when it is articulated by the voice of one who is supposed to be constructed as a woman. For if "straight society is based on the necessity of the different/other at every level," then "woman" becomes the site and signifier of a metadifference that governs the grammar of social domination. Unlike the racial other, "woman" cannot be excluded from the everyday operations or representations of straight society, and the most horrific political solutions—apartheid or the Holocaust—cannot be applied to "women" without destroying the principle of sexual difference on which straight society is founded. The oppression of women depends on the constitution of their ontological difference from men. Women are different, but men "are not different, whites are not different, nor are the masters." While racial and class differences have frequently been called into question by straight society itself, sexual difference remains the stronghold against any challenge to the ontology of difference, so that sexual difference indirectly lends its support to racial and class exclusions by legitimating the principle of difference in itself (natural and self-evident). These are the implications of Wittig's oppositional thinking; and her point is not to reverse, for example, Virginia Woolf's insistence on a recognition of the historical difference between men and women but to insist that this difference is *purely historical and political* (which in my opinion makes her position consistent with the *tendency* of Woolf's later writing). According to Wittig, "There is no such thing as being-woman or being-man. . . . The concept of difference has nothing ontological about it. It is only the way that the masters interpret a historical situation of domination. The function of difference is to mask at every level the conflicts of interest, including ideological ones" ("The Straight Mind" 108). It is against this ontology that Wittig conceives the strategic significance of the lesbian relationship: "'Woman' has meaning only in heterosexual systems of thought and heterosexual economic systems. Lesbians are not women" ("The Straight Mind" 110).

I will not repeat here all the objections and qualifications that have been directed at Wittig's controversial position. Since I want to cite her text as an example of apocalyptic writing, however, there is at least one position I need to address. Diana Fuss has argued on the basis of Wittig's handful of theoretical texts that the term "lesbian" in her work "functions as a transcendental signifier, occupying none other than the place of the Lacanian phallus." It is "ahistorical and amaterialist" and possesses "a certain ideality of the sign." As a result, "Wittig's theory is unable to account for heterosexual feminists except to see them as victims of false consciousness" (43–44). Furthermore, and Fuss makes this point central to her criticism, Wittig seems totally unable to account for the subversive tendencies of male homosexuality, which "comes to function as a repressed other, a subversive category that threatens the stability of her privileged trope 'lesbian' at the same time that it performs the vital (though unacknowledged) function of preventing it from solidifying" (46). In other words, Wittig's radical antiessentialism ends up rooting itself in yet another version of the essentialism it is meant to overthrow.

Fuss's argument is very convincing, but because it is concerned with only the so-called theoretical texts it misses the "theory" implicit in the rhetorical strategies of Wittig's fictional writings. To take Wittig's "theory" as theory in the traditional sense leads to a radical misconstruction of her project, which calls into question those concepts of "history," "culture," and the "real" that theoretical discourses are meant to define and delimit. For this reason, there can be no absolute division between Wittig's "theory" and her "fiction." As rhetorical strategies both are forms of political action aimed at destroying a linguistic hegemony that has no outside and must be challenged from within by destablizing its truth-functions and real-effects. It seems to me that Wittig is concerned with deploying the political significance of the sign "lesbian" and not with privileging the actual "experience" of being a lesbian. She does not privilege that "experience" over the "experience" of being a male homosexual or a heterosexual woman. These "experiences" remain irreducible and incommensurable, however (even the word "experience" is misleading in creating the illusion of a transparent relation between the human subject and the outside world), until humans intervene with language to delineate the order of sexual difference. Within this order, Wittig concludes that "lesbian is the only concept I know of which is beyond the categories of sex (woman and man), because the designated subject (lesbian) is *not* a woman, either economically, or politically, or ideologically. For what makes a woman is a specific social relation to a man, a relation that we have previously called servitude." A lesbian escapes servitude by "refusing to become or to stay heterosexual" ("One Is Not Born a Woman" 53). But what about male homosexuals? Don't they refuse to become or to stay heterosexual? Perhaps so, but this refusal does not necessarily entail a rejection of the system of sexual difference that defines "woman" as a position of servitude in relation to "man." For a man who accepts or leaves unquestioned the class relations that exist between men and women, a break with heterosexuality as a sexual preference can coexist with the choice and support of the heterosexual system of power. If male power depends on the heterosexual system that defines women as and confines them to an obligatory reproductive function, then a homosexual man who enjoys the privileges of that power implicitly supports the dominance of heterosexual social relations despite his "different" sexual preference. A woman who chooses lesbianism, on the other hand, chooses a cultural relation that rejects the heterosexual system of power. She rejects her own self-definition as "a woman," that is, as a being for reproduction. She rejects "servitude." (I do not mean, of course, that there are no lesbians who support the heterosexual system of power. It is always possible to wear more than one social mask, to engage in more than one cultural relation. Such is the nature of contradiction.) Although the concept of the lesbian must arise out of a concrete history (even if it is the history of a silence), it is not necessarily limited to that history. "Lesbian" cannot be a subcategory of "woman," which suggests perhaps that any subject can become a lesbian. Fuss says, "It may well be that Wittig is leaving open the possibility for a male subject, 'gay' or 'straight,' to fill the category 'lesbian,' but this intriguing line of inquiry is not, unfortunately, pursued" (46).

I would suggest that it is pursued but not in the way Fuss expects. Neither the male nor the female subject could fill the category lesbian and remain male or female. But does this mean that the concept "lesbian" articulates a social space beyond "male" and "female" which both men and women can enter? If we say yes, we ignore the actual history of the lesbian concept and the way it has been applied to specific historical women. We make lesbianism into another version of androgyny, which is never meant to designate a concrete historical class or formation but an idealized concept of sexual identity. "Androgyny" really does function like a transcendental signifier because it imagines an end to sexual opposition without calling into question the category of sex itself. The term "lesbian" refers to a concrete form of human relationship, *with a history*, which falls outside the laws of heterosexual society. For Wittig, the term "women" has a social meaning but not an ontological one. "Women" are an oppressed class, "which is to say that the category 'woman' as well as the category 'man' are political and economic categories not eternal ones." The only way to free women from oppression is "to suppress men as a class, not through a genocidal, but a political struggle. Once the class 'men' disappears, 'women' as a class will disappear as well, for there are no slaves without masters." The social class "women" must be dissociated, however, from the myth "woman": "For 'woman' does not exist for us: it is only an imaginary formation, while 'women' is the product of a social relationship" ("One Is Not Born a Woman" 50–51). Lesbianism, as Wittig understands it, does not refer to a sexual preference but to an act of rebellion against class domination. Lesbians refuse to be "women" for "men." They refuse to serve "either economically, or politically, or ideologically" the heterosexual system of values. Speaking as a lesbian, Wittig claims, "We are escapees from our class in the same way as the American runaway slaves were when escaping slavery and becoming free" ("One Is Not Born a Woman" 53). You may want to disagree with Wittig's historical interpretation of lesbianism, but I don't think it makes much sense to say that she proffers it as a transcendental signifier like the phallus. She does not foreclose the possibility of relationships between "men" and "men" or between "men" and "women" beyond the category of sex; but she insists that in the current historical context the only concept she knows of that gives a name to what such a relationship would be is "lesbian." This formulation does not mean that "men" can be "lesbians" in the historical sense. But it does mean that whatever relationships "men" or "women" can have beyond the category of sex find a concrete realization in lesbianism and surely in other relationships for which we have no name at the present time. For Wittig, "lesbianism" has not ontological but practical historical value. She writes, "A lesbian society *pragmatically* reveals that the division from men of which women have been the object is a political one and shows how we have been ideologically rebuilt into a 'natural group'" ("One Is Not Born a Woman" 47, my emphasis).

In *The Lesbian Body*, Wittig directly confronts the fiction of the subject which the apocalyptic tone unveils. This work assumes that once we have deconstructed the "natural" authority of the patriarchal subject, once we have overturned and displaced the binary relation between *origin* and *fiction* which lends metaphysical support to the institution of the subject, we are left with "the task of defining the subject in materialist terms." It is no longer possible to rely on absolute distinctions between essence and existence, truth and fiction, literal and figurative. A new subject must be constructed on the basis of a language that has been emptied (relatively speaking) of metaphysics (and this is all that the term "materialist" should signify in this context). According to Wittig, "For women to answer the question of the individual subject in materialist terms is first to show, as the lesbians and feminists did, that supposedly "subjective," "individual," "private" problems are in fact social problems, class problems; that sexuality is not for women an individual and subjective expression, but a social institution of violence" ("One Is Not Born a Woman" 53). Nevertheless, the construction of class consciousness does not mean the negation of subjectivity:

> For once one has acknowledged oppression, one needs to know and experience the fact that one can constitute oneself as a subject (as opposed to an object of oppression), that one can become *someone* in spite of oppression, that one has one's own identity. There is no possible fight for someone deprived of an identity, no internal motivation for fighting, since although I can only fight with others, first I fight for myself. ("One Is Not Born a Woman" 51)

It may seem initially that Wittig simply reinstitutes the ideology of the subject that in some way is the crucial ground of oppression. Can there be subjects without objects, without exclusions, without hierarchical relationships? Judith Butler argues that, by insisting on the category of the subject as the necessary ground of women's liberation, Wittig adheres to "a metaphysics of substance that confirms the normative model of humanism as the framework for feminism" (20). Fuss makes a similar point: "Phrases such as 'that is the point of view of a lesbian' or 'a lesbian subject as the absolute subject' are troubling because, in or out of their textual contexts, they suggest that a lesbian is innocent and whole, outside history, outside ideology, and outside change" (43). This sounds like a legitimate critique until we take a step back and try to reconstruct how Wittig understands the concept of the subject. For it is Wittig's assumption that part of what oppression means, particularly as it concerns the construction of subjects in language, is the denial of the universal to "women." "The universal," she says, "has been, and is continually, at every moment, appropriated by men." Through the denial of their access to the universal in language, "women" are denied access to the subject position. The universal in this context should be understood as nothing more than the ontological emptiness of language that makes possible the emergence of the subject in the first place (and on this point Wittig refers directly to the philosophical linguistics of Emile Benveniste):

> It is when starting to speak that one becomes "I." This act—the becoming of *the* subject through the exercise of language and through locution—in order to be real, implies that the locutor be an absolute subject. For a relative subject is inconceivable, a relative subject could not speak at all. I mean that in spite of the harsh law of gender and its enforcement upon women, no woman can say "I" without being for herself a total subject—that is, ungendered, universal, whole. Or, failing this, she is condemned to what I call parrot speech (slaves echoing their masters' talk.) Language as a whole gives everyone the same power of becoming an absolute subject through its exercise. But gender, an element of language, works upon this ontological fact to annul it as far as women are concerned and corresponds to a constant attempt to strip them of the most precious thing for a human being—subjectivity. ("Mark of Gender" 66)

Wittig's use of terms should be carefully scrutinized. The so-called "absolute" or "total subject" is "ungendered, universal, whole." It is not-woman, not-man, not-black, not-white. If it is universal and whole, it is also nothing in itself. To state the plain though paradoxical truth, the universal is not-everything: it is total but not totalitarian. Every individual has access to the subject position insofar as language in itself, language as language, which may be a whole but can never be a closed system, is eccentric to the individual and therefore remains irreducible to what we would call physical distinctions. Language in itself cannot be masculine or feminine. It can't be anything but a universal means of communication and social exchange (insofar as the possibility of translation provides an access to the interminable process of language as language and not simply to this particular language). From this perspective, it should be clear why, for Wittig, there can be no such thing as "feminine writing," which she calls "the naturalizing metaphor of the brutal fact of the domination of women." Such a metaphor designates "a sort of biological production peculiar to 'Woman,' a secretion natural to 'Woman'" which suggests "that women do not belong to history, and that writing is not a material production" ("Point of View" 63). For Wittig, gender is neither a natural fact nor a linguistic fact (i.e., a fact about the nature of language). Rather it is an ideology imposed on the users of language from the outside—"an act, a criminal act, perpetrated by one class against another. It is carried out at the level of concepts, philosophy, politics" ("Mark of Gender" 66). The "mark of gender," as she designates it, is the mark of value, the articulation of a system of values. The individual subject as the universal representation of the particular is incommensurable in itself. But concepts such as gender and race subject this universal to the law of value by attributing a fixed meaning to what were incommensurable human differences. The universal becomes the norm and difference marks that which deviates from the norm. Women and people of color are different; white men are the norm. The universal ceases to be the access of all human beings to language and becomes the ideal or standard by which all human beings are measured. Whoever controls the "universal" controls the access to language and subjectivity.

In order to reverse this process, it is necessary to withdraw the universal from the space of value, to destroy its power as the norm, and bring it back to the place of the articulation of the particular. In effect, the minority writer universalizes the particular and reverses its subjection to the norm. To some extent, of course, this reversal involves the production of a new value, since, as Wittig puts it, "a text by a minority writer is efficient only if it succeeds in making the minority point of view universal, only if it is an important literary text" ("Point of View" 66). But the ground of such an act has to be the momentary disruption of the law of value, a disarticulation of the norm through an insistence on the universality of the particular. This is all that Wittig means when she refers to the "point of view of a lesbian" or to the "lesbian subject as the absolute subject." It is impossible to articulate the subjectivity of a lesbian in language without calling into question the normative "category of sex" on which heterosexual society is founded. To universalize the lesbian as a subject does not constitute a new norm or transcendental signifier. It simply demonstrates that there is no "natural" division of Being, no privileged relation to language according to sex. It shows that the assignment of gender to language is a political and not a natural act. When Wittig says that "there is no possible fight for someone deprived of an identity, no internal motivation for fighting," she defines a strategy of empowerment, for the articulation of a voice that has never been heard by heterosexual society. "Wittig's subject," as Linda Zerilli stresses,

> is not so much a return to an ontological right of speech or to a pre-discursive fiction before the intrusion of gender in language. Instead her fiction deploys the universal as, what she herself calls, a "Trojan Horse," a simulacrum of Being and of the universal which not only pulverizes "old forms and formal conventions" but effects as well a radical decentering of the subject as it has been conceptualized by the straight mind. (162; see also Wittig, "The Trojan Horse")

The universal is a simulacrum, a copy of a copy, without any absolute origin. Every construction of the universal is, therefore, a political act, the validity of which can be analyzed only within the framework of a strategy. In Wittig's writing, lesbianism is such a strategy: "The lesbian subject is a thoroughly political subject, a provisional subject, an invented 'epic' subject, which is created . . . as a universal subject without a name, without an Other, and with no recourse to a pre-social, pre-discursive identity" (Zerilli 166). Although Wittig can be faulted for not saying it (and Zerilli calls into question her "disturbingly monolithic view of heterosexuality" [159]), she implies through her fictions that every subject, whatever its political necessity, is provisional.

By writing *The Lesbian Body*, Wittig is making the point not that lesbianism is outside of history and ideology but that the history of the lesbian has been silenced by the norms of patriarchal culture. "Only the woman's movement," she says in the Author's Note to the English translation, "has proved capable of producing lesbian texts in a context of total rupture with masculine culture, texts written by women exclusively for women, careless of male approval" (*Lesbian Body* 9). Wittig wants to articulate the repressed of patriarchal culture, that which has no "authorized" name. She calls it "the lesbian body" and writes of those women whose history has never been written, whose "reality" has never been accepted, because they exceed the categories of heterosexual representations. The "Amazons," as she names these women, "embody" a form of human relationship; they "are women who live among themselves, by themselves and for themselves at all the generally accepted levels: fictional, symbolic, actual." There is no distinction between these three levels because masculine culture has made women's existence "illusionary." As a result, "our reality is the fictional as it is socially accepted, our symbols deny the traditional symbols and are fictional for traditional male culture, and we possess an entire fiction into which we project ourselves and which is already a possible reality. It is our fiction that validates us" (*Lesbian Body* 9–10). The term "fiction" has already been deconstructed for this context, so that it is not opposed to truth or reality but constitutes the ground of struggle for the social construction of reality. "Our reality," that is, the reality of "women" as a class, is fictional insofar as it is the product of a "socially accepted" or hegemonic heterosexuality. "Our symbols," that is, the language and material representations of a counterhegemonic lesbian culture, are read as fictions by the tradition grounded in the norms of heterosexuality. Ironically, rather than reject these fictions, it is necessary to seize upon them, to recognize the identities articulated by them as the basis of a possible reality or, I should say, realities. In other words, "reality" is a fiction that can be transformed from within, a text that can be rewritten. Heterosexual or patriarchal culture is a fiction that denies its own fictionality by insisting on a univocal reality, by excluding or restricting any other form of relation to the "real."

Wittig's concept of the "real" resembles even as it exceeds the Lacanian category. It is not a thing-in-itself but a discursive relation that identifies all "realities" as social constructions. Although Wittig rejects psychoanalysis for its phallocentrism, she borrows many of its insights in displacement from their institutional context. Having said this, it is important not to confuse her concept of "fiction" with the "imaginary." "Woman" as a concept is imaginary because it identifies sex as an ontological category that transcends social relationships. As such, "woman" is a myth. When women see through this myth and understand their position as that of an oppressed class, they directly confront their own fictionality not as an ontological absolute but as a social construction subject to change. They confront the category of sex that produces "men" and "women" as one of the supreme fictions. Overthrowing this fiction, however, is not simply a matter of speaking the truth. An oppressive fiction must be replaced by a liberating fiction; and this means, first of all, deconstructing the binary opposition between language and reality. As Wittig stresses,

In modern theory, even in the assumptions of disciplines exclusively concerned with language, one remains within the classical division of the concrete world on the one hand, and the abstract one on the other. Physical or social reality and language are disconnected. Abstraction, symbols, signs do not belong to the real. There is on one side the real, the referent, and on the other side language. It is as though the relation to language were a relation of function only and not one of transformation.

For Wittig, the "real" is not only that which resists symbolization or that which every symbolization misses (after Lacan). Although the "real" limits language and prevents any final symbolic closure, it is also the space of linguistic action and social process: "Language casts sheaves of reality upon the social body, stamping it and violently shaping it. For example, the bodies of social actors are fashioned by abstract language as well as by non-abstract language. For there is a plasticity of the real to language: language has a plastic action upon the real" ("Mark of Gender" 64). Wittig implies that what is generally thought of as reality is the action of language upon the "real." Although that action is violent, it can result either in a reality that institutionalizes violence by enforcing its univocal authority or in a reality that is plural, that allows for creative play and struggle. Authoritarian reality could be said to repress its fictionality or what Lacoue-Labarthe calls that "reciprocal and insurmountable metaphorical (figural) exchange between the concepts of *origin* and *fiction*" (*Typography* 128). It represses its own truth as a social and linguistic construction. In the struggle for a plural reality, for an end to sexual (political) hegemony, the minority writer has to "assume both a particular *and* a universal point of view" (Wittig, "Point of View" 68). Achieving this fusion in a world where the universal is defined as the signifier of the One (reality, sex, law, truth) requires struggle in both the textual and physical realms (and for Wittig these two orders are implicated in each other and never fully autonomous).

Writing the lesbian body means making "real" and "universal" what has been repressed and oppressed by the history of patriarchy. To Wittig's mind, there is no evading the violence of such a political act: "The fascination for writing the never previously written and the fascination for the unattained body proceed from the same desire. The desire to bring the real body violently to life in the words of the book (everything that is written exists), the desire to do violence by writing to the language which *I* [*j/e*] can enter only by force." Notice that Wittig speaks of *writing to* the language. In effect, her desire emerges from within language as its fundamental division or bifurcation. By insisting on and marking in the text the universality of her subject position (not as a "woman" but as a member of the oppressed class "women," as a lesbian, and as a materialist feminist), she challenges the value and final authority of the masculine universal. Ironically, the universal subject of the lesbian body subverts the ideology of gender by disclosing its link to the principle of univocal language founded on the exclusive authority of a generic masculine subject. According to Wittig, a generic feminine subject "can *only* enter by force into a language which is foreign to it, for all that is human (masculine) is foreign to it, the human not being feminine grammatically speaking but he [*il*] or they [*ils*]." In everyday speech, "women" are able to forget that their identities are submerged in a universal masculine subject. "But the 'I' [*je*] who writes is driven back to her specific experience as subject. The 'I' [*je*] who writes is alien to her own writing at every word because this 'I' [*je*] uses a language alien to her; this 'I' [*je*] experiences what is alien to her since this 'I' [*je*] cannot be '*un* ecrivain'" (Author's Note, *Lesbian Body* 10). Wittig attacks her alienation from language by foregrounding it, by constructing a universal feminine subject that is marked by its division from and refusal of the generic masculine: "*J/e* is the symbol of the lived rending experience which is *m/y* writing, of this cutting in two which throughout literature is the exercise of a language which does not contitute m/e as subject. *J/e* poses the ideological and historic question of feminine subjects" (Author's Note, *Lesbian Body* 10–11). By writing this universal feminine subject, Wittig destroys the metaphysical content of the masculine universal and reduces the "universal" itself to a purely linguistic and material effect. This "universal" is ontologically empty but gives ground to a form of being that is no longer divided into sexual categories. It gives ground to the "real" itself and the multiple realities by which it is articulated. It reveals the plastic force of the political in language. Wittig has not substituted a feminine universal for a masculine universal in a war between different systems of value. Rather she shows that the universal is not a value, a law, or a norm, which are the products of the metaphysical illusion. Emptied of value, the universal represents the possibility of symbolic exchange between multiple and irreducible positions of interest across the field of different languages and cultures through the medium of *language as language*, as a social tie. Wittig's *j/e* refuses the position of *other* in the relations man/woman, subject/object, self/other, only to give ground to an apocalypse, a dis-closure of radical alterity (Lacan's Other or Derrida's totally other), of language's power of transformation through representation.

The Lesbian Body dramatizes this alterity in the mode of its address. Like Woolf's novel *The Waves*, it deconstructs or, we could say, *disseminates* the positions of addresser and addressee so that this relationship is no longer thinkable in terms of a binary opposition. Early on in *The Lesbian Body*, the two categories virtually collapse into each other:

> Il n'y a pas trace de toi. Ton visage, ton corps ta silhouette sont perdus. Il y a un vide à la place de toi. Il y a dans m/on corps une pression au niveau du ventre au niveau du thorax. Il y a un poids dans m/a poitrine. Il y a des phénomènes à l'origine d'une douleur intense. A partir d'eux j/e te quiers mais j/e l'ignore. Par exemple, j/e marche le long d'une mer, j/ai mal dans tout m/on corps, m/a gorge ne m/e permet pas de parler, j/e vois la mer, j/e la regarde, j/e cherche, j/e m//interroge dans le silence dans le manque de trace, j//interroge une absence si étrange qu'elle m/e cause un trou au-dedans de m/on corps. Puis j/e sais de façon absolument infaillible que j/e te quiers, j/e te requiers, j/e te cherche, j/e te supplie, j/e te somme d'apparaître toi qui es sans visage sans mains sans seins sans ventre sans vulve sans membres sans pensées, toi au moment même où tu n'es pas autre chose qu'une pression un insistance dans m/on corps. Tu es couchée sur la mer, tu m/e rentre par les yeux, tu viens dans l'air que j/e respire, j/e te requiers de te laisser voir, j/e te demande de te laisser toucher, j/e te sollicite de sortir de cette non-présence où tu t'abîmes. Tes yeux il se peut sont phosphorescents, tes lèvres sont pâles m/a très désirée, tu m/e tourmentes d'un lent amour. (*Le corps lesbien* 31)

> There is no trace of you. Your face your body your silhouette are lost. In your place there is a void. In m/y body there is a pressure at the level of the belly at the level of the thorax. There is a weight on m/y chest. Initially these phenomena are intensely painful. Because of them *I* seek you but without knowing it. For instance, *I* walk beside the sea, m/y entire body is sick, m/y throat does not allow m/e to speak, *I* see the sea, *I* gaze at it, *I* search, *I* question m/yself in the silence in the lack of traces, *I* question an absence so strange that it makes a hole within m/y body. Then *I* know in absolutely infallible fashion that *I* am in need of you, *I* require your presence, *I* seek you, *I* implore you, *I* summon you to appear you who are featureless without hands breasts belly vulva limbs thoughts, you at the very moment when you are nothing more than a pressure an insistence within m/y body. You lie on the sea, you enter m/e by the eyes, you arrive in the air *I* breathe, *I* summon you to show yourself. *I* solicit you to emerge from this non-presence which engulfs you. Your eyes perhaps are phosphorescent, your lips are pale m/y much desired one, you torment m/e with a slow love. (*Lesbian Body* 37)

Because this poem does not occupy a privileged place in the series, it should not be read as the origin of desire or the crisis of desire or the end of desire. It is rather an aspect, a moment, an instance of desire. The speaking subject confronts its own absence from itself and from the other (woman) as one possibility of relationship. As Marthe Noel Evans observes, "There is no need to decide whether the 'you' in the text represents a real other person, the reader, or the author's ideal self. In fact, the effort to separate out those instances of address is futile, as they are all inextricably linked to each other by their common erasure from and in language" (195). The speaker confronts the absence of traces as the sign of the "real" body that has not been written. If there is a void or blank space in the symbolic, this is not necessarily the sign of the body's repression. On the contrary, the body's repression results from its representation within the heterosexual order of value that blinds the subject to the "real" absence of traces by substituting the wholeness of its symbols for the irreducible and unrepresentable wholeness of the body. The "real" wholeness of the body lies in its untranslatable finitude. The body has never been experienced more intensely than in this pain or sorrow of what is not written or marked. Signifying this pain becomes a political act, a gesture toward constructing the lesbian body. What the subject seeks without knowing it, what it questions in the silence of the unrepresented, is the body unmarked by gender. The hole within the body is the whole of the body; for there is no lack in the body itself, only in language. Confronting this body, experiencing this body as an absence of language, breaks the law of gender and moves toward a rewriting of the body outside the category of sex. The body is summoned into language even as its absence is signified. This "featureless" or universal body, this pressure within the body, signifies that the body *is*; it solicits the *being* of the body or calls the body into *being*. This language says, "Come." It is a form of love outside the heterosexual or patriarchal systems of value—outside value systems altogether. There is no hierarchy here, no distribution of power, no natural authority to govern and determine the meaning of love. There is no self and other in this exchange—no man, no woman. This love is "slow" because it has no climax, no pleasure index, no economy.

The other in Wittig's book is unnamable, irreducible. The subject (*j/e*) "shall not utter your adorable name. Such is the interdict you have laid on m/e, so be it. *I* [*j/e*] shall recount only how you come to seek m/e in the very depths of hell" (*Lesbian Body* 19). Hell (or the "dark continent" as it is sometimes referred to in these texts) is the "female" body marked and coded by the ideology of patriarchal (and implicitly imperialist) culture. Wittig never simply dismisses this culture or imagines that it can be wished away through a few linguistic reforms. The ground of revolution and social change is never the dream of some perfect society in the future but the insistence of a desire that somehow fissures the productions of the dominant culture in the present. As a writer, Wittig's task is to expand these fissures, to disrupt violently the smooth surface of hegemonic representations. Her speaker cannot utter the name of the other (woman) because this act would reify the difference between self and other which the lesbian subject is meant to disrupt. To name the other as a whole would once again belie the "real" alterity of the body by substituting a univocal symbol for a complex process whose very finitude exhausts the power of naming. The only way to signify this radical alterity is to foreground the disjunction between language and the "real" by demonstrating the exhaustion of language in the act of naming the body. The list of names that interrupts the text at intervals has exactly this function. Although the list begins and ends with "LE CORPS LESBIEN," the parts that are named are the parts of every female body and demonstrate the irreducibility of that body by dramatizing the arbitrariness of the terms that cut it up and divide it into parts. Even the term "LESBIAN BODY" is only one more name and cannot begin to summarize or gather up all the names and all the possibilities of naming. In the last complete prose poem before the final segment of the list, Wittig's "lesbian" subject says,

> A travers les facettes de m/es yeux j/e n'ai pas une vision unitaire de tons corps, tu es diversifiée, tu es différée, j//englobe tout à coup des indices de tes bras des fragments de ton ventre une partie d'épaule une de tes nymphes, j/e te vois partout à la fois, une ivresse m/e prend, j/e t'appréhende en miettes innombrable, j/e me perds dans ta géographie. (*Le corps lesbien* 172–73)

> Through the facets of m/y eyes *I* have no unitary vision of your body, you are diversified, you are different, *I* suddenly embody signals from your arms fragments of your belly part of a shoulder one of your labia, *I* see you everywhere at once, an intoxication grips m/e, *I* apprehend you in innumerable morsels, *I* lose m/yself in your geography. (*Lesbian Body* 152)

Wittig's style performatively illustrates the violence of language, the plastic force of which constructs the body socially but then can imprison it by insisting on a natural link between the sign and the referent. Such an *ideological* effect abstracts the body and the language of its construction from history. Challenging this "natural" representation of the body, which implies a "natural" set of relations between bodies, requires that one explore the capacity of language for violence that exceeds the natural order. The violence of linguistic categories "works specifically, as it did for black slaves, through an operation of reduction, by taking the part for the whole, a part (color, sex) through which the whole human group has to pass as through a screen" (Wittig, "Category of Sex" 68). The "natural" female body has been constructed through a process of symbolization—by passing the whole body through a screen of value. Reversing this process requires an insurrection of the parts, a transformation of synecdoche into metonymy so that no part has precedence over any other. The list performs this function to some extent by displaying a potentially unlimited partitioning of the female human body. The (dis)organization of the book into a disconnected series of 110 prose poems further dramatizes the arbitrariness of any narrative completion. Within individual poems, Wittig allegorically deconstructs the "natural" female body by showing the mutilation of the parts that results from the construction of a symbolic whole:

> Elles m//attirent jusqu'à tes morceaux dispersés, il y a un bras, il y a un pied, le cou et la tête vont ensemble, tes paupières sont fermées, tes oreilles détachées sont quelque part, tes globes oculaires ont roulé dans la boue, j/e les vois côte à côte, tes doigts sont coupés et jetés en un endroit, j//aperçois ton bassin, ton buste est ailleurs, il manque quelques fragments d'avant-bras, les cuisses et les tibias. (*Le corps lesbien* 86)

> The women lead m/e to your scattered fragments, there is an arm, there is a foot, the neck and head are together, your eyelids are closed, your detached ears are somewhere, your eyeballs have rolled in the mud, *I* see them side by side, your fingers have been cut off and thrown to one side, *I* perceive your pelvis, your bust is elsewhere, several fragments of forearms the thighs and tibiae are missing. (*Lesbian Body* 79–80)

As in *Les Guérillères*, "elles" is translated as "the women," which fails to capture Wittig's effect in using the "feminine" pronoun as a universal. This effect is important to the passage, for a few lines later the speaker pronounces "a ban on the recording of your death so that the traitress responsible for your being torn to pieces may not be alerted" (*Lesbian Body* 80). The traitress, I suspect, is not a person or subject but a myth, that is, "woman" herself or gender as an ontological category. The imaginary body constructed by this category covers the "real" bodies of individual "women" and in the process mutilates those bodies by subjecting them to a phallocentric system of values. The parts of the (female) body are subordinated to its overall function as an instrument of male sexuality in a heterosexual relationship. In this way, the parts are rendered obscene. Any discourse that confronts this mutilation by lifting the veil of ideology is necessarily apocalyptic, as Derrida's reading of the Greek verb *apokalupto* suggests:

> I disclose, I uncover, I unveil, I reveal the thing that can be a part of the body, the head or the eyes, a secret part, the genitals or whatever might be hidden, a secret, the thing to be dissembled, a thing that does not show itself or say itself, that perhaps signifies itself but cannot or must not first be handed over to its self-evidence. *Apokekalummenoi logoi* are indecent remarks. So it is a matter of the secret and the *pudenda*. ("Apocalyptic Tone" 65).

In truth, the apocalyptic words seem indecent or obscene—the parts of the human body seem mutilated and disgusting—only from the perspective of the hegemonic system of values. Outside of that framework, nothing is self-evident. The problematic reception of *The Lesbian Body* by critics who had praised Wittig's earlier work testifies to the difficulty of getting beyond hegemonic values. As Evans explains, Wittig's sympathetic readers were shocked by the book's violence: "Dismemberment, flaying, evisceration are all part of the 'love-making' that takes place between the two nameless protagonists. Body parts are everywhere. It is disgusting. . . . Wittig rips open this stereotypical woman and rubs our noses in her guts" (187). *The Lesbian Body* shows and says everything that the commonplace imagination represses or refuses to contemplate but not as an end in itself. Apocalyptic writing must finally veil as well as unveil, reconstruct as well as deconstruct, the human (female) body. For Wittig, this necessity takes shape as a rewriting of the Osiris myth:

> J/e prononce que tu es là vivante quoique tronconnée, j/e cherche en toute hâte tes morceaus dans la boue, m/es ongles râclent les menues pierres et les cailloux, j/e trouve ton nez une partie de ta vulve tes nymphes ton clitoris, j/e trouve tes oreilles un tibia puis l'autre, j/e te rassemble bout à bout, j/e te reconstitue. . . . m/oi Isis la très puissante j/e décrète que comme par le passé tu vis Osiris m/a très chérie m/a très affaiblie j/e dis que comme par le passé nous pourrons faire ensemble les petites filles qui viendront après nous, toi alors m/on Osiris m/a très belle tu m/e souris défaite épuisée. (*Le corps lesbien* 86–87)

I announce that you are here alive though cut to pieces, *I* search hastily for your fragments in the mud, m/y nails scrabble at the small stones and pebbles, *I* find your nose a part of your vulva your labia your clitoris, *I* find your ears one tibia then the other, *I* assemble you part by part, *I* reconstruct you. . . . *I* Isis the all-powerful *I* decree that you live as in the past Osiris m/y most cherished m/y most enfeebled *I* say that as in the past we shall succeed together in making the little girls who will come after us, then you m/y Osiris m/y most beautiful you smile at me undone exhausted. (*Lesbian Body* 80)

It would appear that Wittig has incorporated a heterosexual myth into her text; but, as Namascar Shaktini points out, the ithyphallic god Osiris "has been lesbianized" by the use of feminine modifiers in the original French (32). This particular moment in the text, however, must be distinguished from others in which the speaker takes over the identity of male mythological figures by feminizing their names: Ulyssea for Ulysses, Zeyna for Zeus, Achillea for Achilles, and so forth. According to Evans, the latter technique reverses the exclusion of women from universal (male) history: "Wittig suggests that behind these male figures lies a lost female past that can be retrieved" (196). I am not convinced that Wittig is that optimistic about the recovery of the "real" history of women, but it is certainly a political act on her part to disrupt the male-centered mythologies not by inverting them with female-centered mythologies but by forcing into them universal "feminine" signifiers. For Wittig's political goal is never to reinforce the mark of gender but to destroy it by universalizing its grammatical function. Her use of the Osiris myth makes this point especially clear. For once it is not the speaker who assumes the identity of the formerly male god but her other, her lover, her body. She does not alter the spelling of the name Osiris but nevertheless transforms the universal significance of this god by writing the modifiers with feminine endings. The myth of Osiris is no longer about man or woman; it goes beyond the category of sex. As Shaktini reminds us, after the mutilation of Osiris, Isis was able to recover all the parts of his body except the penis, for which she made a substitute, an image: "The phallus produced is a simulacrum, an artifact crafted by Isis who then attributes to it a sacred meaning" (33). In effect, the missing part becomes a metaphor of the whole, a symbol of magical power and authority. According to Esther Harding, the public rituals of Isis and Osiris centered on the phallus, and it was said that "Isis conceived by means of this image and bore a child" (quoted by Shaktini 33–34). Wittig reinterprets this myth

not as the mutilation and reassembly of the male body but as the construction of the "female" body through mutilation by the fiction of the
phallus. In destroying that fiction, she not only reconstructs the "female"
body as lesbian but makes possible a "male" body that is not subjected to
the phallus as signifier. Although I agree with Shaktini that Wittig effectively diplaces the phallic subject, I don't support her claim that "lesbian
metaphor must overwrite phallogocentric metaphor, just as, historically,
phallogocentric metaphor had to overwrite an earlier symbolic system"
(32). Wittig works against what I would call the imperialism of the metaphor, which erases the "real" body (ultimately, I would suggest, both
male and female). The phallus as simulacrum or rhetorical figure produces and governs the ideology of sexual difference by reducing the human body as the incommensurate to the law of a unitary representation.
As Dianne Griffin Crowder suggests, Wittig reverses the "metaphorizing
process of male love poetry" since "metaphor is always in some sense a
denial of the word that is replaced by another. But metaphor disguises this
absence with the presence of the substituted term. Because Wittig's writing is political, she consistently marks the absent term, calling it to our
attention to force us into an evaluation of the ideological implications of
'absence' from discourse and language" (128). When Wittig constructs
the lesbian body, there is no part to represent the whole, there is no
privileged signifier. The lesbian body is not metaphysical; and consequently even those parts of the human body that are not listed (for
example, the penis) are not excluded from the universal. Although Wittig
might object to my formulation, it follows from her writing practice that
the universal as metonymy operates within the economy of the not-
everything, the *pas-tout*. But what the sign of negation signifies here is not
the incompletion of the "real" (male or female) body but the incompletion of language. It is language—it is the symbolic—that is not everything.

Wittig demonstrates what I mean in the poem about the institution of
a new language based upon the "pure and simple disappearance of the
vowels":

Il faut que tu m//écrives l'information pour que j//en comprenne le
sens. Tes lèvres ta langue modulent le nouveau langage aux sons gut-
turaux, les consonnes prononcées les une contre les autres bousculées
produisent des grognements des rauquements des râclements de cordes
vocales, ta voix inexpérimentée dans cette prononciation s'accélère ou
se ralentit et cependant tu ne peux pas t'arrêter de parler. L'effet

nouveau du mouvement de tes joues et de ta bouche la difficulté des sons à se frayer un passage hors de ta bouche sont si comiques que le rire m//étouffe, j/e tombe à la renverse, les larmes m/e coulent, j/e te regarde immobile muette, le rire m/e gagne de plus en plus, tu te trouves brusquement contaminée, tu éclates, tes joues se colorent, tu tombes à la renverse tandis qu'on entend leurs clameurs au dehors leurs interpellations de longues phrases incompréhensibles prononcées par l'une d'entre elles et reprises par de nombreuses autres répétées sans cesse. (*Le corps lesbien* 116)

You must write down the news for m/e if *I* am to understand its meaning. Your lip your tongue modulate the new language in guttural sounds, the uttered consonants jostled one against the other produce gruntings gratings scrapings of the vocal cords, your voice untried in this pronunciation speeds up or slows down and yet you cannot stop talking. The novel effect of the movement of your cheeks and mouth the difficulty the sounds have in making their way out of your mouth are so comical that *I* choke with laughter, *I* fall over backwards, m/y tears stream, *I* regard you still and silent, *I* am increasingly overcome by laughter, suddenly you too are affected, you burst out, your cheeks colour, you fall over backwards as the women's clamour is heard outside their interpellations the long incomprehensible phrases prononced by one of them and repeated interminably by many others. (*Lesbian Body* 103–4)

In a sense, Wittig is suggesting in this passage that if there is an alternative to patriarchal language it lies not in the direction of a natural "woman's language" but in the material alteration of the language that has been handed down to women and men. Such an alteration does not appeal to metaphyscial essence; it is a political act. Patriarchal-heterosexual culture has centered on the male sex, which it identifies as the One sex to the exclusion of "women" as a class. Women as such provide the background or matrix to such a culture. They constitute the margin. Such an order is justified through an appeal to nature, God, metaphysics. In an analogous way, Western languages such as French and English center on the vowels, which nevertheless need the articulation of the consonants in order to make whole words. Within the fiction of *The Lesbian Body*, the vowels have been removed from language just as the "men" have been removed from society. All that is left are the margins. But there is no metaphysical justification of these orders. There is nothing naturally feminine about a language of consonants; nor is a lesbian society a "natural" society of women. Thus, all that is revealed by the removal of the vowels from language is the arbitrariness of the sounds that compose a language in the first place, their lack of any metaphysical authority. This new language becomes the object of laughter not because it has been made the language of the other sex but because it has been made Other. The repression has been lifted on the material constitution of language itself. In fact, this new language is not simply the object but the subject of laughter; for Wittig has evoked the same *oui rire* (the *affirmation in laughter*) that Derrida hears in Joyce (see "Ulysses Gramophone"). Wittig's text is laughing at itself. After all, the language with which Wittig tells us about this new language of the lesbian society is not a language from which the vowels have been removed; but it is a language that has exposed itself, displayed its materiality, made itself obscene. Similarly, in evoking a world from which men have been removed, Wittig employs a language that requires her to disfigure the sign of her own subjectivity (*j/e*) in order to reclaim the universal in language for herself as a member of the social class "women." Though Wittig calls the patriarchal language "alien," the new language—not only the language she writes about but the language she writes—is also "alien" but in a different sense. It is a language that knows its incompleteness, that knows its inadequacy to the "real" it calls into being.

From this moment of the laughter-of-language-at-language emerges the apocalyptic tone of Wittig's writing. For in this *affirmation in laughter*, the identity of the subject collapses, and we no longer know who is speaking—in what language they are speaking—to whom and for whom they are speaking. This apocalyptic tone, this vibration or laughter, discloses the ontological emptiness of language—including the mark of gender—which calls out to being and invites it to come. It does not call out to "you" or "me" but to the beings that inhabit those positions. Derrida suggests that the apocalyptic tone would be "a transcendental condition of all discourse, of all experience itself, of every mark or every trace" ("Apocalyptic Tone" 87). I have called this transcendental or "quasitranscendental" condition alterity or, after Lacan, the big Other. Though I have also stressed that such a condition is beyond value, my meaning has never been that this "beyond" refers to a "thing" or a "place." There is only a relation and a moment of rupture that makes possible the revaluation or transvaluation of value. In the context of her writings and political struggles, I have to agree with Wittig when she says that "no Thought of the Other or Thought of Difference should be possible for us, for 'nothing human is alien' to the One or to the Other" ("Homo Sum" 10). And yet I think there is a thought of radical difference, of incommensurable difference, that may be the only way of defeating the metaphysics of difference and saving the particular from the alienation of value. There is a way of thinking the Other that we must hang onto for a while longer, a way of thinking that the Other—the big Other or radical alterity—*is* the intersubjective link that constitutes the human. There is no alienation of the Other for there is no Other of the Other. While it is essential that we construct new values, new subjects, new sites for being, it must never be forgotten that no value, no identity, and no truth in language can escape the structure of fictionality. Everything is subject to change. When language seems to collapse into the sound of its own laughter, something is heard, something that has no name, something for the ear of the Other in us. As with Wittig's new language, every language explodes when its apocalyptic tone is heard:

> Les résonances insolites de la langue transformée à présent répétée par de plus en plus de voix produisent des ondes incontrôlables des mouvements d'air des masses de nuages. On entend un roulement sourd, les éclairs se succèdent aveuglant, l'orage éclate avec un fracas tel qu'il couvre d'un seul coup le bruit des milliers de voix. (*Le corps lesbien* 117)

> The unwonted resonances of the now transformed language repeated by more and more voices produce uncontrollable waves movements of air masses of clouds. A heavy rumbling is heard, lightning flashes follow each other blindingly, the storm breaks with such a din as at once to cover the sound of the thousand of voices. (*Lesbian Body* 104)

The apocalyptic tone is "a pure differential vibration, without support, unbearable." It says *Yes*; it says *Come*. It lifts the veil of social categories in order to make visible the repression that all "true" subjects share. In this way, it makes possible not the end of repression but the transformation of its material form. The din of the storm is the "differential vibration" of the voices, the languages, the others that are the true subjects.

The word "come" is not magical. What matters is not some mystery of the word, which could never be anything more than another version of logocentrism. What matters is the relation to language that these words articulate; what matters is their pedagogical effect. One need not accept Nietzsche's metaphysics of the will (of which music or tone is the symbolic expression) to be fascinated by the implications of his theory of *the duality in the essence of language*. Words certainly produce meanings and values, but there are *other* effects that seem irreducible to the production model. Before there are meanings, before there are acts of communication, language exists as a tone; and this tone constitutes the social tie. Before the Eurocentric, patriarchal subject can hear the message of the postcolonial or the feminist writer, it has to recognize the tone of their discourse, the symbolic exchange that calls out to the Other in the subject—that displaces authority with alterity. To go back to my earlier example from Faulkner's *Absalom, Absalom!*, when Judith Sutpen hands Charles Bon's letter over to Quentin Compson's grandmother, she transfers not the message but the tone. The act is not really a communication but an appeal, a call. And it is not, strictly speaking, a call to another person who stands opposed to me as my *alter ego*, the other in the narrow sense (for Lacan, the *a'*). Her act appeals to the big Other, intersubjectivity itself, in which she, Charles Bon, and Mrs Compson are constituted as subjects. It is important that, within the frame of the novel, Mrs Compson is someone whom Judith does not really know. Like the analyst, she stands in the place of the Other, where she can facilitate a symbolic exchange. With reference to another letter, the "purloined" one in Edgar Allan Poe's short story, Lacan remarks in his seminar on the ego, "The letter is here synonymous with the original, radical, subject." In the scene in which the letter is stolen by the minister before the king and the queen, the fourth character is not the person who sends the letter: "He has only fictional importance, whereas the letter is indeed a character" (*The Ego* 196). The "original, radical, subject" is not the person but the signifier that determines personhood as a position for some other signifier. In Faulkner's novel or in Poe's story, the radical subject is the Other, that is, the letter that articulates "persons" as a set of positions. In the "Seminar on 'The Purloined Letter'" revised for the *Ecrits*, Lacan stresses that the letter is "the *true subject* of the tale," and "since it can be diverted, it must have a course *which is proper to it*: the trait by which its incidence as signifier is affirmed" ("Seminar on 'The Purloined Letter'" 43). But it seems necessary to go further (as Derrida's critique of Lacan would demand [*The Post Card* 413–96]) and say that it is always possible that the *true subject* has already been diverted from its proper course— that this possibility of diversion has already contaminated the concept of the proper in advance. Indeed, it may be that the "proper" course of the subject can be articulated only in the imaginary register, where, so to speak, it is pinned to an ego, to something fantastic. The *true subject* lies elsewhere, diverted from its structural end (the ego, the category of sex, racial difference), toward the Other, the totally other, the symbolic not as a system but as the underivable, only derivable—interminable—process.

The true subject is an effect of symbolic exchange. It is the answer to an appeal or call that says, "Come." The pedagogical effect "comes." It is not produced but *seduced*. With some hesitation, I use the latter term in Baudrillard's sense: as opposed to production, seduction leads to "the opposite of the psychoanalytic distinction between manifest and latent discourse." In classical psychoanalysis, "latent discourse diverts manifest discourse not *from* its truth but *towards* it and makes it say what it did not wish to say." In seduction, on the contrary, "the manifest discourse, the most 'superficial' aspect of discourse, . . . acts upon the underlying prohibition (conscious or unconscious) in order to nullify it and to substitute for it the charms and traps of appearances" ("On Seduction," *Selected Writings* 149). The phrase "charms and traps," like the use of the word "seduction" itself, betrays a lingering nostalgia in Baudrillard's work for the very depths of meaning it seeks to destroy. Whether we speak of appearances, the rhetorical dimension of language, the material signifier, text-inscribed blankness, or language as the Other (and I am not equating these phrases, for each has its specificity)—we aim at a material practice beyond value, underlying value, rupturing value. Whenever a discourse says "come," it opens itself to the Other, to the alterity and the materiality of language; it subverts meaning with tone. This "come" is an effect. It throws the subject who hears it up against the wall of language. It destroys the ego (*moi*) and the self-certain knowledge to which it is the ground of production. The "effect" of "come" is pedagogical because it brings the human subject into a direct confrontation with its own alterity. It cannot know itself, it cannot *be* itself, without reinstituting or teaching itself. The self and its knowledge is a social construction derived from a material practice. But it is perpetually undone by those effects that come uninvited, unexpected. Pedagogy that would do more than produce information in the imaginary register must direct the learning subject toward a critical relation to knowledge by allowing the unexpected to emerge in teaching and writing. Literature can offer examples of such an effect, but it cannot offer a formula for its production.

Such an effect emerges from what Baudrillard calls "the primitive seduction of language": "the original way in which . . . [a discourse] absorbs meaning and empties itself of meaning in order better to fascinate others" ("On Seduction," *Selected Writings* 150). This fascination directs us to a revelation. It makes apparent, or brings to the surface, the voice of the other within us. It makes us/it delirious. It brings us to the verge of cultural revolution. Such a revolution should not be thought of as a single event in human history, for it is rather the potentiality for total history contained in each event. In such a moment or event, history fascinates and seduces us with its call and appeal. William Blake spoke for such revolutionary time in the second book of *Milton*:

> There is a Moment in each Day that Satan cannot find
> Nor can his Watch Fiends find it, but the Industrious find
> This Moment & it multiply. & when it once is found
> It renovates every Moment of the Day if rightly placed[.]
> (136)

The pedagogical effect is such a moment in discourse. It takes place when the human relation to language—and to those cultural systems that operate like a language—is transformed into an event through the emergence of the unexpected. In every communication, something happens in excess, beyond the exchange of information. Something says, "Come." The tone of this call cannot be reduced to objectivity, to system, to structure, to value. The subject who hears it is not you or me but the intersubject. This hearing is symbolic exchange. This event is the apocalypse that annuls abstract time and unveils the face of total history.

Works Cited

Achebe, Chinua. *Morning Yet on Creation Day*. London: Heinemann, 1975.
———. *Things Fall Apart*. London: Heinemann, 1976.
———. *Hopes and Impediments: Selected Essays, 1965–1987*. London: Heinemann, 1988.
Ahmad, Aijaz. "Jameson's Rhetoric of Otherness and the 'National Allegory,'" *Social Text* 17 (1987): 3–25.
Althusser, Louis. *Lenin and Philosophy and Other Essays*. Trans. Ben Brewster. London: NLB, 1971.
Armah, Ayi Kwei. *The Beautyful Ones Are Not Yet Born*. London: Heinemann, 1975.
———. *Two Thousand Seasons*. Chicago: Third World, 1979.
Atherton, William. *The Books at the Wake: A Study of Literary Allusions in James Joyce's "Finnegans Wake."* Carbondale: Southern Illinois University Press, 1974.
Attridge, Derek. "Finnegans Awake: The Dream of Interpretation," *James Joyce Quarterly* 27.1 (1989): 11–29.
Baudrillard, Jean. *The Mirror of Production*. Trans. Mark Poster. St. Louis: Telos, 1975.
———. *L'échange symbolique et la mort*. Paris: Gallimard, 1976.
———. "Beyond the Unconscious: The Symbolic," *Discourse* 3 (1981): 60–87.
———. *For a Critique of the Political Economy of the Sign*. Trans. Charles Levin. St. Louis: Telos, 1981.
———. *Selected Writings*. Stanford: Stanford University Press, 1988.
Benjamin, Walter. *Illuminations*. Trans. Harry Zohn. New York: Schocken, 1969.

_____. *The Origin of German Tragic Drama*. Trans. John Osborne. London: NLB, 1977.

Benstock, Shari. "The Genuine Christine: Psychodynamics of Issy." In *Women in Joyce*. Ed. Suzette Henke and Elaine Unkeless. Urbana: University of Illinois Press, 1982. Pp. 169–96.

_____. "Apostrophizing the Feminine in *Finnegans Wake*," *Modern Fiction Studies* 35.3 (1989): 587–614.

Bhabha, Homi K. "Articulating the Archaic: Notes on Colonial Nonsense." In *Literary Theory Today*. Ed. Peter Collier and Helga Geyer-Ryan. Ithaca: Cornell University Press, 1990. Pp. 203–18.

_____. "DissemiNation: Time, Narrative, and the Margins of the Modern Nation." In *Nation and Narration*. Ed. Homi K. Bhabha. London: Routledge, 1990. Pp. 291–322.

Bishop, John. *Joyce's Book of the Dark: "Finnegans Wake."* Madison: University of Wisconsin Press, 1986.

Blake, William. *The Complete Poetry and Prose*. Ed. David V. Erdman. Rev. ed. Berkeley: University of California Press, 1982.

Bourdieu, Pierre. *Distinction: A Social Critique of the Judgement of Taste*. Trans. Richard Nice. Cambridge: Harvard University Press, 1984.

Brantlinger, Patrick. *Rule of Darkness: British Literature and Imperialism, 1830–1914*. Ithaca: Cornell University Press, 1988.

Brennan, Timothy. *Salman Rushdie and the Third World: Myths of the Nation*. New York: St. Martin, 1989.

Bürger, Peter. *Theory of the Avant-Garde*. Trans. Michael Shaw. Minneapolis: University of Minnesota Press, 1984.

Burke, Kenneth. *A Rhetoric of Motives*. Berkeley: University of California Press, 1969.

Butler, Judith. *Gender Trouble: Feminism and the Subversion of Identity*. New York: Routledge, 1990.

Conrad, Joseph. *Heart of Darkness*. Ed. Robert Kimbrough. 3d ed. New York: Norton, 1988.

Crane, Hart. *The Complete Poems and Selected Letters and Prose*. Ed. Brom Weber. Garden City, N.Y.: Anchor, 1966.

Cronin, Richard. "The Indian English Novel: *Kim* and *Midnight's Children*," *Modern Fiction Studies* 33.2 (1987): 201–13.

Crowder, Diane Griffin. "Amazons and Mothers? Monique Wittig, Hélène Cixous, and Theories of Women's Writing," *Contemporary Literature* 24.2 (1983): 117–44.

de Certeau, Michel. "Lacan: An Ethics of Speech." In *Heterologies: Discourse on the Other*. Trans. Brian Massumi. Minneapolis: University of Minnesota Press, 1986. Pp. 47–64.

de Man, Paul. "The Resistance to Theory," *Yale French Studies* 63 (1982): 3–20.

Derrida, Jacques. *Of Grammatology*. Trans. Gayatri Chakravorty Spivak. Baltimore: Johns Hopkins University Press, 1976.

_____. *Writing and Difference*. Trans. Alan Bass. Chicago: University of Chicago Press, 1978.

_____. "Living On: Borderlines." *Deconstruction and Criticism*. Ed. Harold Bloom. New York: Seabury, 1979. Pp. 75–175.

_____. *Dissemination*. Trans. Barbara Johnson. Chicago: University of Chicago Press, 1981.

_____. *Positions*. Trans. Alan Bass. Chicago: University of Chicago Press, 1981.

_____. "Of an Apocalyptic Tone Recently Adopted in Philosophy," *Semeia* 23 (1982): 63–97.

_____. "*Geschlecht*: Sexual Difference, Ontological Difference," *Research in Phenomenology* 13 (1983): 65–83.

_____. "The Principle of Reason: The University in the Eyes of Its Pupils," *Diacritics* 13 (1983): 3–20.

_____. "Des tours de Babel." In *Difference in Translation*. Trans. and ed. Joseph F. Graham. Ithaca: Cornell University Press, 1985. Pp. 165–207.

_____. "Pas." In *Parages*. Paris: Galilée, 1986. Pp. 19–116.

_____. "*Geschlecht* II: Heidegger's Hand." In *Deconstruction and Philosophy*. Ed. John Sallis. Trans. John P. Leavey, Jr. Chicago: University of Chicago Press, 1987. Pp. 161–96.

_____. "Interview." In *Criticism in Society*, by Imre Salusinszky. New York: Methuen, 1987.

_____. *The Post Card: From Socrates to Freud and Beyond*. Trans. Alan Bass. Chicago: University of Chicago Press, 1987.

_____. "Like the Sound of the Sea Deep within a Shell: Paul de Man's War," *Critical Inquiry* 14 (1988): 590–652.

_____. "Ulysses Gramophone: Hear Say Yes in Joyce." In *James Joyce: The Augmented Ninth*. Ed. Bernard Benstock. Baltimore: The Johns Hopkins University Press, 1988. Pp. 27–79.

Edelman, Lee. *Transmemberment of Song: Hart Crane's Anatomies of Rhetoric and Desire*. Stanford: Stanford University Press, 1987.

Eliot, T. S. "Tradition and the Individual Talent." In *Selected Essays*. New York: Harcourt, Brace, 1950. Pp. 3–11.

Evans, Martha Noel. *Masks of Tradition: Women and the Politics of Writing in Twentieth-Century France*. Ithaca: Cornell University Press, 1987.

Fanon, Frantz. *The Wretched of the Earth*. Trans. Constance Farrington. New York: Grove, 1968.

Faulkner, William. *Absalom, Absalom! The Corrected Text*. New York: Vintage International, 1990.

_____. *As I Lay Dying: The Corrected Text*. New York: Vintage International, 1990.

Felman, Shoshana. *Jacques Lacan and the Adventure of Insight: Psychoanalysis in Contemporary Culture*. Cambridge: Harvard University Press, 1987.

Fish, Stanley. *Is There a Text in This Class? The Authority of Interpretive Communities*. Cambridge: Harvard University Press, 1980.

Fogel, Daniel Mark. *Covert Relations: James Joyce, Virginia Woolf, and Henry James*. Charlottesville: University Press of Virginia, 1990.

Forster, E. M. *A Passage to India*. New York: Harcourt, Brace, and World, 1952.

Fraser, Robert. *The Novels of Ayi Kwei Armah: A Study in Polemical Fiction*. London: Heinemann, 1980.

Fuss, Diana. *Essentially Speaking: Feminism, Nature, and Difference*. New York: Routledge, 1989.

Gasché, Rodolphe. *The Tain of the Mirror: Derrida and the Philosophy of Reflection.* Cambridge: Harvard University Press, 1986.

Gifford, Don. *Ulysses Annotated.* 2d ed. Berkeley: University of California Press, 1988.

Glasheen, Adaline. *Third Census of "Finnegans Wake": An Index of the Characters and Their Roles.* Berkeley: University of California Press, 1977.

Gordon, John. *"Finnegans Wake": A Plot Summary.* Syracuse, New York: Syracuse University Press, 1986.

Graff, Gerald. *Professing Literature: An Institutional History.* Chicago: University of Chicago Press, 1987.

Gramsci, Antonio. *An Antonio Gramsci Reader: Selected Writings, 1916–1935.* New York: Schocken, 1988.

Groden, Michael. *"Ulysses" in Progress.* Princeton: Princeton University Press, 1977.

Gugelberger, Georg M. *Marxism and African Literature.* London: James Currey, 1985.

Habermas, Jürgen. *The Philosophical Discourse of Modernity: Twelve Lectures.* Trans. Frederick Lawrence. Cambridge: MIT, 1987.

Harlow, Barbara. *Resistance Literature.* New York: Methuen, 1987.

Hart, Clive. *Structure and Motif in "Finnegans Wake."* Evanston, Ill.: Northwestern University Press, 1962.

Hayman, David. *The "Wake" in Transit.* Ithaca: Cornell University Press, 1990.

Head, Bessie. *A Question of Power.* New York: Pantheon, 1973.

Irigaray, Luce. *This Sex Which Is Not One.* Trans. Catherine Porter, with Carolyn Burke. Ithaca: Cornell University Press, 1985.

Jakobson, Roman. "Two Aspects of Language and Two Types of Aphasic Disturbances." In *Selected Writings,* vol. 2: *Word and Language.* The Hague: Mouton, 1971. Pp. 239–59.

Jameson, Fredric. *The Political Unconscious: Narrative as a Socially Symbolic Act.* Ithaca: Cornell University Press, 1981.

——. "Postmodernism, or the Cultural Logic of Late Capitalism," *New Left Review* 146 (1984): 53–92.

——. "Third-World Literature in the Era of Multinational Capitalism," *Social Text* 15 (1986): 65–88.

——. "*History and Class Consciousness* as an 'Unfinished Project,'" *Rethinking Marxism* 1.1 (1988): 49–72.

JanMohamed, Abdul R. *Manichean Aesthetics: The Politics of Literature in Colonial Africa.* Amherst: University of Massachusetts Press, 1983.

——. "The Economy of Manichean Allegory: The Function of Racial Difference in Colonialist Literature." In *"Race," Writing, and Difference.* Ed. Henry Louis Gates. Chicago: University of Chicago Press, 1985. Pp. 78–106.

Jay, Gregory. *America the Scrivener: Deconstruction and the Subject of Literary History.* Ithaca: Cornell University Press, 1990.

Joyce, James. *Finnegans Wake.* New York: Viking, 1959.

——. *A Portrait of the Artist as a Young Man: Text, Criticism, and Notes.* Ed. Chester G. Anderson. New York: Viking, 1968.

——. *Ulysses: The Corrected Text.* Ed. Hans Walter Gabler, with Wolfhard Steppe and Claus Melchior. New York: Random House, 1986.

Kellner, Douglas. *Jean Baudrillard: From Marxism to Postmodernism and Beyond*. Stanford: Stanford University Press, 1989.

Krause, David. "Reading Bon's Letter and Faulkner's *Absalom, Absalom!*" *PMLA* 99.2 (1984): 225–41.

Kristeva, Julia. *Semeiotiké: Recherches pour une semanalyse*. Collection Points. Paris: Seuil, 1969.

———. *Powers of Horror: An Essay on Abjection*. Trans. Leon S. Roudiez. New York: Columbia University Press, 1982.

Kronick, Joseph G. "Dr. Heidegger's Experiment," *boundary 2* 17.3 (1990): 116–53.

Lacan, Jacques. *Ecrits*. Paris: Seuil, 1966.

———. *Encore*. Book 20 of *Le séminaire*. Ed. Jacques-Alain Miller. Paris: Seuil, 1975.

———. *"Ecrits": A Selection*. New York: Norton, 1977.

———. "Le sinthome," *Ornicar?* 10 (1977): 5–12.

———. *Feminine Sexuality: Jacques Lacan and the "Ecole Freudienne"*. Ed. Juliet Mitchell and Jacqueline Rose. New York: Norton, 1985.

———. "Joyce le symptome I." In *Joyce avec Lacan*. Ed. Jacques Aubert. Paris: Navarin, 1987. Pp. 21–29.

———. *The Ego in Freud's Theory and in the Technique of Psychoanalysis, 1954–1955*. Book 2 of *The Seminar*. Trans. Sylvana Tomaselli. New York: Norton, 1988.

———. "Seminar on 'The Purloined Letter.'" In *The Purloined Poe: Lacan, Derrida, and Psychoanalytic Reading*. Ed. John P. Muller and William J. Richardson. Baltimore: The Johns Hopkins University Press, 1988. Pp. 28–54.

Lacoue-Labarthe, Philippe. *Typography: Mimesis, Philosophy, Politics*. Introduction by Jacques Derrida. Ed. Christopher Fynsk. Cambridge: Harvard University Press, 1989.

———. *Heidegger, Art, and Politics: The Fiction of the Political*. Trans. Chris Turner. Oxford: Basil Blackwell, 1990.

Lazarus, Neil. *Resistance in Postcolonial African Fiction*. New Haven: Yale University Press, 1990.

Lévi-Strauss, Claude. *Introduction to the Work of Marcel Mauss*. Trans. Felicity Baker. London: Routledge and Kegan Paul, 1987.

Lyotard, Jean-François. *The Postmodern Condition: A Report on Knowledge*. Trans. Geoff Bennington and Brian Massumi. Minneapolis: University of Minnesota Press, 1984.

———. *The Differend: Phrases in Dispute*. Trans. George Van Den Abbeele. Minneapolis: University of Minnesota Press, 1988.

———. *Heidegger and "the Jews."* Trans. Andreas Michel and Mark S. Roberts. Minneapolis: University of Minnesota Press, 1990.

Macey, David. *Lacan in Contexts*. London: Verso, 1988.

Marcus, Jane. *Virginia Woolf and the Languages of Patriarchy*. Bloomington: Indiana University Press, 1987.

Matthews, John T. *The Play of Faulkner's Language*. Ithaca: Cornell University Press, 1982.

McCannell, Juliet Flower. *Figuring Lacan: Criticism and the Cultural Unconscious*. Lincoln: University of Nebraska Press, 1986.

McGann, Jerome J. *Social Values and Poetic Acts: A Historical Judgment of Literary Work.* Cambridge: Harvard University Press, 1988.

McGee, Patrick. *Paperspace: Style as Ideology in Joyce's "Ulysses."* Lincoln: University of Nebraska Press, 1988.

———. "Joyce's Pedagogy: *Ulysses* and *Finnegans Wake* as Theory." In *Coping with Joyce: Essays from the Copenhagen Symposium.* Ed. Morris Beja and Shari Benstock. Columbus: Ohio State University Press, 1989. Pp. 206–19.

McHugh, Roland. *Annotations to "Finnegans Wake."* Baltimore: The Johns Hopkins University Press, 1980.

Meisel, Perry. *The Absent Father: Virginia Woolf and Walter Pater.* New Haven: Yale University Press, 1980.

Miller, Christopher L. *Blank Darkness: Africanist Discourse in French.* Chicago: University of Chicago Press, 1985.

———. *Theories of Africans: Francophone Literature and Anthropology in Africa.* Chicago: University of Chicago Press, 1990.

Minow-Pinkney, Makiko. *Virginia Woolf and the Problem of the Subject.* Brighton: Harvester, 1987.

Moi, Toril. *Sexual/Textual Politics: Feminist Literary Theory.* London: Methuen, 1985.

Moreland, Richard. *Faulkner and Modernism: Rereading and Rewriting.* Madison: University of Wisconsin Press, 1989.

Morris, Wesley, with Barbara Alverson Morris. *Reading Faulkner.* Madison: University of Wisconsin Press, 1989.

Ngara, Emmanuel. *Art and Ideology in the African Novel: A Study of the Influence of Marxism on the African Novel.* London: Heinemann, 1985.

Ngũgĩ wa Thiong'o. *Petals of Blood.* London: Heinemann, 1977.

———. *Writers in Politics.* London: Heinemann, 1981.

———. *Devil on the Cross.* London: Heinemann, 1982.

———. "The Tension between National and Imperialist Culture," *World Literature Written in English* 24.1 (1984): 3–9.

———, "On Writing in Gĩkũyũ," *Research in African Literatures* 16.2 (1985): 151–56.

———. *Decolonising the Mind: The Politics of Language in African Literature.* London: James Currey, 1986.

———. Interview by Hansel Nolumbe Eyoh, *The Journal of Commonwealth Literature* 21.1 (1986): 162–66.

———. *Matigari.* London: Heinemann, 1989.

Nietzsche, Friedrich. "On Music and Words." In *The Complete Works of Friedrich Nietzsche,* vol. 2: *Early Greek Philosophy and Other Essays.* Trans. Maximilian Mügge. London: Macmillan, 1924. Pp. 27–47.

———. "On Truth and Lie in an Extra-moral Sense." In *The Portable Nietzsche.* Ed. and trans. Walter Kaufmann. New York: Viking, 1954. Pp. 42–47.

Olney, James. *Tell Me Africa.* Princeton: Princeton University Press, 1973.

Ouologuem, Yambo. *Bound to Violence.* Trans. Ralph Manheim. London: Heinemann, 1977.

Parameswaran, Uma. "Handcuffed to History: Salman Rushdie's Art," *Ariel* 14.4 (1983): 34–45.

Porter, Carolyn. *Seeing and Being: The Plight of the Participant Observer in Emerson, James, Adams, and Faulkner.* Middletown, Conn.: Wesleyan University Press, 1985.

Ragland-Sullivan, Ellie. *Jacques Lacan and the Philosophy of Psychoanalysis.* Urbana: University of Illinois Press, 1986.

Riddel, Joseph. "Hart Crane's Poetics of Failure," *ELH* 33.4 (1966): 473–96.

Rose, Danis, and John O'Hanlon. *Understanding "Finnegans Wake": A Guide to the Narrative of James Joyce's Masterpiece.* New York: Garland, 1982.

Rushdie, Salman. *Midnight's Children.* New York: Avon, 1982.

——. "The Empire Writes Back with a Vengeance," *London Times,* July 3, 1982: 8.

——. "Author from Three Countries," *New York Times Review of Books,* Nov. 13, 1983: 3, 22–23.

——. "Outside the Whale," *Granta* 11 (1983): 123–41.

——. "A Pen against the Sword: In Good Faith," *Newsweek,* Feb. 12, 1990: 52–57.

Said, Edward W. *Orientalism.* New York: Pantheon, 1978.

——. "Intellectuals in the Post-colonial World," *Salmagundi* 70–71 (1986): 44–81.

——. "Representing the Colonized: Anthropology's Interlocutors," *Critical Inquiry* 15 (1989): 205–25.

Schor, Naomi. "This Essentialism Which Is Not One: Coming to Grips with Irigaray," *Differences* 1.2 (1989): 38–58.

Scott, Bonnie Kime. *Joyce and Feminism.* Bloomington: Indiana University Press, 1984.

Shaktini, Namascar. "Displacing the Phallic Subject: Wittig's Lesbian Writing," *Signs* 8.1 (1982): 29–44.

Smith, Barbara Herrnstein. *Contingencies of Value: Alternative Perspectives for Critical Theory.* Cambridge: Harvard University Press, 1988.

Soyinka, Wole. *Season of Anomy.* London: Rex Collins, 1973.

——. *Myth, Literature, and the African World.* Cambridge: Cambridge University Press, 1976.

——. "Seminar on *Aké* with Wole Soyinka," *Southern Review* 23.3 (1987): 511–26.

Spivak, Gayatri Chakravorty. "Can the Subaltern Speak?" In *Marxism and the Interpretation of Culture.* Ed. Cary Nelson and Lawrence Grossberg. Urbana: University of Illinois Press, 1988. Pp. 271–313.

——. *The Postcolonial Critic: Interviews, Strategies, Dialogues.* New York: Routledge, 1990.

——. "Poststructuralism, Marginality, Post-coloniality, and Value." In *Literary Theory Today.* Ed. Peter Collier and Helga Geyer-Ryan. Ithaca: Cornell University Press, 1990.

Sundquist, Eric. *Faulkner: The House Divided.* Baltimore: Johns Hopkins University Press, 1983.

Valente, Joseph. "Hall of Mirrors: Baudrillard on Marx," *Diacritics* 15 (1985): 54–65.

White, Hayden. *The Content of the Form: Narrative Discourse and Historical Representation.* Baltimore: Johns Hopkins University Press, 1987.

Williams, Raymond. *Keywords: A Vocabulary of Culture and Society.* London: Oxford University Press, 1976.

———. *Marxism and Literature.* London: Oxford University Press, 1977.

———. "The Future of Cultural Studies." In *The Politics of Modernism: Against the New Conformists.* Ed. Tony Pinkney. London: Verso, 1989.

Wilson, Deborah. "The Fin and the Fish: Virginia Woolf's Images of Artistic Vision and Power," unpublished essay.

Wittig, Monique. *The Lesbian Body.* Trans. David Le Vay. Boston: Beacon, 1986. First published as *Le corps lesbien.* Paris: Minuit, 1973.

———. "The Straight Mind," *Feminist Issues* 1.1 (1980): 103–11.

———. "One Is Not Born a Woman," *Feminist Issues* 1.2 (1981): 47–54.

———. "The Category of Sex," *Feminist Issues* 2.2 (1982): 63–68.

———. "The Point of View: Universal or Particular?" *Feminist Issues* 3.2 (1983): 63–69.

———. "The Trojan Horse," *Feminist Issues* 4.2 (1984): 45–49.

———. "The Mark of Gender." In *The Poetics of Gender.* Ed. Nancy K. Miller. New York: Columbia University Press, 1986. Pp. 63–73.

———. "Homo Sum," *Feminist Issues* 10.1 (1990): 3–11.

Woolf, Virginia. *A Room of One's Own.* New York: Harcourt Brace Jovanovich, 1957.

———. *The Waves.* New York: Harcourt Brace Jovanovich, 1959.

———. *Three Guineas.* New York: Harcourt Brace Jovanovich, 1966.

———. *The Diary of Virginia Woolf.* Ed. Anne Olivier Bell. 4 vols. New York: Harcourt Brace Jovanovich, 1977–1982.

———. "A Woman's College from Outside." *The Complete Shorter Fiction of Virginia Woolf.* Ed. Susan Dick. New York: Harcourt Brace Jovanovich, 1985. Pp. 139–42.

———. *Moments of Being.* Ed. Jeanne Schulkind. 2d ed. London: Hogarth, 1985.

Yingling, Thomas E. *Hart Crane and the Homosexual Text: New Thresholds, New Anatomies.* Chicago: University of Chicago Press, 1990.

Zerilli, Linda. "The Trojan Horse of Universalism," *Social Text* 25/26 (1990): 146–70.

Index

abject (abjection), 85–86, 89, 111
Achebe, Chinua, 3, 126, 134, 145, 173;
    No Longer at Ease, 148–49; *Things
    Fall Apart,* 135–39, 148
Acker, Kathy, 3, 171
Ahmad, Aijaz, 149–50
Alighieri, Dante, 2
allegory, 149, 151–52, 159, 162, 171;
    manichean, 161
Althusser, Louis, 40, 172
ambivalence, 16, 22, 26–29, 32–34,
    37, 45, 47, 57, 62, 88, 99, 103, 143,
    156, 169
androgyny, 107, 183
apocalyptic tone, 174–75, 177–78,
    180, 184, 199–200
Aristotle, 43, 69, 76
Armah, Ayi Kwei, 154; *The Beautyful
    Ones Are Not Yet Born,* 156–57;
    Two Thousand Seasons, 157, 159–60
Atherton, William, 86
Attridge, Derek, 79–81

Bakhtin, Mikhail, 108
Bataille, Georges, 20
Baudrillard, Jean, 17–20, 22–31, 43–
    44, 61, 63, 65, 71, 88, 90, 202
Beckett, Samuel, 3, 5
Benjamin, Walter, 23, 43, 45–46, 108,
    137, 160; theory of allegory, 151–55;
    theory of translation, 166, 169

Benstock, Shari, 82, 86, 101
Benveniste, Emile, 185
Berkeley, George, 6
Bhabha, Homi K., 134, 137, 155–56
Bildung, 176
Bishop, John, 79
Blake, William, 203
Bloom, Harold, 99
Boucicault, Dion, 86
Bourdieu, Pierre, 2, 13, 28–29, 43–44, 120–21, 124
Brantlinger, Patrick, 126–29
Brennan, Timothy, 145
Bürger, Peter, 3, 151–52
Burke, Kenneth, 70
Butler, Judith, 96, 184

canon, 2, 30, 62, 155, 161, 166
canonization, 62, 120
class, 2, 10–11, 25, 29, 42, 50, 57, 60, 105, 113–14, 120–21, 125, 149, 154, 164, 169, 173, 175, 181–84, 186, 188–89, 198–99
Conrad, Joseph, 61, 136–38, 143, 163, 173; *Heart of Darkness,* 53, 57–58, 112, 118, 126–34, 136, 138–39, 142, 177
counterhegemonic, 120–21, 124, 188
Crane, Hart, 32–38, 40
criticism, 40, 121, 150, 170; historical, 18; ideologies of, 39; as judgment, 28–32; literary, 2, 13, 170; responsibility of, 14–15; as symbolic exchange, 40
Cronin, Richard, 140
Crowder, Diane Griffin, 197
cultural critique, 3
cultural revolution, 31, 114, 202
Cultural Studies, 15–16

Dante. *See* Alighieri
Dasein, 179
death: alterity of, 64, 88; as difference, 85; dissemination as signifier of, 35; drive, 51, 85, 131; as goal of human desire, 143; as Other, 85; and symbolic exchange, 34; totality as form of, 41; and utopia, 41; wish, 57
de Certeau, Michel, 75–78
decolonization (decolonizing), 62, 133, 145, 157
deconstruction (deconstructive), 3–4, 6–11, 15, 20, 25, 61, 97, 176

Deleuze, Gilles, 121–23
de Man, Paul, 24–25
Derrida, Jacques, 6–11, 14, 16, 20, 22, 27, 33, 36–37, 55, 75, 99–101, 105, 123, 125, 167, 169, 173–75, 178–79, 195, 199, 201
difference, 57, 81, 95, 180–81; being as, 92; class, 50, 180; cultural, 98, 124, 132–34, 137, 155–56, 167; of cultural knowledge, 155; death as, 85; erasure of, 130; future of, 115; genus of, 180; ideological, 167; as incommensurable in social processes, 95; metaphysical, 133; metaphysics of, 200; ontological, 173, 175, 180–81; originary, 97–99, 105; as positivity, 67; pure, 85, 89, 91; racial, 130, 132, 177, 180, 201; radical, 77, 199–200; sexual, 35, 67, 69, 74, 77, 79, 97, 99, 104–7, 120, 125, 130, 173–74, 179–80, 182, 197; signified by translation, 166; social, 42, 56, 124, 133; Thought of, 199–200; and universal, 186; Woolf's theory of, 97–99, 104–7, 114–15
differend, 167
dissemination, 11, 27, 35, 38, 88

economy: of big Other, 90; of equivalences, 88, 174; of ethnocentric subject, 122; general, 20, 25, 77–78; of language, 25, 84; linguistic, 84; manichean, 133; of not-all, 78–79, 90; patriarchal, 77; phallic, 68, 83–84, 90; phallocentric, 84; phallogocentric, 79; of pleasure and pain, 95, 114; of presence and absence, 52; restricted, 20, 25; visual, 91; of writing, 77
écriture feminine (feminine writing), 102, 185
Edelman, Lee, 33, 35–36
Eliot, T. S., 30–31, 99, 148
essentialism, 97; biological, 66; gender, 145; Irigaray's, 69; Marxist, 18; Wittig's, 181
Evans, Marthe Noel, 192, 195–96

Fanon, Frantz, 155
Faulkner, William: *Absalom, Absalom!,* 41, 44–63, 126, 201; *As I Lay Dying,* 49
Felman, Shoshana, 72–73

feminism, 97
Fish, Stanley, 2
Fogel, Daniel Mark, 99, 115
Ford, John, 12
Forster, E. M., 61, 139; *A Passage to India*, 132–35, 140
Foucault, Michel, 121–23
Fraser, Robert, 159
Freud, Sigmund, 19, 39, 69, 88, 106, 149
Fuss, Diana, 69, 181–82, 184

Garcia Marquez, Gabriel, 171
Gasché, Rodolphe, 16, 176, 180
gender, 11, 13, 42, 50, 70, 91, 114, 121, 125, 145, 179, 186–87, 192, 199; ideology of, 186, 190; law of, 185, 192, 196; as ontological category, 194
general text, 7, 16
Geschlecht, 179
Gifford, Don, 6
Gilbert, Sandra, 99, 101
Glasheen, Adaline, 92
Goethe, Johann Wolfgang von, 151
Gordon, John, 83
Graff, Gerald, 2
Gramsci, Antonio, 29, 157, 169
Groden, Michael, 8
Gubar, Susan, 99, 101
Gugelberger, Georg M., 153

Habermas, Jürgen, 9–11, 44
Harding, Esther, 196
Hardy, Thomas, 61
Harlow, Barbara, 170
Hart, Clive, 79
Hayman, David, 79
Head, Bessie, 154; *A Question of Power*, 160–61
Hegel, Georg Wilhelm Friedrich, 23, 50, 152, 160
hegemony (hegemonic), 13–14, 23, 27, 29, 57, 63, 76, 80, 119, 120–21, 124–26, 130, 133–35, 139–40, 144–45, 150–57, 159–60, 165, 167–71, 180–81, 188–89, 193, 195
Heidegger, Martin, 179
historical materialism, 22–23
historicism, 23, 43
history (History): Benjamin on, 23, 160; as concrete relation to death, 152; and context, 8, 15; as decline,

152; as discourse of the Other, 143; indeterminate, 50; Lacan on, 68; language as incomplete body of, 36; as letter, 45; literal truth of, 47; marked by alterity, 59; as narrative form, 69; Other of, 123; overdeterminations of, 109; personal, 143; as process without telos, 40; as situated discourse, 123; Subject of, 11; as system of values, 45; total, 23–24, 39, 42, 59, 202–3; universal, 13; unwritten, 57; from viewpoint of victors, 80
Hyde, Douglas, 6

ideology, 14, 169, 172, 195; American, 62; of art, 34; colonial(ist), 159, 161; Eurocentric, 129; European, 25; fascist, 104; of gender, 190; gender as, 186; of imperialism (imperialist), 112, 117, 119, 129; nationalist, 149; patriarchal, 89, 97, 106–7; of patriarchal culture, 192; poetic, 36; of poetic genius and literary imagination, 37–38; of progress, 57; racist, 60; of sexual difference, 120, 197; of subject, 184; transparency of, 119; Western, 130, 153
imaginary, 43, 51, 54, 56–57, 61, 66, 69–72, 89–92, 121, 141, 188, 201–2; feminine, 66–68; masculine, 68, 90
imperialism (imperialist), 11, 14, 53–54, 112, 117–19, 122–23, 125–27, 129–34, 136, 139–41, 144–45, 151, 154, 156, 161, 164, 170, 173, 178, 192; aesthetic, 170; of metaphor, 130, 132, 136, 178, 197
incommensurate, 20, 29, 37–39, 42, 49, 57, 63, 197
influence, 97–99, 109, 115
interpellation, 172–74
interpretive community, 2, 10, 163
intersubject, 9, 11–12, 203
intersubjectivity, 10–11, 46, 71, 73, 201
Irigaray, Luce, 64–69, 73–74, 77–78, 84–85, 113–14

Jakobson, Roman, 25, 107
James, Henry, 61, 99
Jameson, Fredric, 41–42, 126–28, 149–52, 170–71
JanMohamed, Abdul, 130, 132, 134–36, 138, 152–53, 161

Jay, Gregory S., 10–11, 18
Jha, Prabhakara, 170
jouissance, 65, 70, 74, 76–78, 82–85, 87, 89–95, 111, 114, 143, 175
Joyce, James, 1–9, 99–101, 139, 153, 199; *Finnegans Wake*, 3, 29, 61, 64–65, 78–83, 85–93, 126, 141; *A Portrait of the Artist as a Young Man*, 90; *Ulysses*, 3–9, 61–62, 80, 91, 96, 111, 126, 141

Kant, Immanuel, 171, 178
Kellner, Douglas, 18–19
Krause, David, 49
Kristeva, Julia, 26–27, 85–86, 89–90, 97
Kronick, Joseph, 179

Lacan, Jacques, 11, 13, 22, 27, 41, 54, 57, 61, 64–78, 83–84, 88–89, 91–92, 99, 107, 111–12, 152–53, 171, 176, 181, 189–90, 199, 201; *Encore*, 64, 68–70, 73–78, 84, 89, 91–92, 96
Lacoue-Labarthe, Philippe, 175–78, 189
language: as communication system, 73; as (discourse of the) Other, 74, 108, 123, 153, 169, 202; disfigurative power of, 27; as event, 72; foreignness of, 137; as form of class relationship, 10; gender in, 186–87; *jouissance* of, 65, 111; "as language," 36, 43, 108, 185; Levi-Strauss on origin of, 20–21; literary, 43, 144; material dimension of, 108, 124; metaphoric and metonymic poles of, 25; Nietzsche on, 173, 200; ontological emptiness of, 185, 199; ordinary or normal, 24, 26–27, 70; patriarchal, 77, 84–85, 90, 102, 130, 198–99; phallocentric (economy of), 84, 130; poetic, 25–28; as process, 27, 62, 108; restricted and general economy of, 25; rhetorical dimension of, 24–25, 176, 202; as social tie, 31, 43, 63, 190; as structure, 72; as symbolic exchange, 72; as value, 24, 36
Lawrence, D. H., 61
Lawrence, T. E., 118–19
Lazarus, Neil, 157, 160
Leclaire, Serge, 85

lesbian (lesbianism), 14, 181–84, 186–87
letter: alterity of, 83; diachrony of, 45; as event, 51; history as, historical, 45–46; *litteral* truth of, 79; of past, 59; place of, 90; proper name as, 87–89; as social tie, 87; as subject, 201; as *sumbolon*, 51; as waste, litter, 78, 81, 89, 112
Levi-Strauss, Claude, 20–22, 50, 72
literature, 1–2, 24–25, 27–28, 30, 78, 156, 170, 202; as form of value, 3; as institution, 3, 25, 97; as lapsus, 78
logocentrism (logocentric), 18, 77, 86, 200
logos, 36–37, 65–66, 120
Lukács, Georg, 41, 127
Lyotard, Jean-François, 20, 96, 159, 167, 170, 179

McCannel, Juliet Flower, 73
Macey, David, 67, 83, 85
McGann, Jerome J., 38–40
McHugh, Roland, 81–82
Marcus, Jane, 101–2, 108–9
Marx, Karl, 18–19, 23, 149, 152
Marxism, 22–23, 100–101
master narrative, 52, 56, 59, 152, 156, 158–59
Matthews, John T., 55–57
Mauss, Marcel, 18–20
Meisel, Perry, 97–99, 105, 115
Miller, Christopher, 132, 150–52, 158
Milton, John, 1–2
mimesis, 67, 176–77
modernism (modern, modernist), 3, 9, 15, 41, 61–63, 96, 99–102, 114, 120, 125–27, 133–34, 139, 145, 149, 170, 173, 177
Moi, Toril, 96–97
Moreland, Richard, 45, 49, 51
Morris, Wesley, 46–47, 55–57
Morrison, Toni, 3

nationalism, 133, 140–41, 145
nationality, 11, 13, 175
Ngara, Emmanuel, 159
Ngũgĩ wa Thiong'o, 147–48, 154–55, 160–71, 173; *Devil on the Cross (Caitaani Mũtharabainĩ)*, 162–67; *Matigari*, 168–69; *Petals of Blood*, 160–61
Nietzsche, Friedrich, 123, 173–75, 200

object a, 66, 71, 74–75, 77–78, 80
O'Hanlon, John, 82–83
Olney, James, 158
Orientalism, 116–17, 119
Other, 11–12, 16, 27, 65, 70, 72–74,
   76–79, 80, 83–85, 87–90, 92–93,
   95–96, 107–14, 119, 123, 125, 132,
   143, 152–53, 166–67, 169, 171,
   174, 179, 190, 199–202
Ouologuem, Yambo, 154, 160; *Bound
   to Violence (Le devoir de violence)*,
   157–59

Parameswaran, Uma, 144
pas tout, 64, 67–68, 197
Pater, Walter, 97, 99, 115
pedagogical effect, 63, 121, 123, 200,
   203
pedagogy, 2–3, 8–9, 12, 15, 170, 202
phallocentrism (phallocentric), 35, 55,
   65, 67–68, 84, 91, 130, 188
phallogocentrism, 77
phallus, 35, 66–67, 70, 73–74, 76–77,
   84–85, 87, 89, 92–93, 112, 114,
   181, 183, 196–97
Plato, 36–37, 177
Poe, Edgar Allan, 201
poetic effect, 27, 29, 31, 33, 40, 63
poetry, 24–28, 40, 43, 63; as form of
   life, language game, 40; as an institution, 26; as "poetry," 28; and symbolic exchange, 27, 32; and utopian
   revolt, 24
political correctness, 15
Porter, Carolyn, 49–50, 52, 55
postcolonialism (postcolonial), 15,
   123–26, 135, 139, 144, 145–49,
   154, 156, 158, 160, 162–63, 165,
   167, 170–71, 173, 201
postmodernism (postmodern, postmodernist), 3, 15, 96, 126–27, 139, 145,
   149, 161, 170, 172
Pound, Ezra, 99, 101
production: Baudrillard's concept of,
   24, 44, 61, 63, 71, 202; as form of
   value, 61, 63; metaphor, 61–63; mirror of, 61–62, 71, 73, 89, 122, 124
proper name, 45, 87–88
psychoanalysis, 68–69, 75, 88, 92, 96,
   99–101, 188, 202
Pynchon, Thomas, 3

race, 11, 13, 42, 121, 141, 175, 178–
   79, 186
racism (racist), 50, 53, 60, 126, 133–
   34, 139–40, 160
Ragland-Sullivan, Ellie, 66–67
real, the, 23, 41, 57, 68–69, 81, 84, 90,
   120, 134, 143–44, 180–81, 188–94,
   196–97, 199
Reed, Ishmael, 3, 171
reification, 55, 127
Riddel, Joseph, 36, 38, 40
Rodney, Walter, 159
Rose, Danis, 82–83
Rushdie, Salman, 147–48, 171, 173;
   Midnight's Children, 139–45; *The
   Satanic Verses*, 144, 147; *Shame*, 147

Said, Edward, 53, 116–19,131, 133
Salusinszky, Imre, 8–9, 11
Sartre, Jean-Paul, 41
Saussure, Ferdinand de, 19
Schor, Naomi, 67, 69
Scott, Bonnie Kime, 91
Shaktini, Namascar, 196–97
Showalter, Elaine, 96
Smith, Barbara Herrnstein, 19–20
social process, 20, 43, 60–61, 95, 124,
   189
Soyinka, Wole, 153–54; *Season of Anomy*, 154, 160–61
spacing, 6–7
Spivak, Gayatri, 13, 120–25, 160, 167,
   178
style: Achebe's, 136–37; Baudrillard's,
   18; beautiful, 41; Conrad's, 127,
   136–37, 139, 143, 173, 177;
   Crane's, 34; disfigurations or disloca-
   tions of, 88; ecstasy of, 93; in/of excess, 77–78; India's, 145; Lacan's,
   65, 75–78, 91; modernist will-to-,
   126–27, 134, 145, 177; of Other,
   78; pure, 173; of realism, 135; rhetorical, 6; transmitted by psychoanalysis, 96; of *The Waves*, 111;
   Wittig's, 193; of women, 77–78;
   Woolf's, 94–95
subaltern, 122, 144
subject: alterity of, 11; authorial, 62;
   autonomy of, 28, 52, 121, 124; bourgeois, 71; collective, 87, 160; colonial, 130, 155; as construction of,
   constituted by interests, 13–15; cri-

subject (*cont.*)
  tique of, 13; dissemination of, 11;
  European, 118–19, 122–23, 129–30,
  133, 137; hegemonic, hegemonized,
  124–25; homosexual, 34; ideology
  of, 184; imperialist, 122; lesbian,
  182, 184, 186–87, 193; neocolonial,
  155, 157–58; of oppressed, 121–22,
  124; patriarchal, 45, 117, 184, 201;
  phallic, 197; third-world, 122–23,
  125; transcendental, 52; true, 12, 16,
  71, 73, 200–202; typography of,
  175–77
Sundquist, Eric, 58
Swift, Jonathan, 82, 86
symbolic, the, 18, 21–22, 27–29, 31,
  49, 57, 76–77, 81, 90, 92, 94, 96,
  106–7, 113, 125, 127, 161, 192,
  197, 201
symbolic exchange, 11, 18–20, 22, 29,
  31–32, 34, 40, 46, 51, 58, 63, 65,
  72, 88, 95, 123, 140, 146, 167–68,
  171, 173–74, 190, 201–3

taste, 28–29
textuality, 3, 7, 16, 18, 126
truth: as absence of meaning, 71; alterity of, 74; and apocalyptic tone,
  175; exclusion of women from, 53;
  as expression of reason, 178; as function of poetic form, 45; historical, 17,
  59; homoerotic, 53; of incommensurate, 63; and metaphor, 37; as Other,
  87; universal, 62; as woman, 69–70;
  as writing, 69

unconscious, the, 8, 14, 74, 83, 88, 96,
  118, 161, 174
undecidability (undecidable), 3, 6, 9,
  14, 22, 56, 82, 111, 176
universal, the, 69–70, 73, 185–87,
  189–90, 194, 197, 199
university, 62, 100–102, 104–5, 112–
  14
utopia, 22–23, 26–27, 32, 41, 63, 80,
  113, 123

Valente, Joseph, 17–18
value: aesthetic, 30, 46, 60, 62, 155; ar-

tistic, 28, 38; commodity, 46; critique
  of, 17–19; didactic, 63; as distinction, 2, 29; ethical, 60; exchange,
  26–27, 60, 161, 174; hegemonic sys-
  tem/order of, 155, 195; heterosexual
  system/order of, 183, 192; institution
  and reproduction of, 62; language as,
  24, 36; law of, 27, 31, 43, 56, 63,
  72, 144, 186; linguistic, 24, 26; literary, 2, 36; literature as form of, 3;
  Marxist theory of, 18; of other, 10–
  11; other of, 20; phallocentric system
  of, 195; poetic, 37–38; as process,
  19; production as form of, 61, 63; as
  product of system, 60; as progress,
  24; representation as, 39; sign, 27;
  social, 12, 24, 95, 118, 121; structural code of, 26; symbolic, 121;
  transvaluation of, 17, 199; use, 26–
  27, 60
Volosinov, V. N., 43

Walker, Alice, 3
White, Hayden, 68–69
Williams, Raymond, 43–44, 60
Wilson, Deborah, 110
Wittgenstein, Ludwig, 40
Wittig, Monique, 70, 73, 171, 180–
  200; *The Lesbian Body,* 184, 187–
  200; *Les Guérillères,* 194
Woolf, Virginia, 61–62, 94–120, 125–
  26, 139, 178, 180–81; *A Room of
  One's Own,* 95, 100–102, 104–9,
  114, 147;*Three Guineas,* 98, 102,
  104–5, 108, 114–15; *To the Lighthouse,* 94–95, 110; *The Waves,* 61,
  94–95, 102–3, 110–14, 116–20,
  125, 128, 190; "A Woman's College
  from Outside," 102–4, 109
writing, 6, 24, 36–37, 40–41, 64–65,
  68–69, 77–78, 81, 85–86, 89, 97,
  100, 123, 126–27, 144, 156, 158,
  173

Yeats, W. B., 40, 148
Yingling, Thomas, 33–36, 38

Zerilli, Linda, 187

Library of Congress Cataloging-in-Publication Data

McGee, Patrick, 1949–
    Telling the other : the question of value in modern and
postcolonial writing / Patrick McGee.
        p.   cm.
    Includes bibliographical references and index.
    ISBN 0-8014-2749-5 (alk. paper). — ISBN 0-8014-8027-2
(pbk. : alk. paper)
    1. Literature, Modern—20th century—History and criticism—
Theory, etc.   2. Canon (Literature)   I. Title.
PN771.M4   1992
809'.04—dc20   91-48247